KB197050

영어회화 만능수첩

→ 바로보고 바로말하는 **현지영어회화사전**

CHRIS SUH

MENT⊘RS

바로보고 바로말하는 현지영어회화사전
영어회화 만능수첩

2025년 01월 13일 인쇄
2025년 01월 20일 발행

지 은 이 Chris Suh
발 행 인 Chris Suh
발 행 처 **MENT⊙RS**
경기도 성남시 분당구 황새울로 335번길 10 598
TEL 031-604-0025 FAX 031-696-5221
mentors.co.kr
blog.naver.com/mentorsbook
* Play 스토어 및 App 스토어에서 '멘토스북' 검색해 어플다운받기!
등록일자 2005년 7월 27일
등록번호 제 2009-000027호
I S B N 979-11-94467-29-8
가   격 18,600원(MP3 무료다운로드)

SMART ENGLISH | SECTION

Situation English

01

상황영어회화

Chapter **01** 교통 | 도로

01 교통 차가 너무 막혀

I'm stuck in traffic 길이 막혀 꼼짝못해

I got stuck in traffic on the way 도중에 차가 막혔어

Traffic is very heavy today 오늘 차가 너무 막혀

This is quite a traffic jam 교통이 꽉 막혔네

Traffic was bumper-to-bumper 차가 엄청 막혔어

It's a one-way street 일방 도로야

It's a right-turn-only lane 우회전 전용차선야

This is a toll road 유료도로야

Why don't you slow down a bit? 좀 천천히 가자

I got caught speeding 속도위반으로 걸렸어

I was busted for speeding 속도위반하다 걸렸어

I just got my license 방금 면허증 땄어

Don't fall asleep at the wheel 운전 중에 졸지 마라

Be sure to drive carefully 운전 조심하고

Want me to take the wheel? 내가 운전할까?

Fill it up 기름 가득 넣어줘요

Where can we fill it up? 어디서 기름넣지?

I ran out of gas 기름이 떨어졌어

Can you give me $10 worth of gas? 10달러어치 기름 넣어줄래요?

Would you change the oil, please? 엔진오일 갈아줄래요?

The engine won't start 차가 시동이 안 걸려요

Is it all right to park on the road? 도로에 주차해도 괜찮아?

Is there any gas station near here? 주변에 주유소 있어?

The brakes don't work 브레이크가 말을 안들어

I've got a flat 타이어가 빵구났어

Something's wrong with this car 이 차에 뭐 좀 문제가 있어

My car broke down. Would you come right away and check it? 차가 고장났는데 와서 확인 좀 해봐요

02 교통 태워다 줄게

I'll give you a ride 태워다 줄게

Do you want a ride? 태워다 줄까?

How about a ride? 태워줄래?

Are you going my way? 혹시 같은 방향으로 가니?, 같은 방향이면 태워줄래?

Hop in 어서 타

Where can I get a taxi? 택시 어디서 타나요?

Where's the taxi stand? 택시승강장이 어디예요?

Is there a taxi stand near here? 택시승강장이 이 근처에 있나요?

Can you get me a taxi, please? 택시 좀 잡아줄래요?

Can you call a cab for me? 택시 좀 불러줄래요?

Where to? 어디로 모실까요?

Where're you going? 어디 가세요?

(Take me) To this address, please 이 주소로 가 주세요

I'd like to go to this address 이 주소로 갈려고요

Please take me here 이쪽으로 가 주세요

Please take me to the airport 공항으로 갑시다

Here're twenty dollars, and keep the change
여기 20달러예요, 거스름돈은 가져요

Please stop just before that traffic light 신호등 바로 전에 세워주세요

Pull over here 여기 세워줘요

Let me out of here 여기서 내릴게요

I get off here 여기서 내릴게요

필수활용어구

road sign 도로 표지판 | intersection 교차로 | shortest way 지름길 | road map 도로지도 | route map 노선도 | ten-minute walk 걸어서 10분 거리 | toll road 유료도로 | traffic light 교통신호등 | parking lot 주차장 | opposite side 반대편

Are we almost there? 거의 다 왔나요?

I have to get there by 8 o'clock. Could you hurry up?
8시까지 가야 되는데 서둘러 줄래요?

Clear the way! 비켜주세요!

Step aside 비켜주세요

Coming through 좀 지나갈게요

차를 렌트할 때

03 교통 차를 렌트하려고요

I'd like to rent a car, please 차를 렌트하려고요

I'd like to rent this car for 10 hours
10시간 동안 이 차를 렌트하려고요

Where can I rent a car?
차를 어디서 렌트할 수 있어요?

Where's the nearest rent-a-car company?
가까운 렌터카 회사가 어디죠?

What's the rental fee? 렌탈비가 얼마예요?

Here is my international driving license 여기 국제 운전면허증 요

How much is the rate? 요금이 얼마예요?

Please show me the price list 가격표를 보여주세요

I only drive an automatic car 오토 차만 운전해요

With automatic transmission, please 오토차로 주세요

Do you deliver the car to my hotel? 호텔로 차를 갖다 주나요?

Where do I return the car? 차를 어디에 반납하나요?

Do I have to return the car filled with gas? 기름채워 반납해야 하나요?

Does this price include the insurance fee? 보험포함된 가격인가요?

Please give me insurance coverage 보험들어주세요

I'd like to buy insurance 보험가입할게요

Full insurance, please 보험 다 들어주세요

Please tell me who I contact if I have troubles
문제발생하면 누구와 연락해야 하죠?

Where should I call, if I have any trouble?
문제생기면 어디에 연락해야죠?

How long will you need it? 얼마동안 쓰실 건가요?

Which model do you like? 어떤 모델을 좋아하세요?

An automatic, medium-sized car 중형의 오토차로 해주세요

Can I leave the car at my destination? 목적지에 차를 두어도 됩니까?

버스나 전철을 타거나 내릴 때

04 교통 버스 정거장이 어디예요?

Where's the bus stop? 버스 정거장이 어디예요?

Which way is the bus stop? 버스 정거장이 어느 편에 있나요?

May I have a subway route map? 지하철 노선도 좀 주세요

Do you have a train schedule? 열차시간표 있어요?

Is there a direct train to New York? 뉴욕행 직행열차 있어요?

Where is the ticket counter? 매표소가 어디인가요?

A single ticket to New York, please 뉴욕행 편도 주세요

How much is the (bus) fare? 요금이 얼마예요?

How much to downtown? 시내까지 얼마인가요?

Which train should I take to Kangnam?
강남가려면 어떤 전철을 타야 돼요?

Which train goes to Kangnam?
어느 전철이 강남가요?

Which bus goes to the center of town?
어떤 버스가 시내중심으로 가나요?

What time is the last train to Suwon?
수원행 막차는 몇 시에 있어요?

Which bus goes to Chicago?
어떤 버스가 시카고로 가나요?

Is this a right train for Boston?
이게 보스톤 가는 기차 맞나요?

Does this train stop at Incheon?
이 전철이 인천에서 서나요?

Does this bus go to Sears Tower? 이 버스가 시어스 타워에 가나요?

How many stops are there to Kyungbokgung?
경복궁까지 몇 정거장예요?

How many stops to the museum? 박물관까지 몇 정거장입니까?

Where am I supposed to change[transfer]? 어디서 갈아타야 하나요?

You can change to Line #3 at Yaksu 약수역에서 3호선으로 갈아타세요

Take this train 이 열차를 타세요

Take the orange train 오렌지 색 열차를 타세요

How often do trains come? 열차 배차시간이 어떻게 돼요?

The trains come every ten minutes 열차들은 10분마다 와요

Could you tell me when to get off? 어디서 내려야하는지 알려줄래요?

It's four stops from here 여기서부터 4정거장에서요

After the next stop 다음 정거장 후예요

What's the next stop[station]? 다음 정거장은 어디예요?

The next stop is Sadang 다음 정거장은 사당이예요

Do I have to transfer? 갈아타야 합니까?

You have to change trains at the next station
다음 정거장에서 갈아타야 돼요

What time does the bus for New York leave?
뉴욕행 버스가 언제 출발해요?

필수활용어구

be looking for …을 찾고 있다 | walk down …을 따라 걸어가다 | be[get] lost 길을 잃다 | go back 되돌아가다 | get (to) + 장소 …에 가다, 도착하다(arrive at) | get off (기차 등 대중 교통 수단에서) 내리다 | take the subway 지하철을 타다 | be close to + 장소 …에 가깝다 | go straight 곧장 가다 | switch buses 버스를 갈아타다 | make a turn 방향을 틀다 | turn around (반대쪽으로) 방향을 바꾸다 | turn the corner 모퉁이를 돌다 | follow …를 따라 가다 | head …로 향해 가다 | be located 위치하다 | show A the way A에게 길을 안내하다 | write the directions down 가는 방법을 적다

I went past my stop 내릴 곳을 지나쳤어요

How can I go back to East Hill station?
이스트 힐 역으로 어떻게 다시 돌아가요?

I'd like a hotel near the station 역에서 가까운 호텔로 가주세요

What time does the next bus leave? 다음 버스가 언제 출발합니까?

What time does the last train leave? 막차가 언제 출발합니까?

Is there any seat in the non-smoking car?
비흡연석에 다른 좌석 있어요?

길을 잃었을 때 길 물어보기

05 교통 여기가 어디죠?

Where am I? 여기가 어디죠?

Where am I on this map? 지도상에 제가 어디 있는 거죠?

I can't understand where I am on this map
지도상에 어딘지 모르겠어요

Well, this is Baker St., which is right here on the map
글쎄요, 이곳이 베이커 가(街)니까, 지도에서는 바로 여기네요

What's the name of this street?
이 거리명이 어떻게 됩니까?

I think I'm lost 길을 잃은 것 같아요

Excuse me, but I'm lost
실례합니다만, 길을 잃어서요

I'm trying to go to COEX, but I think I'm lost
코엑스가려는데 길을 잃은 것 같아요

I got lost 길을 잃었어요

I seem to have lost my way 제가 길을 잃은 것 같아요

Is this the right road to reach Wall Street?
이 길이 월스트리트로 가는 길 맞나요?

Is this the right way to go to Mapo?
이 길이 마포가는 길 맞아요?

Does this road go to the station? 이 길이 역으로 향하나요?

Am I on the right road for the Korean Stock Exchange?
증권거래소 가는 길 맞나요?

Which way is it to the Blue House? 어느 길이 청와대로 가나요?

Could you draw me a map? 약도 좀 그려줄래요?

길을 몰라 알려주지 못할 때

06 도로 여기가 초행길이라서요

I'm a stranger here myself
여기가 초행길이라서요, 여기는 처음 와봐서요

I'm sorry, but I'm a stranger here too
미안하지만 저도 여긴 잘 몰라요

Sorry, I'm new here too
미안하지만 저도 여기가 초행길이어서요

I'm not familiar with this area 이 지역은 잘 몰라요

Where do you want to go? 어디에 가실 건데요?

Where is it that you are heading? 어디 가는 길인데요?

Are you lost? 길을 잃었나요?

I think you're heading in the wrong direction
방향을 잘못 잡은 것 같은데요

If you get lost, just give me a call
혹 길을 잃어버리면 전화주세요

Why don't you ask someone else?
다른 사람한테 물어보세요

I'm sorry, but I'm not from Seoul
미안하지만 서울 사람이 아니라서요

I'm not a local 이 지역 사람이 아니에요

I'm not from around here 나도 잘 몰라요

This is my first time here too 여기 나도 처음야

Wait a minute, let me ask someone for you
잠깐, 딴사람한테 물어볼게요

보충설명 특히 길 안내해줄 영어가 안될 때는 "I'm sorry, but I can't speak English very well"
혹은 "I'm sorry, but my English isn't very good" 이라 먼저 한 다음 "Could you ask

someone else?" 나 "You'd better check with someone else" 라고 하면 된다

Can you tell me how to get to the nearest subway station?

구체적으로 길을 알려달라고 할 때

07 **도로** 가장 가까운 지하철역 좀 알려줄래요?

가장 가까운 지하철역 좀 알려줄래요?

Can you tell me the way to Maxim?
맥심사 가는 길 좀 가르쳐 줄래요?

Do you know the shortest way to the mall?
쇼핑몰가는 지름길 아세요?

Do you know any good outlet malls in Buffalo?
버팔로에 좋은 아웃렛몰 좀 알아?

Where is the nearest post office? 가장 가까운 우체국이 어디예요?

I'm looking for the convention center 컨벤션 센터를 찾고 있는데요

I'm trying to find the National Art Gallery 국제 미술관에 가려구요

How long does it take to get to the stadium?
경기장까지 시간이 얼마나 걸리죠?

How do[can] I get there? 거기에 어떻게 가죠?

Is it within walking distance? 걸어서 가도 돼나요?

Can I get there by bus? 버스로 갈 수 있나요?

How far is it to Busan? 부산까지 얼마나 걸려요?

How far is it from the subway to the museum?
전철역에서 박물관까지 얼마나 걸려요?

I was wondering if you could tell me where to get off the train 어느 역에서 내려야 하는지 알려줄래요?

How far is it from here? 여기서 얼마나 먼가요?

필수활용어구

in the wrong direction 잘못된 방향으로, 틀린 방향으로 | timetable 시각표 | direct
bus 직행버스 | fare 요금 | express charge 급행요금 | conductor 승무원 |
dining car 식당차 | sleeping car 침대차 | upper[lower] berth 상층[하층]침대

Is it far (from here)? (여기서) 멀어요?

Is Busan far? 부산이 멀리 있나요?

Is it close[near] to Kyungbu Highway? 경부고속도로까지 가까워?

Am I near[close to] Busan? 부산에 가까이 왔나요?

What's the fastest way to get there?
거기까지 가는데 뭐가 가장 빠른 길이야?

What's the best way to get there? 거기 가는데 가장 좋은 방법은 뭐야?

Which way is shorter? 어느 길이 더 빨라?

Is it on the right or left? 오른편에 있나요, 왼편에 있나요?

Go down this street and turn to the left

구체적으로 길 알려주기(1)

08 | **도로** 이 길로 내려가서 왼쪽으로 도세요

이 길로 내려가서 왼쪽으로 도세요

Go straight for two blocks 두 블록 더 곧장 가요

Go straight on the highway for ten kilometers
고속도로를 타고 10킬로 곧장 가요

Go east for two blocks and then turn right
동쪽으로 2블록 간후 우회전해요

Keep going straight until you reach the church 교회까지 곧장 가요

Take this road for about five minutes and it's on your left
이 길로 5분가면 왼편에 있어요

Take[Follow] this road 이 길을 따라가요

Take this road until it ends and then turn right
이 길 끝에서 우회전해요

Take Line #3 and get off at Shinsa Station

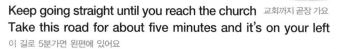
필수활용어구

How far is it from A to B? A에서 B까지 얼마나 멉니까? | How long does it take to + V? ⋯하는 데 시간이 얼마나 걸리죠? | How do I get to + 장소? ⋯에 어떻게 가나요? | Do you know how to get to + 장소? ⋯에 어떻게 가는지 아세요? | how to get to + 장소 ⋯에 가는 방법 | the fastest way to + 장소 ⋯에 가는 가장 빠른 방법

3호선 타고 신사역에서 내려요

Take the subway for one stop and get off at Yoksam Station 지하철로 한 정거장 가서 역삼역에서 내려요

Take the subway from Bloor Station and get off at King Station 블로어 역에서 지하철을 타고 킹 역에서 내리면 되요

Take bus number 65 and get off at the third stop
65번 타고 3번째 정거장에서 내려요

Turn right at the first traffic light 첫번째 신호등에서 우회전해요

Turn left[right] at the first intersection 첫번째 교차로에서 좌(우)회전해요

Turn to the left when you come to a post office
우체국에서 좌회전해요

Go back that way for ten minutes and take the road on your left 왔던 길을 10분정도 되돌아간 다음 왼쪽 도로를 타세요

It's a ten minute walk from here 여기서 걸어서 10분 거리에 있어요

┌─────────────────────────────┐
│ 구체적으로 길 알려주기(2)
└─────────────────────────────┘

09 | 도로 여기서 걸어서 10분 거리에 있어요

보충설명 걸어서 5분 거리는 five-minute walk로 five와 minute 사이에 '-'를 붙여야 하지만 현대의 바쁜 영어에서는 생략하여 five minute walk로 쓰기도 한다.

It's about 10 minutes on foot 걸어서 10분 정도 걸려요

Even on foot, it's no more than 10 minutes 걸어도 10분 이상 안 걸려요

It should take 20 minutes by car 차로 20분 정도 걸릴 거예요

The museum is ten kilometers west of City Hall
박물관은 시청 서쪽 10킬로 지점에 있어
보충설명 'A' is + 거리 + west[east] of~ 'A'가 …의 서(동)쪽 거리만큼에 있어

The hospital is a five minute walk from the bus stop
병원은 정거장에서 걸어서 5분걸려
보충설명 'A' is + 시간 + walk[ride] from~ 'A'가 …에서 걸어서[차타고] ~분[시간]거리야

It's not far from here 여기서 멀지 않아요

It's not (that) far (그렇게) 멀지 않아요

It's on the right 오른편에 있어요

It's around the corner, to your left 왼편 모퉁이를 돌면 있습니다

It's just down the hall to your left 복도를 내려가다 보면 왼편에 있어요

You'll see it on your right side 당신 오른편에 있을거예요

You can't miss it 쉽게 찾을 수 있을 거예요

I'm going in that direction 저도 그 쪽으로 가는 중이에요

I'm going there myself 저도 그리로 가는 중이에요

I'll show you the way myself 제가 직접 안내할게요

Let me show you the way 제가 길을 알려드릴게요

Do you want me to take you there? 제가 거기까지 모셔다 드릴까요?

Chapter **02** 공항 | 비행

01 탑승 6/13일로 예약하고 싶은데요

I'd like to make a reservation for June 13th
6월 13일로 예약하고 싶은데요

Smoking or non-smoking?
흡연석으로 하시겠어요, 비흡연석으로 하시겠어요?

I would prefer non-smoking
비흡연석으로 주세요

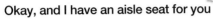

Okay, and I have an aisle seat for you
알겠습니다, 통로측으로 드리죠

Are there any seats left on the 10 o'clock flight to LA?
10시 LA행 좌석 남았나요?

Could you tell me if you have any seats available to Miami?
마이애미행 비행편에 남아있는 좌석이 있습니까?

I have a couple of seats left on this afternoon flight
오늘 오후 비행편에 두 자리가 남아 있습니다

I'm on the waiting list 난 대기자 명단에 있어요

Round trip or one-way? 왕복권요 아니면 편도요?

I'd like a round-trip ticket to New York 뉴욕행 왕복 항공권 주세요

When would you like to depart and return?
언제 출발해서 언제 돌아오실 생각이십니까?

I'd like to leave this Monday and return on Sunday
이번 월요일에 출발해서 일요일에 돌아오려구요

All of the flights are full 모든 항공편이 예약만료되었어요

필수활용어구

book a flight 비행편을 예약하다 | change[cancel] one's flight 비행편 예약을 변경 [취소]하다 | one-way ticket 편도 항공권(cf. round-trip ticket 왕복항공권) | open ticket 비행편 시간을 필요에 따라 변경할 수 있는 항공권 | reconfirm 예약을 확인하다 | reserve a seat for a flight to …행 비행기 좌석을 예약하다 | return date 돌아오는 날짜(cf. date of departure 출발일) | no-show 비행편을 예약하고 탑승하지 않는 사람 | boarding pass 탑승권 | international flights 국제선 | domestic flights 국내선 | transit passenger 비행기 환승객(cf. transit lounge 환승 대기실)

All of the other flights were booked solid
다른 항공편이 다 예약되었어요

Do you know when the next flight leaves?
다음 비행기는 언제죠?

How much is business class? 비즈니스 클래스 요금이 얼마죠?

Do you want first class, business or coach class?
일등석, 비즈니스 아니면 보통석으로 드릴까요?

I'm booked on AA Flight 567 to NY 뉴욕행 AA567편을 예약했는데요

I'd like to change my flight 비행편을 바꾸고 싶습니다

May I change my return date to May 7th?
돌아오는 날짜를 5/7일로 변경해줄래요?

Could I please have your name, flight number and date of departure? 성함과 비행편 번호를 말씀해 주시겠습니까? 그리고 출발일도요

Unfortunately, there are no seats available at this moment, but I could put you on a waiting list 안됐지만 지금 현재로서는 남아있는 좌석이 없습니다. 대기자 명단에라도 올려드릴까요?

What is your flight number? 비행편 번호가 어떻게 되시죠?

It is 845, to New York 845번, 뉴욕행입니다

Your reservation is confirmed, but the flight may be delayed because of bad weather 예약이 확인되었습니다. 그런데 날씨가 나빠서 늦게 출발할지도 모르겠어요

I'd like to reconfirm my flight 예약을 확인하려구요

I want to reconfirm my reservation 예약을 확인하려구요

I'd like to change my reservation, please 예약을 변경하려구요

I'd like to cancel my reservation for the flight on March 5th to Seoul, flight number KW 009, and change it to March 7th, flight number KW 008 instead, please 서울행 3월 5일 비행편 KW009 예약을 취소하고 대신 3월 7일 KW008편으로 바꿔주세요

02 탑승 탑승수속 카운터로 어떻게 가죠?

Can I change my reservation to a later[earlier] flight?
예약을 좀 늦은[빠른] 비행편으로 바꿀 수 있나요?

How can I get to the check-in counter (for Japan Air Lines)? (일본항공) 탑승수속 카운터로 어떻게 가죠?

You need to go up one level and it is on the north side of the building 한 층 올라가면 건물 북쪽 편에 있습니다

Is the flight leaving on time? 비행기가 제 시간에 출발하나요?

Do you have any luggage to check? 부치실 짐이 있으십니까?

How many pieces of luggage are you checking in?
부칠 짐이 몇 개죠?

How many bags do you want to check?
몇 개 가방을 부칠 건가요?

I would like to check three pieces 세 개를 부치려고 하는데요

Is that your carry-on? 저게 갖고 타실 짐인가요?

How many pieces of carry-on are you going to take?
몇 개를 갖고 타실 건가요?

You're only allowed two, but you may be able to take one as a carry-on 두 개까지만 부치실 수 있습니다. 하지만 하나는 휴대 수하물로 들고 타도 됩니다

Your luggage is over the maximum weight
짐이 수화물 제한한도를 초과했습니다

Fortunately, your bags are within the maximum allowable weight 손님의 짐이 무게 한도를 넘지 않아서 다행입니다

How much over is it? 얼마나 넘었죠?

It's five kilograms over the weight allowance
5킬로 초과하셨네요

I'll put a fragile sticker on it for you
짐에 취급주의 스티커를 붙여 드리죠

I'm just taking my carry-on 비행기에 들고 탈 짐밖에 없습니다

03 탑승 금속물건은 전부 받침대에 꺼내 놓으세요

Please place all metal objects in the tray
금속물건은 전부 받침대에 꺼내 놓으세요

Do I need to take off my belt because of its metal buckle?
금속으로 된 버클이 달린 혁대도 풀어놓아야 하나요?

You can collect your belongings on the other side of the machine 운반대 저쪽 끝에서 손님의 개인 소지품을 찾아가시면 됩니다

Do you have any prohibited items with you?
금지품목을 소지하고 계세요?

Did anyone ask you to bring anything into the country for them? 누군가가 손님에게 뭔가 가져다 달라고 부탁한 게 있습니까?

No, these are all my own personal belongings
아뇨, 이것들은 전부 다 제 개인 물품들입니다

You can't bring your pet with you
애완동물은 데리고 탈 수 없어요

Would you mind letting me check your bag? 손님 가방 속을 확인해 봐도 될까요?

What's this red stuff? 이 빨간 건 뭐죠?

That's hot pepper paste, a kind of Korean traditional sauce. Is it one of the prohibited items? 고추장입니다. 한국 전통 소스의 일종이죠. 그게 금지 품목입니까?

필수활용어구

check-in 탑승수속(cf. check in 탑승수속을 하다) | **carry-on (baggage)** 기내 휴대 수하물 | **excess baggage charge** 화물 중량초과 요금 | **free (baggage) allowance** 무료로 부칠 수 있는 짐의 한도 | **personal belongings[effects]** 개인 소지품 | **luggage cart** 화물 운반용 수레 | **prohibited item[articles]** 소지 금지품목 | **baggage claim area** 수화물 찾는 곳 | **baggage check** 탑승 전 짐을 부칠 때 받은 수화물표 | **carousel** 수화물 운반대. 공항에서 승객들이 짐을 찾아갈 수 있도록 회전하는 수화물 운반대를 말한다 | **lost luggage counter** 화물 분실 신고대 | **security check** 보안 검색 | **walk-through detector** 소지 금지품목을 검사하기 위해 걸어서 통과하는 검색장치 (cf. hand-held detector 손에 들고 쓰는 검색장치)

I'm afraid that this is not permitted
이건 가져가실 수 없겠는데요

Your plane is now boarding
손님 비행기가 지금 탑승 중입니다

Your plane is now boarding at gate 3
손님 비행기는 지금 3번 게이트에서 탑승 중입니다

You must proceed to boarding gate 3 immediately
지금 곧바로 3번 탑승구로 가셔야 합니다

Could you tell me how to get to Gate 3? 3번 게이트로 어떻게 가죠?

Where's the boarding gate? 탑승구가 어딥니까?

Excuse me. How do I get to Gate 43?
죄송하지만 43번 게이트를 어떻게 가죠?

Which gate is for the flight to Washington?
워싱톤 행 비행편은 어느 게이트로 가야 하나요?

I think if you follow those signs you'll get there
저 표시들을 따라가시면 그리 가실 수 있을 거예요

What time do you start boarding? 탑승은 언제 하나요?

Has this flight begun boarding? 이 항공편 탑승 시작했나요?

기내에서 이런저런

04 **기내** 월스트리트 한 부 좀 줄래요?

Could I get a copy of the Wall Street Journal?
월스트리트 한 부좀 줄래요?

Unfortunately, we don't have any left 죄송합니다만, 남은 게 없습니다

What other papers do you have? 다른 신문은 어떤 게 있죠?

What are my choices for breakfast? 아침 메뉴가 어떤 게 있죠?

We have a vegetarian omelet or ham and eggs

필수활용어구

in-flight service 기내 서비스(cf. in-flight movie 기내 상영영화) | **flight attendant** (기내) 승무원 | **air duty-free shopping guide** 기내 면세품 안내책자 | **airsickness bag** 비행기 멀미용 봉투 | **refreshments** 비행 중에 제공되는 간단한 음식과 음료

야채 오믈릿과 햄에 계란을 곁들인 요리가 있습니다

I'd like the ham and eggs please 햄과 계란 요리가 좋겠군요

Do you want some coffee or something with that?
커피 같은 것도 함께 드릴까요?

What would you like for dinner, beef or fish?
저녁으로 고기와 생선 중 어느 걸로 하실래요?

What would you like to drink? 뭘 드실래요?

I'd like a glass of milk 우유 한 잔 주십시오

Coffee, please 커피 주세요

With sugar and cream? 설탕과 프림 넣고요?

Can I have some water? 물 좀 줄래요?

Can I have some medicine? 약 좀 줄래요?

Could you tell me how to fill out this form? 이 서식 쓰는 거 알려줄래요?

Can you help me with this form? 이 서식 쓰는 것 좀 도와줄래요?

Will you show me how to turn on the light?
불 어떻게 키는지 알려줄래요?

Would you like me to close the shutter? 창문가리개를 내려 드릴까요?

Could I please get a blanket? 담요 한 장 갖다주시겠어요?

This isn't your seat, I'm afraid 잘못 앉으신 것 같은데요

The earphones aren't working 이어폰이 작동 안돼요

**This is my first time flying and I want to know where the
washroom is** 이번에 비행기를 처음 타보는데요, 화장실이 어딘지 모르겠네요

Can I use the washroom now? 지금 화장실을 사용해도 되나요?

**You'll have to wait until the plane takes off and the captain
shuts off the fasten-seat-belt sign** 비행기가 이륙해서 기장님이 안전벨
트를 묶고 있으라는 신호를 끄고 난 후에 이용하시면 됩니다

**I can't believe how cheap the prices are. I'm going to get a
bottle of whisky and some perfume** 가격이 정말 싸군요. 위스키 한 병
하고 향수를 좀 살게요

**How would you like to pay for that? You may use your
credit card** 지불은 어떻게 하시겠습니까? 신용카드를 사용하셔도 됩니다

I'd like to pay in cash. How much is it? 현금으로 할게요. 얼마죠?

05 기내 곧 이륙하겠습니다

- Attention, this is the head flight assistant.
- We're about to leave the boarding gate to take off and you must put your chair into the upright position.
- Kindly ensure that your seat belts are fastened.
- Our flight attendants will now go over the safety features of this aircraft.

- 알려드립니다. 저는 객실장입니다.
- 이제 곧 탑승구를 떠나서 이륙할 예정이오니 좌석 등받이를 곧바로 세워주십시오.
- 안전벨트를 매시기 바랍니다.
- 저희 승무원들이 이제 비행기의 안전 사항들을 점검하도록 하겠습니다.

- This is the Captain speaking.
- The flight has been delayed due to the large number of people who were late from a connecting flight.
- We expect we will be in the air in less than thirty minutes.

- 기장이 알려드립니다.
- 연결 비행편에서 늦어지는 승객들이 많은 관계로 비행기 출발이 지연되고 있습니다.
- 30분 안에 이륙할 것으로 예상됩니다.

- Good evening and welcome on board Flight 301 to Chicago.
- Please ensure that your carry-on luggage is stored in the overhead bins.
- Once we have reached our cruising altitude we will be serving refreshments.

- 안녕하십니까, 시카고 행 301 비행편에 탑승하신 것을 환영합니다.
- 개인 수하물은 머리 위쪽 보관함에 넣어주시기 바랍니다.
- 운항 고도에 도달하고 나면 간단한 음식을 제공해 드리겠습니다.

- We have just landed at Chicago's O'hare Airport.
- We were going to stay on the ground for two hours.
- But the control tower has advised us that we can expect that our layover will be longer, due to the rainy conditions that Chicago is experiencing at this time.

- 저희 비행기는 지금 막 시카고 오헤어 공항에 착륙했습니다.
- 이곳에서 두 시간 동안 머무를 예정이었습니다.
- 하지만 관제탑에서 시카고에 지금 비가 내리고 있어서 기착 시간이 좀더 길어질 수도 있다고 저희에게 알려왔습니다.

- Once again welcome aboard Flight 524 to Boston, we have reached our cruising altitude of 32,000 feet.
- Our current speed is about 700 km/h and we have a strong tailwind which should allow us to arrive ahead of schedule.

- 보스톤 행 524 비행편에 탑승하신 것을 거듭 환영합니다. 비행기는 지금 운항 고도인 3만 이천피트에 도달해 있습니다.
- 현재 속도는 약 시속 700킬로미터이며 강한 뒷바람을 받고 있어서 예정보다 일찍 목적지에 도착할 것입니다.

- We're about to make our descent into Tokyo's Narita Airport.
- Passengers are reminded to give their blankets, pillows and headsets to the flight attendants.
- The captain has put on the fasten-seat-belt sign and passengers should put their chairs into the upright position.

■ 이제 곧 도쿄 나리타 공항에 착륙하겠습니다.

■ 승객들께서는 잊지 마시고 담요, 베개, 그리고 헤드폰을 승무원에게 반납하시기 바랍니다.

■ 안전벨트를 매라는 신호에 불을 들어왔으므로 승객들께서는 좌석 등받이를 곧게 세우시기 바랍니다.

비행기 갈아타지 못했을 때

06 환승 연결 비행편을 타려고 하는데요

I need to catch my connecting flight 연결 비행편을 타려고 하는데요

I missed my connecting flight to NY 뉴욕행 연결 비행편을 놓쳤어요

I missed AA 456 to New York because of the delay of plane from Incheon 인천출발 비행편 연착으로 뉴욕행 AA456를 놓쳤어요

I need to catch my connecting flight. Could you tell me where gate K is? 비행기를 갈아타려는데요. K탑승구가 어디 있는지 알려줄래요?

That gate is not in this terminal, it's in Terminal Two K 탑승구는 이 터미널에 없구요, 제 2 터미널에 있어요

I missed my connecting flight to NY 뉴욕행 연결 비행편을 놓쳤어요

Do you happen to know when the next available flight leaves? 혹시 다음 비행기는 언제 있는지 아세요?

Let me check. It looks like we can put you on a flight in about an hour 확인해보죠. 한 시간 후쯤 출발하는 비행기에 자리를 마련할 수 있을 것 같네요

필수활용어구

be delayed (비행편의 출발이) 지연되다 | **departure time** 비행기 출발시간 | morning[afternoon] flight 아침[오후] 비행편 | **domestic[international] line** 국내[국제]선 | take off (비행기가) 이륙하다(↔touch down, land) | **ahead of schedule** 예정보다 빨리(↔behind schedule) | boarding time 탑승시간 | **departure time** 출발시간 | delayed arrival 연착

07 입국 친척들을 좀 만나려고 왔어요

May I see your passport, please? 여권 좀 보여주시겠습니까?

Good morning, may I have your ticket and your passport, please? 안녕하세요, 비행기표와 여권을 주시겠습니까?

We are on a group tour. So the tour conductor has all our tickets 단체여행중입니다. 여행가이드가 우리 티켓을 모두 갖고 있어요

Would you show me the return ticket? 돌아갈 항공권 보여주시겠어요?

Do you have a return ticket? 돌아갈 항공권 있어요?

How long are you planning to stay in the US? 미국엔 얼마나 머물 계획예요?

Where will you be staying? 어디 머무를 예정입니까?

I plan to stay for a week 일주일간 머물겁니다

I'm going to stay for a couple of months 몇 달간 머물려구요

I'm planning to stay for three weeks and then I'm leaving the country 3주간 있다가 떠날 생각이에요

What's the purpose of your visit? 방문 목적이 뭡니까?

What brought you here? 여기 오신 이유는 요?

What's the nature of your visit to the US? 미국엔 무슨 일로 오셨나요?

I'm here to see some of my relatives 친척들을 좀 만나려고 왔어요

I'm visiting on business 업무차 왔어요

I'm going to New York on business 업무차 뉴욕에 왔습니다

Business 업무차요

I'm here on business 사업차 왔어요

I'm here on vacation 휴가차 왔어요

I came here to study 공부하러 왔습니다

I will stay with my friend in New York 뉴욕의 친구와 함께 머물겁니다

I'm going to stay in New York, but I haven't decided the hotel yet 뉴욕에 머물거지만 아직 호텔을 정하진 않았습니다

I'll attend a language school 어학원을 다닐겁니다

I'll visit a friend in Chicago 시카고에 있는 친구를 만나러 왔어요

Sightseeing 관광요

Can you tell me where you're going to stay?
여행 기간 동안 어디에 계실 건가요?

Can you tell me where you're going to be staying for the duration of your trip? 여행 기간 동안 어디에 계실 건가요?

Where are you staying? 어디 머무실거예요?

I'm staying at the Intercontinental Hotel
인터콘티넨탈 호텔에 머물거예요

My company has booked me a room at the Park Plaza Hotel and I'll be staying there for the next week 회사에서 파크
플라자 호텔에 방을 예약해둬서 다음 주에는 거기에 있을 거예요

I'm staying at a home in Washington. Here's the address of my host family 워싱톤의 집에서 머물겁니다. 이게 내가 머물 집의 주소입니다

신고할 물건 확인할 때

08 | **입국** 신고할 물건이 있습니까?

(Do you have) Anything to declare? 신고할 물건이 있습니까?

I am bringing some traditional Korean food with me
한국 전통 음식을 좀 가지고 들어왔는데요

I bought it at the duty-free counter in the airport in Seoul. It's a gift for my friend 서울에 있는 공항 면세점에서 샀어요. 친구에게 줄 선
물입니다

I have two gifts for friends 친구에게 줄 선물이 2개 있습니다

What is the approximate value? 대략 값어치가 어떻게 됩니까?

필수활용어구

immigration 입국 심사 | immigration office 입국관리사무소 | declare (세관에) 신
고하다(cf. custom declaration 세관 신고서) | clear customs 세관을 통과하다 | fill
out a form 양식서를 작성하다 | disembarkation[entry] card 입국 신고서 |
customs declaration form 세관신고서 | nationality 국적 | family name 성 |
first name 이름

What is their value? 가격이 어떻게 돼요?

How much money do you have? 돈은 얼마나 소지하고 있습니까?

I have about $2,000 dollars 한 2천 달라 갖고 있습니다

I have this camera that I bought for my friend
내가 친구줄려고 산 카메라입니다

How much did you pay for it?
얼마주고 사셨습니까?

I can't find my baggage
내 가방을 못 찾겠어요

You need to go to the lost luggage counter
수화물 분실신고대로 가보세요

Are you sure that you checked thoroughly around the carousel? 수하물 회전 운반대 주변을 샅샅이 찾아보셨어요?

I waited for an hour and there were no bags on or around the carousel 한 시간이나 기다렸지만 운반대 위는 물론이고 그 주변에도 없었다구요

If that's the case, you need to go to the lost luggage counter which is located at the end of this hall 그렇다면 이 복도 끝에 있는 수화물 분실 신고대로 가보세요

I'm still suffering from jet lag 아직 시차가 적응이 안되었어요

I left something on the plane 비행기에 뭘 두고 왔어요

호텔에서 공항으로 갈 때

09 **입국** 베드포드 호텔에 어떻게 가는지 알려주시겠어요?

Excuse me. Could you tell me how to get to the Bedford hotel? 실례합니다. 베드포드 호텔에 어떻게 가는지 알려주시겠어요?

You have a couple of choices, you can take an airport limo or a taxi 두 가지 방법 중에 고르시면 돼요. 공항 리무진 버스나 택시 타는 거죠

What time does the limo leave? 리무진 버스는 몇 시에 출발하나요?

In about ten minutes. When your limo comes to get you, the driver will help you with your luggage 한 10분쯤 후에요. 리무진을 탈 때 운전사가 짐을 실어줄 거예요

Do you have any tags? 짐에 붙일 만한 꼬리표 있나요?

I was wondering if you could tell me where the taxi stand is? 택시 승차장이 어디에 있는지 알려주실래요?

I think that it's at the other end of the terminal. Just follow the signs and you'll find it 터미널 맞은 편에 있는 거 같아요. 저 표지판들만 따라가다 보면 나올 거예요

I need to get to the Delta Inn 델타 인으로 가려고 하는데요

How long will it take for us to reach the Inn? 가는 데 얼마 걸리죠?

Do you need to put anything in the trunk? 짐을 트렁트에 넣으실래요?

Well, here we are. Let me unload your luggage for you 자, 다 왔습니다. 짐을 내려 드리죠

How much is the fare? 요금이 얼마죠?

Here's twenty dollars, and keep the change 여기 20달러예요. 거스름돈은 가지세요

I need to get to the Delta Inn 델타 인으로 가려고 하는데요

Can you tell me how to get to the Ford Hotel? 포드호텔에 어떻게 가는지 알려줄래요?

Where can I get a taxi to the Inter Continental Hotel? 인터콘티넨탈에 가려면 어디서 택시를 타야 돼요?

Would you take us to the Inter Continental Hotel? 인터콘티넨탈로 데려다 줄래요?

Chapter **03** 호텔 | 관광

01 **호텔** 오늘 밤 방 있나요?

I'd like a twin room for three night, please
3일 묵을 트윈룸을 부탁해요

Is there a room available for tonight? 오늘 밤 방 있나요?

Do you have a room for tonight? 오늘 밤 방 있어요?

What kind of room do you want? 어떤 종류의 방을 드릴까요?

Can you recommend any other hotel? 다른 호텔 추천해주실래요?

Would you refer me to another hotel? 다른 호텔 추천해줄래요?

How many nights? 몇 일밤 묵을 실건가요?

Let me just check to see if a room is available for you
이용할 수 있는 방이 있는지 금방 확인해보도록 하죠

Just one night. How much does it cost?
하룻밤요. 얼마입니까?

What is the rate for a single room per night?
싱글룸으로 하룻밤 얼마입니까?

I want to stay for two nights 2박 3일 묵을 겁니다

Is there a cheaper room? 더 싼 방이 있나요?

Can I change my room? 방을 바꿀 수 있어요?

We have a single for 40 dollars per night
싱글룸은 하룻밤에 40달러입니다

I'd like the most inexpensive room you have for three nights 3박 4일 묵을 건데 가장 저렴한 방을 주세요

I'd like a room with an ocean view 바닷가가 보이는 방을 주세요

This room is too small. I'd like to change to a larger room, please 이 방은 너무 작네요. 큰 방으로 바꿔주세요

필수활용어구

information desk 안내 데스크 | (airport) limo 공항 리무진 버스(=limousine) |
shuttle bus 일정한 장소를 왕복 운행하는 셔틀 버스 | tag[label] 꼬리표(를 붙이다) |
taxi stand 택시 승차장

I'd like to change to a double room, please 더블룸으로 바꿔주세요

Where is the fire exit? 비상구가 어디인가요?

02 호텔 예약을 했는데요. 저는 김성수라고 합니다

Does this rate include breakfast? 이 요금에 조식이 포함되어 있나요?

Check in, please 체크인 해주세요

I'd like to check in 체크인 할게요

When's the checking time? 체크인 타임이 언제인가요?

What time can I check in? 언제 체크인 하나요?

Your room won't be ready until 1 o'clock 한 시에 입실가능합니다

Can you keep my bags until I check in?
체크인 할 때까지 가방 좀 맡아주세요

The travel agency made a reservation for me
여행사가 예약을 해놨어요

I have a reservation 예약을 했는데요

I've reserved a single[double] 싱글(더블)룸 예약했습니다

I have a confirmed reservation 예약 확인했는데요

I reserved a room for tonight 오늘 밤 예약했는데요

I have a reservation. I'm Sung-su Kim 예약했는데 김성수라고 합니다

Hi, my name is Ki-su Park and I'm here to check in
안녕하세요, 저는 박기수라고 하는데요. 첵인을 하려구요

I have your reservation. Are you still planning to stay the third night? 예약되어 있네요. 3일간 묵기로 되어 있는데, 변함없으신가요?

Yes, we have your name. Welcome to our hotel
네, 예약되어 있네요. 저희 호텔에 오셔서 반갑습니다

Sorry, but I can't find your name 죄송하지만, 성함이 없는데요

Your room number is 505. Here is the key
505호실 입니다. 여기 열쇠있습니다

Take my baggage, please 가방 좀 들어줘요

Can you keep my valuables? 귀중품을 맡길 수 있어요?

I'd like the key to room 1024, please 1024호 열쇠 좀 주세요

I'd like to leave my room key, please 키를 맡겨놓을려구요

Where is the dining room? 식당이 어디예요?

Where can I get some beer? 맥주는 어디서 살 수 있어요?

Could you recommend a place that will deliver to the hotel? 호텔로 시켜먹을 만한 곳을 추천해주실래요?

What time do you serve breakfast?
아침은 몇 시에 먹을 수 있습니까?

What time does the dining room open? 식당은 언제 문 열어요?

You can call down to the reception at any time by dialing 0 on your phone 방 전화기의 0번을 누르시면 언제든 접수창구와 통화하실 수 있습니다

> 호텔에서 지내면서

03 호텔 문이 잠겨서 못 들어가요

I'd like a wake-up call, please 모닝콜 좀 부탁해요

A wake-up call, please 모닝콜 요

What time do you want the call? 몇 시에 전화해드릴까요?

I need to be woken up at 6:00 am. I'm a heavy sleeper so you may have to let it ring for a while 아침 6시에 일어나야 해요. 전 깊게 잠들기 때문에 꽤 전화벨을 울려야 할지도 모르겠어요

필수활용어구

check-in counter 호텔에 도착하여 체크인절차를 밟는 곳 | reservation [confirmation] slip 예약확인표 | suite 호텔에서 침실 외에 거실·응접실 등이 딸려 있는 방 | room won't be ready until + 시간 …시 이후에 방에 들어갈 수 있다 | room service 룸 서비스. 객실로 음식을 직접 가져다 주는 서비스[사람] | access one's e-mail 이메일에 접속하다 | maintenance 호텔 내의 각종 시설을 보수, 정비하는 「관리부」 | send A up …를 올려보내다 | wake-up call 모닝콜 | heavy sleeper 깊게 잠드는 사람 | tip 팁 (을 주다), 봉사료 | check out 체크아웃하다, 호텔에서 계산을 하고 나가다 | concierge 호텔 관리인[안내인] | available 이용할 수 있는. 호텔의 경우 「방이 남아 있어 투숙할 수 있는」이란 의미 | ~ nights ~박 | registration card 숙박계 | room rate 객실료

Room service, please 룸서비스 좀 부탁해요

Hello. This is room 510. I'd like to order something to eat, but I'm not sure which menu to use 여보세요. 510호실인데요. 식사주문을 하려구요. 그런데 어떤 메뉴판을 보고 골라야 할지 모르겠어요

Please bring me a pot of coffee 커피포트 좀 갖다줘요

Laundry service, please 세탁서비스 좀 부탁해요

Could you recommend a place that will deliver to the hotel? 호텔로 시켜먹을 만한 곳을 추천해주실래요?

Antonio's Pizza is really good, the number is 967-1111 앤토니오 피자가 아주 맛있어요. 전화번호는 967-1111입니다

I was wondering if you could recommend a restaurant at the hotel 호텔에 있는 식당 좀 추천해주실 수 있을까요?

The restaurant on the second floor is well known for its Indian food 2층에 가시면 인도 음식을 잘하는 식당이 있어요

I'd like to know how I can access my e-mail 이메일에 접속할 수 있는 방법을 알고 싶은데요

Are there any messages for me? 혹 메시지 온 거 있습니까?

If you have your own computer you can plug it into the jack beside the phone line 컴퓨터를 가지고 계시면 전화선 옆에 있는 잭에 꽂으시면 됩니다

This is room 501. There is no hot water 501호인데 온수가 안 나와요

The TV doesn't work in my room TV가 작동 안돼요

I'm calling from room 478 and the air conditioner won't seem to shut off 여긴 478호실인데요. 에어컨이 꺼지질 않아요

I pushed the button, but cool air doesn't come out 버튼을 눌렀는데 찬 공기가 안 나와요

Could you send someone up? 사람 좀 보내줄래요?

Please send someone to help me 사람 좀 보내서 저 좀 도와주세요

Could you send someone to fix it? 사람 좀 보내 고쳐줄래요?

My room hasn't been cleaned yet 방이 청소가 덜 됐네요

I'm afraid the sheets are not clean 시트가 깨끗하지 않아요

I locked myself out 문이 잠겨서 못 들어가요

I went out without the key, so I'm locked out of my room
열쇠를 두고 나와 방에 못 들어가요

I left[forgot] my key inside my room
방에 열쇠를 두고 나왔어요

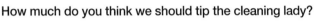

I don't know how to use the card key
이 카드키를 어떻게 사용하는지 모르겠어요

I forgot my room number 방번호를 잊었어요

I'm lost. I want to go back to room 203
길을 잃었어요. 203호로 가려는데요

How much do you think we should tip the cleaning lady?
청소부 팁 얼마 줘야 돼?

There is no shampoo in the bath room 욕실에 샴푸가 없어요

It's too noisy to sleep in this room 이 방은 자기에 너무 시끄러워요

The hot water doesn't come out 온수가 안 나와요

Can I control the air conditioning in the room?
방에서 에어컨 조정할 수 있어요?

Could you please explain to me about these switches?
이 스위치에 대해 설명해줄래요?

The elevator stopped. Help me! 엘리베이터가 멈췄어요. 도와주세요!

What kind of facilities are there in the hotel?
호텔에 어떤 시설들이 있나요?

Could you charge it to my room?
이거 제 방으로 청구해주세요

체크아웃 일자 변경

04 호텔 하룻밤 더 묵어도 돼요?

I need to stay another day 하루 더 묵으려고 하는데요

Unfortunately, I need to leave today instead of tomorrow
유감스럽게도 내일이 아니라 오늘 떠나게 되었습니다

My name is Mr. Jung and I was staying in room 307.
Unfortunately, I need to leave today instead of tomorrow

이름은 '정'이고 307호에 묵었는데 유감스럽게도 내일이 아니라 오늘 떠나게 되었습니다

It's Mr. Suh in room 301, I need to stay another day
301호의 '서' 라고 하는데요, 하루 더 묵으려고 해서요

This is Mr. Kim, room 890, and I'd like to check out on the 11th instead of 10th 890호의 김입니다. 10일이 아닌 11일에 체크아웃을 하려 합니다

I'm Mr. Jung, room 304, and I'd like to stay until 30th instead of 20th 304호의 정인데요 20일 대신 30일까지 머물려고요

This is Mr. Choi, room 405. I'll be checking out about 10:30. Could you send someone up for my bags? 405호의 최입니다. 10시30분에 체크아웃하려는데 가방 들어 줄 사람 좀 올려주실래요?

I'd like to stay two more nights, please 이틀 더 묵을게요

Can I stay one more night? 하룻밤 더 묵어도 돼요?

체크아웃하면서

05 호텔 체크아웃합니다. 505호실 장입니다

I'd like to check out now 체크아웃을 하고 싶은데요

Check out, please 체크아웃 할게요

Could you tell me your room number please?
방 번호를 말씀해 주시겠습니까?

I was staying in room 501
501호에 묵었습니다

I'm checking out. Room 505, Mr. Jang
체크아웃합니다. 505호실 장입니다

Here's your bill 청구서 여기 있습니다

I'll get your bill for you 계산서를 갖다 드리겠습니다

How would you like to pay for the room, Mr. Kim?
어떻게 지불하고 싶으십니까, 김 선생님?

There seems to be some mistake, you have charged me for all four nights 좀 잘못된 게 있는 것 같군요. 4일밤 묵은 걸로 청구하셨네요

I'll be paying with traveler's checks 계산은 여행자 수표로 할게요

Can I pay for that all on one bill?
나중에 전부 다 한 청구서로 계산할 수 있나요?

Please get a taxi for me at 10 am 아침 10시까지 택시불러 주세요

I'm checking out. This is the key 체크아웃합니다. 여기 열쇠요

I didn't use anything from the refrigerator
냉장고에 있는 거 아무 것도 이용하지 않았어요

I didn't use the fridge 냉장고 사용하지 않았어요

I left something in the room. Can I go back in?
방에 뭔가 두고 왔는데, 들어가도 돼요?

What time does the limo leave? 리무진 버스는 몇 시에 출발하나요?

Is it possible to use a limousine bus to the airport?
공항까지 리무진 버스 이용가능해요?

How often does the limousine leave for the airport?
공항가는 리무진 버스는 얼마나 자주 오나요?

When does the next limousine leave?
다음 리무진 버스는 언제 출발해요?

I had a wonderful time at this hotel, thank you
이 호텔에서 멋진 시간 보냈어요. 고마워요

This is a very good hotel 아주 좋은 호텔입니다

I like this hotel very much 이 호텔이 정말 좋아요

I enjoyed the stay so much 호텔에 머물면서 아주 좋았어요

관광할 때

06 관광 시카고에서 볼 좋은 곳 알아

Where's the tourist information center?
관광안내센터가 어디에 있어요?

Can I get a tourist information guide?
관광정보가이드를 구할 수 있을까요?

May I have a city map?
시내 지도를 얻을 수 있어요?

Where is the gift shop? 기념품 점이 어디에 있어요?

Is there a souvenir shop in the hotel? 호텔에 기념품 점이 있어요?

Please tell me about some interesting places in this town
시내에 볼만한 곳 좀 알려줘요

I was hoping that you could suggest an interesting place close by 주위에 가볼 만한 곳을 권해 주셨으면 하는데요

What do you recommend for sightseeing?
관광지로 어디를 추천하시겠어요?

Do you know any good places to stay[see, eat] in Chicago?
시카고에서 머무를[볼, 먹을] 좋은 곳 알아?

What is the best place to visit in this town?
이 마을에서 가장 방문하기 좋은 곳은 어디 인가요?

What are your interests? 어디가 관심있어요?

Are there any sightseeing buses? 관광버스가 있어요?

Is there a sightseeing bus tour? 관광버스투어가 있어요?

What kinds of tours are there? 어떤 종류의 관광이 있나요?

Tell me about the day trip, please 당일 여행에 대해 말해주세요

Can I buy a ticket on the day of the tour?
당일 여행 티켓을 살 수 있을까요?

Which tour returns by five p.m.?
오후 5시에 돌아오는 관광투어가 어떤 겁니까?

Is there any famous places to visit around here?
이 근처에 방문할 유명한 곳이 있습니까?

I'd like to join the tour 그 관광투어를 하고 싶어요

Is there a sightseeing tour bus for the town?
시내 관광투어버스가 있나요?

What kind of places do we visit on this tour?
이 투어에서는 어느 곳을 방문하나요?

Which is the most popular tour?
가장 인기있는 관광투어가 어떤 건가요?

Do you have a night time tour? 밤시간 관광투어가 있나요?

Can I find another tour to join now?
지금 할 수 있는 또 다른 투어가 있나요?

Can I go to the Niagara Falls in this tour?
이번 투어에서 나이아가라 폭포에 갈 수 있나요?

Are meals included in the tour price?
투어비용에 식사가 포함되어 있나요?

I'd like a tour by a taxi 택시타고 둘러볼려고요

I'd like a guide 가이드가 필요해요

I want a Korean-speaking guide
한국말하는 가이드가 필요해요

What a beautiful view! 참 멋진 광경야!

Nice place! 멋진 곳이네요!

When does the museum open? 박물관은 언제 문 열어요?

Are they open on Saturdays? 토요일 날에도 문 여나요?

I want to stay longer 더 머물려고요

Let's leave now 지금 나가자

May I take a picture? 사진 찍어도 돼요?

Would you mind posing with me? 저와 사진 찍어도 될까요?

Can I take a picture with you? 당신과 사진을 찍어도 될까요?

**We'd like to take a picture of you and us together. Is it all
right?** 우리 함께 사진 찍어요? 괜찮겠어요?

Can I take a picture of this building? 이 건물 사진 찍어도 되나요?

I'd like two tickets for today's game 오늘 게임 표 2장 주세요

Two tickets, please 2장 요

Are there any seats available? 좌석 남아 있나요?

Do you have time for shopping? 쇼핑할 시간이 있나요?

What does it cost for one person? 일인 당 비용이 어떻게 돼나요?

How late are you open? 언제까지 여나요?

What's the admission charge? 입장료가 얼마인가요?

Where can I see 'Phantom of the Opera?'
어디서 오페라의 유령을 볼 수 있을까요?

Where can I get a ticket? 어디서 표를 살 수 있습니까?

I'd like a seat on the first base side 1루석 쪽에 표를 주세요

Is there any good movie showing? 좋은 영화하는 것 있어요?

Is there any movie theater near here? 이 근처에 좋은 영화관 있나요?

What kind of movies are showing? 무슨 종류의 영화가 하나요?

I prefer some comedies 난 코미디를 좋아해

Do you come here often? 여기 자주 오나요?

This is my second visit here 여기 두번째 방문예요

I'm a tourist 관광객입니다

I'm from Korea and this is my second time in Boston
한국에서 왔고 보스톤은 두번 째 방문입니다

I'd like to get a hair cut 머리를 깍아주세요

Would you like to have a perm? 파마하시겠어요?

What are the games for beginners at the Casino?
카지노에서 초보자에게 좋은 게임이 뭐가 있나요?

Which is better for a start? 시작하기에 어떤 것이 좋은가요?

Slot machine. Put a coin into a slot. That's all
슬롯머신요. 구멍에 코인을 넣기만 하면 돼요

Where can I get those chips? 저 칩들은 어디서 살 수 있을까요?

Cash my chips, please 이 칩을 현금으로 바꿔주세요

관광에서 어려움을 겪을 때

07 관광 신용카드를 도난 당했으니 정지시켜주세요

My English isn't good enough 영어가 딸려서요

I'm a beginner in English, so please go slowly when you talk to me 영어초보여서 말하실 때 천천히 해주세요

I don't know how to say it in English
그걸 영어로 어떻게 말하는지 모르겠어요

How do you say 'chobop' in English?
초밥을 영어로 뭐라고 하지요?

What's 'chobop' in English? 초밥이 영어로 뭐야?

What's the English word for 'chobop'?
초밥을 영어로 하면 어떻게 돼?

What do you call this in English? 이걸 영어로 뭐라고 해요?

Where is the lost and found? 분실물보관소가 어디예요?

Call the police! My bag was stolen!
경찰을 불러요! 가방을 도난 당했어요!

Is there a police station close by? 근처에 경찰서가 있나요?

Who should I report it to? 어디에 신고해야 하죠?

I'd like to have a Korean interpreter
한국말 통역하는 사람이 필요해요

I need somebody who understands Korean
한국어를 할 줄 아는 사람이 필요해요

Does anyone here speak Korean?
여기 누구 한국말 하는 사람 있어요?

Where is the Korean Embassy?
한국 대사관이 어디 있어요?

I lost my passport 여권을 잃어버렸어요

I can't find my passport 여권을 못 찾겠어요

I'd like to have my passport reissued 여권을 재발급해주세요

I had my purse stolen 지갑을 분실했어요

I had my credit card stolen, please cancel it
신용카드를 도난 당했으니 정지시켜주세요

Please cancel my credit card 신용카드를 정지시켜주세요

I don't remember where I lost it
어디서 잃어버렸는지 기억이 안나요

I left my suitcase in the taxi 택시에 가방을 두고 내렸어요

Excuse me, but can you make an announcement?
죄송하지만 안내방송 좀 해주시겠어요?

My daughter is missing. I'm sure she's in this department
딸을 잃어버렸는데 백화점에 있을 거예요

Where did you lose her? 따님을 어디서 잃어버렸나요?

필수활용어구

interesting place 흥미로운 곳, 재미있는 곳, 구경할 만한 곳 | traveler's check 여행
자 수표 | beauty parlor 미장원 | admission fee 입장료 | ticket office 매표소 |
fill in 기입하다 | intermission (공연)막간 | checkroom[cloakroom] 소지품보관소

How old does she look? 인상착의를 말해주세요

She has long black hair 검은 머리가 길어요

She wears a blue shirt and skirt 파란 셔츠와 치마를 입었어요

은행이용하기

08 관광 원화를 달러로 바꿔주세요

Where is the currency exchange office? 환전소가 어디입니까?

I'd like to change won to dollars, please 원화를 달러로 바꿔주세요

Yen to dollars, please 엔화를 달러로 바꿔줘요

Could you cash this traveler's check for me?
이 여행자 수표를 현금으로 바꿔줄래요?

I'd like to cash this check 이 수표를 현금으로 주세요

I'd like to cash my traveler's check
여행자 수표를 현금으로 바꿀려고요

Do you have any identification?
신분 증명할 거 뭐 있어요?

Please fill this out 이걸 작성하세요

I'd like to deposit $200 200달러 예금하려고요

I'd like to withdraw $100 100달러 인출하려고요

I'd like to open an account at your bank
여기 은행에 계좌 하나 만들려고요

I'd like to open a savings account
저축계좌 만들려고요

I'd like to close my account and withdraw my money
계좌 끝내고 돈 인출해주세요

Please endorse it 이서하세요

Would you please break this 100 dollar bill for me?
100달러 지폐를 작은 것으로 바꿔줄래요?

I'd like this fifty broken into tens 이 50달러를 10달러지폐로 바꿔줘요

Please make it four tens and ten ones
이걸 10달러짜리 4개와 1달러짜리 10개로 바꿔줘요

Do you have an account with us?
저희 은행 계좌 갖고 계신가요?

I lost my ATM card and need a replacement
카드분실로 재발행해주세요

The ATM in your lobby isn't working
로비에 있는 ATM기가 작동안돼요

What's the interest rate on my savings account?
저축계좌 이자율은 요?

What time does your bank open? 은행은 언제 여나요?

Chapter 04 전화 | 통신

01 통화 워싱톤호텔 전화번호를 알고 싶은데요

I'd like to know the number of the Washington Hotel
워싱톤 호텔 전화번호를 알고 싶은데요

I'd like to talk to Mr. Kim, room number 539
539호실의 김선생님 바꿔주세요

Hello, is this United Airlines?
안녕하세요, 유나이티드 항공사이죠?

Is there a public telephone nearby?
근처에 공중전화가 있나요?

Where is the public phone?
공중전화는 어디 있나요?

Can I make an international call on this phone?
이 전화기로 국제전화가 가능한가요?

I'll connect you with the international operator
해외안내원 연결해드릴게요

Your party is on the line. Please go ahead
상대방이 연결되었습니다. 말씀하세요

I'd like to call to Korea. I'm Mr. Kim In-soo, room 609. The number is 89-2-345-9876 한국으로 전화하려구요. 609호의 김인수입니다. 번호는 89-2-345-9876입니다

I'd like to make a collect call to Korea. I'm Jung Soo-ja, room 421. I'd like to speak to Mr. Park at 89-31-384-3334
한국으로 콜렉트콜 하려고요. 421호의 정수자인데 89-31-384-3334번의 박 선생님 부탁해요

I'd like to make a person-to-person call to Korea. I'm Shin Sun-ho, room 343. I'd like to speak to Ms. Kim at 89-42-342-0987 한국으로 지명통화하려구요. 전 343호의 신선호인데 89-42-342-0987의 김 선생님 연결해주세요

02 **통화** 밀러 씨 좀 바꿔줄래요?

Can[May] I speak to Mr. Miller? 밀러 씨 좀 바꿔줄래요?

I'd like to speak to the branch manager, please
지사장님 연결해줘요

I'm calling to talk to Mr. Kim in the marketing department
마케팅부 김선생님과 통화하려고요

Is Mr. Jones there? 존스 씨 계세요?, 존스 씨와 통화하고 싶은데요?

Is Mr. Jones in? 존스 씨 계세요?

Is Mr. Jones in the office? 존스 씨 사무실에 계세요?

Please give me Jane 제인 좀 바꿔주세요

Mr. Levine, please 레빈 씨 좀 부탁해요

Let me talk to Mr. Levine, please 레빈 씨와 통화할게요

Is this the Astron Insurance Company? 애스트론 보험사인가요?

Is Mr. Kim available? 김 선생님 계세요?

Is Mr. Kim free right now? 김 선생님 지금 통화 돼나요?

Is this Mr. Dennis Smith? 데니스 스미스 씨입니까?

Is this the billing department? 경리부인가요?

Would you put me through to the billing department?
경리부 연결해주세요

Would you transfer this call to extension 104? 104번으로 돌려줘요

Extension 104, please 104번 부탁해요

May I have extension 104? 104번 좀 바꿔줄래요?

I'd like to get through to Mr. Berkman 버크만 씨 좀 통화하려고요

I need to talk to Mr. Harris immediately 해리스 씨와 급히 통화해야 해요

It's me 나야

필수활용어구

operator 전화 교환원 | collect call 수신자 부담 전화 | local call 시내전화 | direct
phone 직통전화 | area code 지역번호 | long distance call 장거리 전화 |
extension 내선 | pay phone[public telephone] 공중전화

03 통화 누구세요?

Who's calling please? 누구세요?

May I ask who's calling? 누구십니까?

Who is this, please? 누구시죠?

NTB Company, may I help you? NTB 회사입니다, 뭘 도와드릴까요?

Marketing department 마케팅 부입니다

This is James Young 제임스 영이에요

This is he 전데요

This is 전데요

Speaking 전데요

It's me, Jane 나야, 제인

How may I direct your call? 어디 연결해드릴까요?

Who do you want to speak to? 어느 분을 바꿔줄까요?

Who would you like to talk to? 어느 분을 바꿔드릴까요?

Who are you trying to reach? 어느 분과 통화하실려구요?

I'll put you through (right away) (바로) 바꿔드리죠

I'll transfer your call 전화 바꿔드릴게요

I'll connect you 연결해 드릴게요

I'll get him for you 바꿔드리죠

Which Mr. Kim do you want to talk to? 어느 미스터 김과 통화하시겠어요?

There are four Kims here 여기에 미스터 김이 4명 있거든요

필수활용어구

I'd like to speak with …와 통화하고 싶어 | May I speak to ~? …를 바꿔주시겠어요? | I'm calling to~ …하려고 전화하는거야 | transfer A to~ A를 …로 연결시켜주다 | leave a message 메시지를 남기다 | have A call …에게 전화하라고 하다 | call back 다시 전화하다 | have a call on the other line 다른 전화가 와있다 | get back to …에게 다시 연락하다

04 **통화** 잠시 기다릴래요?

Hold on 잠깐만요, 끊지말고 기다려요

Hang on 잠시만요

Hold the line, please 잠시만요

Could you hold? 잠시 기다리실래요?

Can you hold the line, please? 잠시만 기다려줄래요?

Wait a minute[second] 잠깐만요

Just a moment[minute; second], please 잠시만요

One moment, please 잠시만요

Would you like to hold (on)? 기다리시겠어요?

Sorry to keep you waiting 기다리게 해서 미안해요

I shouldn't have tied you up so long 너무 기다리게 하는 게 아닌데

I've been on hold for a couple of minutes already
벌써 몇 분 동안 기다렸어요

05 **통화** 너한테 전화왔어

(There's a) Phone call for you 너한테 전화왔어

You have a phone call 전화왔어요

You've got a call from a friend 한 친구가 전화했어요

You are wanted on the telephone
너한테 전화왔어

Some guy just called for you
방금 어떤 사람한테서 전화왔었어

I have a call for you 전화왔어

You have[There's] a call from Mr. Smith of XYZ Company
XYZ회사의 스미스 씨 전화왔어요

Mr. Carter of XYZ is on line 2
2번 라인에 XYZ회사의 카터 씨 전화와 있어요

Mr. Carter for you 카터 씨예요

It's your girlfriend on the line
여자 친구 전화 와 있어요

Excuse me, there's a call on another line 실례지만 다른 전화 와 있어요

전화를 바꿔줄 수 없을 때

06 불통 지금 통화중이신데요

Her line is busy now 지금 통화 중이신데요

(I'm afraid) She's on the other line now 지금 다른 전화 받고 계세요

He's talking to someone else now 지금 다른 분과 얘기 중이세요

I'm sorry, but he has someone with him right now
미안하지만 지금 손님이 와 계신데요

I'm sorry, but she's busy at the moment 미안하지만 지금 바쁘세요

I'm sorry, he's not in right now 미안하지만 지금 안에 안 계세요

He's in, but he's not at his desk right now
안에 계시는데 지금 자리엔 없네요

He's not here now 지금 여기 안 계세요

He's out to lunch now 지금 점심 식사하러 나가셨어요

He hasn't come back from his lunch yet
아직 점심식사에서 안 돌아오셨어요

He's out now 지금 외출 중이에요

He's out of the office right now 지금 외근 중이에요

He's out on business 출장이에요

I'm afraid he's on a business trip 미안하지만 출장 중이신데요

He's away on business for a week 일주일 간 출장 중이세요

He's out of town now 지금 출장 중이에요

He's in a meeting right now 지금 회의 중이세요

The advertising department is meeting now
광고부는 지금 회의 중예요

He's off today 오늘 쉬어요

When do you expect him back? 언제 돌아오실까요?

How soon do you expect him back? 언제쯤 돌아오실까요?

When is he coming back? 언제 돌아와요?

I'm afraid he's left for the day 오늘 퇴근했어요

He won't be back in the office today 오늘 안 돌아오실거예요

He should be back in ten minutes 10분내로 돌아올거예요

He'll be back in the afternoon 오후에 돌아올거예요

Would you like to talk to someone else? 다른 분하고 통화하실래요?

전화연결이 안 되어서 메시지를 주고 받을 때

07 불통 메모 좀 남겨주세요

Could[May] I leave a message? 메모 좀 전해줄래요?

I'd like to leave a message 메모 좀 남길게요

Please take a message 메모 좀 남겨주세요

Could[May] I take a message? 메시지를 전해드릴까요?

Would you like to leave a message? 메시지를 남기시겠어요?

Would you tell him that Jim called? 짐이 전화했다고 전해줄래요?

Do you want him to call you back? 전화하라고 할까요?

Would you like him to call you back? 전화드리라고 할까요?

Just have him call me (back) 그냥 전화 좀 해달라고 해주세요

Please tell[ask] him to call me 내게 전화해달라고 하세요

Please tell him that I'll call him back 내가 전화 다시 할거라고 전해주세요

I'll tell him that you called 전화하셨다고 말할게요

I'll have him call you back 전화드리도록 할게요

I'll tell[ask] him to call you back 전화드리도록 말할게요

How can I get in touch with him? 그 사람 연락처가 어떻게 됩니까?

How can he get in contact with you? 어떻게 당신께 연락드리죠?

Are there any messages? 메시지 뭐 온 거 있어요?

Do you have any messages? 메시지 뭐 있어요?

Any messages or phone calls? 메시지나 전화없었어?

Mr. Miller called you during the meeting 밀러 씨가 회의중 전화하셨어요

May I have your number? 번호 좀 알려줄래요?

Your number, please? 번호 좀 요?

What's your number? 번호 어떻게 돼요?

May I have your name again, please? 성함 좀 다시 말해줄래요?

전화가 잘못 걸렸을 때

08 불통 잘못 거셨네요

How do you spell your name? 성함 철자 어떻게 쓰나요?

Could you please spell your name? 성함 철자 좀 말해줄래요?

(I'm afraid) You have the wrong number 전화 잘못 거셨어요

You must have the wrong number 전화 잘못 하셨어요

I'm sorry, you've got the wrong number 미안하지만 전화 잘못 하셨어요

Sorry, wrong number 미안하지만 전화 잘못 걸었어요

What number are you calling[dialing]? 어디로 전화하셨어요?

What number are you trying to reach? 어느 번호로 전화하신 거예요?

There's no one here by that name 그런 분 여기 안 계세요

There's no Anderson in this office 사무실에 앤더슨이란 사람 없어요

There's nobody named Anderson here
여기 앤더슨이란 이름의 사람은 없어요

혼선이나 전화 상태가 안 좋을 때

09 불통 좀 천천히 말씀해주실래요?

I'm sorry, I must have misdialed 죄송해요 전화 잘 못 돌렸네요

I dialed your number by mistake 다이얼을 잘못 돌렸네요

I'm sorry, I can't hear you (very well) 죄송하지만 (잘) 안 들려요

I'm having trouble hearing you 잘 들리지 않아요

Would you speak more slowly, please? 좀 천천히 말씀해주실래요?

Could you speak a little louder, please? 좀 크게 말씀해줄래요?

Could you repeat that? 다시 한번 말해줄래요?

We have a bad connection 혼선이야

You sound very far away 감이 아주 멀어

There's noise on my line 내 전화선에 소음이 있어

Let me call you from another line 다른 선으로 전화할게

Could you dial again? 다시 걸래요?

The phone went dead 전화가 죽었어

I was cut off 전화가 끊겼어

┌─ 다음에 통화하자고 하면서 전화를 끊을 때 ─┐

10 전화끊기 그만 끊을게

I have to go now 전화 그만 끊어야 겠어

I've got to go 그만 끊을게

It's been good talking to you 통화해서 좋았어요

I'm sorry, I can't talk long 미안하지만 길게 얘긴 못해

(I'll) Talk to you soon 또 걸게, 다음에 통화하자

Talk to you tomorrow 내일 통화하자

Could you call back later? 나중에 전화할래?

Would you mind calling back later? 나중에 전화해도 돼?

Would you call again later? 나중에 전화할래요?

Please call me back in ten minutes 10분 후에 전화 줘

Please call again anytime 아무 때나 전화 다시 해

I'll call back later 나중에 전화할게

I'll call you again 다시 전화할게

I'll catch up with you later 나중에 연락할게

Get back to me 나중에 연락해

필수활용어구

make[place] an overseas call 국제 전화를 하다 | be connected 전화가 연결되다
| hold (전화를 끊지 않고) 기다리다 | have A on the line A로부터 전화가 와 있다 |
answer the phone 전화를 받다 | be set to vibrate (휴대폰을) 진동으로 해놓다 |
text message 문자 메시지 | person-to-person call 지명 통화 전화

I'll get back to you when you're not so busy
너 안 바쁠 때 다시 전화할게

Could I call you? 나중에 전화해도 될까요?

Would you please get off the phone? 전화 좀 끊을테야?

Give me a call[ring; buzz] 전화해

Thank you[Thanks] for calling 전화줘서 고마워

Thank you for your call 전화줘서 고마워

Thank you for returning my call 전화걸어줘서 고마워

핸드폰 영어표현

11 핸드폰 문자메시지로 보내줄게

I'm sorry, but my phone was set to vibrate
미안해요, 진동으로 했놓았거든요

I always have my phone on vibrate
난 핸드폰 항상 진동으로 해놔

My cell phone is on silent mode
내 휴대폰은 진동으로 해놨어

Did you see that I sent you a text message?
제가 보낸 문자 받았어?

I'll send it to you in a text message 문자메시지로 보내줄게

I'm calling you because I saw that you called me
부재중 전화가 와서 전화하는거야

The first name on my speed number is you
스피드 단축번호의 첫 번째 이름은 너야

Call me on you cell phone 핸드폰으로 전화해

She's on a cell phone 핸드폰으로 통화중이야

Why didn't you answer your cell phone? 왜 핸드폰 안 받았어?

I forgot it at home today 집에 놔두고 왔어

I turned my cell phone off 핸드폰 꺼놨어

You're breaking up 소리가 끊겨

My cell phone isn't getting good reception
내 핸드폰 수신상태가 안 좋아

We get bad reception in the elevator
엘리베이터에서는 수신상태가 안 좋아

I've been calling your cell phone 네 핸드폰으로 계속 전화했어

My battery went dead and it stopped working
배터리가 죽어서 작동이 안돼

My battery is dying 배터리가 다해서 끊어지려고 해

You'd better keep your cell phone charged
핸드폰 충전해놓고 다녀

Is your cell phone not working? 핸드폰 안돼?

Your cell phone is ringing 너 핸드폰 온다

I like your ring tone 벨소리 좋네

Do you mind if I answer this call? 이 전화 받아도 돼요?

전화영어에 자주 쓰이는 표현들

12 기타 더 빨리 연락 못줘서 미안해

I'm sorry for calling you this late 너무 늦게 전화해서 미안해

Am I calling too late? 내가 너무 늦게 전화했니?

I hope I'm not disturbing you 방해한 게 아니었으면 해

I'm calling to ask you for a favor 도움 좀 청하려고 전화했어

I'm calling about tomorrow's meeting 내일 회의 문제로 전화한거야

Excuse me, is there someone there who can speak Korean?
실례지만, 한국어하는 사람 있어요?

Are you (still) there? 듣고 있는 거니?, 여보세요?

I called, but your line was busy 전화했는데 통화 중이더라

I was expecting your call 네 전화 기다리고 있었어

He's expecting your call 당신 전화를 기다리고 있었어요

Where can I reach him? 어떻게 그 사람에게 연락하죠?

You can reach me at 011-667-1957 until six o'clock
6시까진 011-667-1957으로 하세요

Hello, I got your message on my answering machine
여보세요, 응답기에 메시지가 있어서

I heard you called this morning 오늘 아침 전화했다고 들었어요

You called? 전화하셨어요?

I'm sorry I wasn't in when you called 전화했을 때 자리 비워서 미안해요

I'm returning your call 전화했다고 해서 하는 거야

I'm sorry I didn't get back to you sooner 더 빨리 연락 못 줘서 미안해

Hello, this is Mr. Fick and I'm returning Mr. Kim's call
픽예요 김선생이 전화했다고 해서요

I'm sorry I've taken so much of your time 너무 오래 붙잡고 있었네요

He won't take my calls 걘 내 전화를 안 받으려고 해

Give me a call 전화해

I've been meaning to call you 안그래도 전화하려고 했어

I have got another call 다른 전화가 왔어

I'm getting another call 다른 전화가 오고 있는데

자동응답기에 메시지를 남기고 들을 때

13 **자동응답기** 메모 남겨주면 바로 연락할게

You've reached Ben Affleck. I can't come to the phone right now. Leave a message, and I'll return your call. Thanks. Have a great day 벤 애플렉입니다. 지금 전화를 받지 못하니 메시지 남겨주시면
전화드리겠습니다. 감사하고 좋은 하루 보내세요

You've reached Stephen King. Please leave a message after the beep 스티븐 킹입니다. 삐 소리 후에 메시지 남겨주세요

This is 459-1905. I'm not in, so please leave a message
459-1905입니다. 집에 없으니 메시지 남겨주세요

Hey, it's Ellie. Leave a message and I'll get back at you when I can 안녕하세요, 엘리입니다. 메시지 남겨주시면 가능할 때 연락드릴게요

Yeah, you got Karl. Leave a message 칼입니다. 메시지 남기세요

We're not home, please leave a message
지금 외출중이니 메시지 남겨주세요

Hey, it's Julie. I needed you to call me about our homework assignment. Please give me a call back 안녕, 줄리야. 학교 숙제 때문

에 전화 좀 해줘. 전화해

This is your mom calling. I just wanted to check in and see how things are going. Your father and I will be home tonight, so give us a call anytime 엄마다. 어떻게 지내는지 궁금해서 전화했어. 아빠하고 함께 오늘 밤 집에 있으니 언제든 전화해라

Hey there, It's me Chris. I'm going to stop by around 8 pm. Is that OK? Let me know. See you 안녕, 나 크리스야. 8시경에 들를게. 괜찮아? 알려줘. 안녕

Hello? It's Christie calling. I want you to come over in a few hours so we can study for our exam together. Would that be alright? Call me and we'll chat about it. Bye bye 안녕? 크리스티야. 몇 시간안에 우리 집에 들러. 숙제 같이 하게. 괜찮겠어? 전화해서 얘기해보자. 안녕

Hello, this is Aaron Hughes. I just wanted to check and find out if you'd like to go out to eat with me tonight 안녕, 아론 휴즈야. 오늘 밤에 함께 외식할 수 있는지 해서 전화했어

Hopefully we can grab some pizza and drinks if you have time. I'll call you about this later on 시간되면 피자하고 음료 좀 같이 먹을까해서. 나중에 전화 다시 할게

이메일 주고 받을 때

14 이메일 시간되면 이메일보내

Let's meet there at the chat room at 9:00 9시에 채팅방에서 만나자

I found your ad on the web and would like to be friends
인터넷에서 광고를 봤는데 친구하고 싶어서요

I'm afraid I sent my e-mail to the wrong address
다른 주소로 이메일을 보낸 것 같아

Please give me your e-mail address 이메일 주소 좀 알려줘

Can you give me her e-mail address?
걔 이메일 주소 좀 알려줄래?

My e-mail address is ENC@gmail.com
내 이메일 주소는 ENC@gmail.com이야

You can e-mail me at ENC@gmail.com
ENC@gmail.com로 메일 보내

I'll let you know my new e-mail address
as soon as I get it 내가 이메일 만들면 바로 새 이
메일주소 알려줄게

I have a new e-mail address because
I've changed my Internet service providers 인터넷 업체를 바꿔서
이메일 주소가 바뀌었어

My e-mail address has been changed to ENC@gmail.com
바뀐 내 이메일 주소는 ENC@gmail.com이야

Please change my address ABC@gmail.com to ENC
@gmail.com 내 이메일 주소를 ABC@gmail.com에서 ENC@gmail.com으로 바
꾸라고

Do e-mail me when you get a chance 시간되면 이메일보내

Thank you for your e-mail of March 17 3월 17일자 이메일 고마워

I'll e-mail you later 나중에 이메일 보낼게

I will send you e-mail again 다시 이메일 보낼게

I received your e-mail of June 21 6월 21일 보낸 이메일 받았어

I'm writing with regard to your e-mail of May 12
보내신 5월 12일자 이메일 건으로 글을 씁니다

I still haven't received any e-mail from you
네게서 아직 아무런 이메일도 못 받았어

Wishing you a very Merry Christmas and the happiest of
New Years 즐거운 성탄절을 맞고 행복한 새해를 맞기를 바래

Best wishes for a Happy Holiday Seasons and much
happiness in the New Year 즐거운 휴일보내고 새해엔 복 많이 받기를 바래

Wishing you a beautiful Holiday Season and a Happy New
Year 휴일 멋지게 보내고 새해 복 많이 받아

Please delete my name from your mailing list
귀사의 발송자명단에서 절 빼주세요

I just wanted to drop you an e-mail to say 'hi'
그냥 인사나 하려고 이메일보냈어

I would like to take this opportunity to thank you for your kindness and hospitality 이 기회를 빌어 당신의 친절과 호의에 감사드립니다

I'm sending a quick e-mail to let you know that I'll be arriving this Sunday 이번 일요일날 도착을 알려주려고 짧게 이메일 보내는 거야

Please forward my e-mail to my new address
내 이메일을 새로운 주소로 전송해줘

I'll be waiting to hear from you 연락기다리고 있을게

Write back when you can 시간되면 연락해

Please write me whenever you can 언제든 시간되면 연락해

I'm looking forward to hearing from you soon
소식 주기를 학수고대하고 있겠습니다

I'm looking forward to your early reply 빨리 답장 주기를 기다릴게요

We look forward to your prompt response 빠른 답신을 기다립니다

Please return e-mail ASAP 가능한한 빨리 이메일 답줘

I still haven't received a response from you
아직 너로부터 답장을 못 받았어

Thank you for your quick response 빨리 답장줘서 고마워

Thank you for your response to my e-mail of October 25
내 10월 25일자 이메일에 답장을 해줘서 고마워요

Thank you so much for your prompt reply to my e-mail of January 11 내 1월 11일자 이메일에 바로 답을 줘서 무척 고마워요

I sent a reply to you 답장 보냈어

I'm sorry I didn't reply to you sooner 빨리 답신을 못해서 미안해요

Sorry for not responding earlier
좀 더 일찍 답을 못줘 미안해

I'm sorry I haven't had time to write earlier, but I've been so busy 좀 더 일찍 소식 못 전해 미안하지만 정말 바빴어

It has taken me so long to respond to you. As you probably know, I'm busy 답장 쓰는데 시간이 너무 걸렸네. 아마 알다시피, 내가 바빠서

Attached please find a detailed statement
상세한 명세서를 첨부했습니다

I'm attaching a file to this e-mail 이 이메일에 파일을 첨부했어
Thank you for your time and thank you for reading this e-mail
시간내줘서 그리고 이 이메일을 읽어주셔서 감사합니다

I can't read the attached file 첨부파일을 읽지 못하겠어

I was unable to log on to the computer 컴퓨터에 로그인이 안됐어

I couldn't get this file to open. It reads 'error reading file.' I downloaded it several times, but the result was the same
파일이 열리지가 않아. "파일읽기에러"라고 적혀있어. 여러 번 다운로드했는데 마찬가지야

I got both of your e-mails and tried to download both files, but neither would download again. I'm not sure what the problem is, because other files that have been sent download OK 네가 보내준 메일 2개를 받았는데 다운로드가 안돼. 문제가 뭔지 모
르겠어. 다른 첨부 파일들은 다운로드 잘 되거든

Let's try sending it to my yahoo e-mail: ENC@yahoo.com. It may be a problem that is specific to hotmail. If that doesn't work, we can cut and paste the file again 내 야휴 이메일인 ENC@
yahoo.com으로 보내봐. 핫메일만의 문제일 수도 있거든. 그래도 안되면 텍스트를 잘라
붙여 보내자

For some reason the attachment wouldn't open. Could you send the general contents within an e-mail? 어떤 이유에선
가 첨부파일이 열리지 않아. 이메일에 텍스트로 보내줄래?

I'm sorry for not answering sooner. For some reason, there was a problem accessing my hotmail account the last few times I used the Internet 더 빨리 답 못해 미안. 어떤 이유에선
가 인터넷을 하는데 핫메일 계정이 열리지 않았어

Have you gotten any of my e-mails? I sent several but they have been returned to me saying the message delivery was delayed. I'm not sure if any got through to you  내가 보낸 이메일 받아봤어? 여러 번 보냈는데 발송이 지연되었다는 메시지와 함께 되돌아 와. 네가 받은 게 있는지 모르겠네

I got a notification that the e-mail I sent you had been delayed, so I'm sending it again 내가 보낸 이메일이 지연되었다고 해서 다시 보내는 거야

I am sorry I did not send it sooner. I am traveling in Paris this week, and it has been difficult to find Internet access 좀 더 빨리 보내지 못해 미안. 이번 주에 파리 여행을 하고 있어 인터넷이 되는 곳을 찾기가 어려웠어

I just got home from a trip Montreal tonight and saw your e-mail. Unfortunately, there was no chance to check e-mail when I was traveling in Canada 오늘 밤에 몬트리올에서 집에 돌아와 네 메일을 봤어. 안타깝게도 캐나다를 여행하면서 네 메일을 확인할 기회가 없었어

Starting on Sunday, I have tried to send this to you 4 times, and I'm not sure why it keeps getting rejected. Anyhow, hopefully it will reach you through your other e-mail address 일요일부터 이걸 보내려고 4번이나 해봤는데 왜 거절되어 오는지 모르겠어. 어쨌거나 네 다른 이메일 주소로 받아볼 수 있기를 바래

They went to my junk e-mail instead of my regular inbox 이메일들이 받은메일함이 아니라 스팸메일박스로 갔어

It seems like your ENC@nate.com account is working OK now. I haven't had any messages returned from it lately 네 ENC@nate.com 계정은 잘 되는 것 같아. 최근엔 반송되는게 없었어

I'm glad the files have gotten through to you. I've been sending to both of your e-mail addresses, but lately, most of the files to ENC@gmail.com seem to be getting returned. I guess the ENC@yahoo.com address is working well 파일들을 네가 받아봤다니 다행야. 네 계정 두 곳으로 보냈는데 ENC@gmail.com은 계속 반송

되는 것 같아. ENC@yahoo.com이 잘 되는 것 같아

I tried to send you this e-mail a few days ago but it keeps returning to my inbox. Please let me know if it gets to you 몇 일 전에 이 이메일을 보내려고 했는데 내 받은메일함으로 자꾸 돌아와. 혹시 받았으면 알려줘

I didn't get an e-mail from you, so I'm not sure if you received these files when I resent them to you yesterday. Anyhow, this is the third time I'm sending them, so I hope they get through to you 너한테서 이메일이 오지 않아 어제 내가 다시 보낸 이 파일들을 네가 받았는지 모르겠어. 어쨌든 3번째 이것들을 보내는데 네게 도착하기를 바래

I just sent you a file. Please check to see that you got it 방금 파일을 보냈는데 제대로 받았는지 확인해봐

I just wanted to confirm that I got your file today and will be working on it 오늘 네 파일 받아서 작업하고 있다는 걸 알려주려고

I didn't get back until very late Sunday night, and couldn't check e-mail until yesterday 일요일 저녁 늦게서야 도착했고 어제야 이메일을 확인할 수 있었어

Chapter 05 음식 | 식당

01 식당 가장 가까운 한국식당이 어디예요?

Is there a good restaurant? 좋은 식당이 있나요?

Is there a Korean restaurant close by?
근처에 한국 식당이 있습니까?

Where is the closest Korean restaurant?
가장 가까운 한국식당이 어디예요?

Which restaurant do you recommend?
어느 식당을 추천해주실래요?

Can you recommend a good restaurant for local food?
이 지역 음식을 먹을 좋은 식당을 추천해주실래요?

Which is the closest Japanese restaurant from here?
여기서 가장 가까운 일본 식당이 어느 곳인가요?

Could you recommend a good restaurant near here?
근처에 좋은 식당 추천해줄래요?

Is there a Mexican restaurant around here?
이 근처에 멕시코 식당 있나요?

Are there any restaurants still open near here?
근처에 아직 문 연 식당 있나요?

I'd like to take her out for dinner on the weekend
주말에 걔 데리고 가서 저녁먹고 싶어

I'd like to take you to try some Italian food
널 데리고 가서 이태리음식 맛보자

Would you like to join us for some cocktails?
함께 칵테일 좀 마실테야?

Is this a self service restaurant? 셀프서비스 식당인가요?

필수활용어구

delicatessen 델리카트센, 조제(調製) 식품점 | automat 간이식당 | cafeteria 카페테리아 | ethnic restaurant 민속음식점 | lunch counter 간이식당 | today's special 오늘의 요리 | seasoning 조미료, 양념 | condiments 조미료 | flavored 맛을 낸, 맛이 있는 | table d'hote 정식 | delicious 음식이 맛있는 | hot 뜨거운, 톡 쏘는 | salty 짠 | spicy 향료를 넣은, 매운(hot) | sour 시큼한, 신 | bitter 쓴

02 식당 예약을 안 했는데 자리 있나요?

I didn't make a reservation. Can I get a seat?
예약을 안 했는데 자리 있나요?

Is there a table available? 자리 있어요?

Can I take this seat? 이 자리에 앉아도 돼요?

All the seats are taken right now 모든 자리가 다 찼어요

No tables are available now 앉을 자리가 없는데요

How long do we have to wait for a table?
자리나려면 얼마나 기다려야 하나요?

What time can I get a table? 언제 자리가 나죠?

How long is the wait? 얼마나 기다려야 하나요?

How long do we have to wait? 얼마동안 기다려야 합니까?

Is the wait long? 오래 기다려야 합니까?

I'll be in the bar until I can get a seat 자리 날 때까지 바에 있죠

I've been waiting for 30 minutes 30분간 기다렸는데요

We'd like to have seats together, please 함께 앉을 자리를 주세요

03 식당 오늘 밤 4명 예약하려구요

Do I need a reservation? 예약이 필요합니까?

Is it necessary to make a reservation? 예약을 해야 하나요?

I'd like to reserve a table for seven 일곱 명 예약하고 싶은데요

What time can we make a reservation for? 몇 시에 예약할 수 있나요?

I'd like to make a reservation for four tonight
오늘 밤 4명 예약하려구요

I'd like to make a reservation for 6 o'clock 6시에 예약할게요

I'd like to make a reservation for tonight 오늘 밤에 예약할게요

All the tables are reserved for that time
그 시간에는 예약이 다 찼습니다

After eight will be fine 8시 이후에는 괜찮습니다

How many of you, sir? 몇 분이십니까?

For how many people? 몇 명이세요?

Three persons at 7 p.m. 7시에 3명입니다

Would you like a table by the window?
창가자리를 원하세요?

I'd like to reserve a table near the window 창가에 예약하고 싶어요

I'd like to get a table in the corner 구석자리를 주세요

Would you like smoking or nonsmoking? 흡연석 아니면 금연석으로요?

I'd like to have a non-smoking seat 비흡연석으로 주세요

I'm sorry. We're all booked up tonight
미안하지만 오늘밤은 예약 다 끝났어요

I'm sorry. We're quite full tonight 미안하지만 오늘 밤은 다 찼습니다

I'm sorry, but I have to cancel my reservation
죄송하지만 예약 취소해야 될 것 같아서요

Please cancel my reservation for tonight
오늘밤 예약 취소해주세요

어떤 음식을 먹을지 물어보기

04 음식 뭘 드시겠어요?

What would you like (to have)? 뭘 드시겠어요?

What will you have? 뭘 할래요?

What are you going to have? 뭘 들래?

What are you having? 넌 뭐 먹을래?

What's yours? 네 거는 뭔데?, 즐겨 마시는 게 뭔데?

What would you like to have for an appetizer?
애피타이저로 뭘 할래요?

What would you like to have for dinner this evening?
오늘 밤 저녁식사로 뭐 할래요?

What do you want to eat for lunch today? 오늘 점심 뭐 먹을래?

What's your favorite food? 어떤 음식을 좋아하세요?

I'd like to have some seafood 해산물을 먹고 싶어요

Is there any special dish that you like? 뭐 특별히 좋아하는 음식 있어?

Which do you prefer to have, Italian or Mexican food?
이태리 아니면 멕시코음식이 좋아?

Would you like some coffee? 커피 좀 들래요?

Would you care for some coffee? 커피 좀 들래요?

How about some coffee? 커피 어때?

Let's have a light meal 간단한 식사로 하자

I don't care for heavy foods 배불리 먹는 건 싫어

I don't have any strong likes or dislikes
특별히 좋아하거나 싫어하는 거 없어

Sushi is my favorite dish 스시는 내가 가장 좋아하는 음식이야

Raw fish is my least favorite food
날 생선은 내가 가장 좋아하지 않은 음식이야

I'm sick of hamburgers 햄버거는 싫증나

I don't have much of an appetite 식욕이 별로 없어

식당에서 손님에게 음식 주문을 주고 받을 때

05 **음식** 스테이크를 어떻게 해드릴까요?

Are you ready to order? 주문하시겠어요?

Are you ready for dessert? 디저트 준비하시겠어요?

May I take your order? 주문 받을까요?

What's your order? 뭘 주문하시겠습니까?

What would you like to order? 뭘 주문하시겠습니까?

Which dressing would you like with your salad?
샐러드에 무슨 드레싱을 해드릴까요?

We'll wait. Please call us when you're ready
기다리겠습니다. 준비되시면 부르세요

What can I get you, sir? 뭘 갖다 드릴까요, 손님?

What'll it be? 뭘로 드시겠어요?

Would you care for dessert? 디저트 드시겠어요?

Have you chosen your dessert? 디저트를 고르셨나요?

How would you like your steak? 스테이크를 어떻게 해드릴까요?

How would you like your steak cooked[prepared]?
스테이크를 어떻게 해드릴까요?

How would you like it done? 그걸 어떻게 해드릴까요?

How do you like your coffee? 커피 어떻게 해드릴까요?

What do you take in your coffee? 커피에 뭘 넣으시나요?

Would you care for a glass of wine with your dinner?
저녁식사에 와인 한 잔 할래요?

Is that all? 그게 전부입니까?

Would you like to order something else, or will that be all?
다른 주문하실래요 아님 다 됐나요?

Is there anything else you'd like? 다른 거 뭐 더 필요한 거는 요?

Anything else? 다른 건요?

Anything else you want?
다른 거 더 필요한 건요?

That's all (for me) (전) 됐어요

That's it 됐어요

That will be all 그게 다예요

My order[dishes] hasn't come yet 주문이 아직 안 나왔어요

We're still waiting for our food 아직 음식이 안 나왔어요

This is not what I ordered 내가 주문한 게 아닌데요

I didn't order this 이거 주문 안 했는데요

필수활용어구

grilled salmon 그릴 새우 | fried prawns 새우튀김 | abalone 전복 | clam 대합 | cod 대구 | crab 게 | crawfish 가재 | escargot 달팽이 | herring 청어 | lobster 바닷가재 *shrimp 새우 | mackerel 고등어 | mussel 홍합 | octopus 문어 *squid 오징어 | oyster 굴 | plaice 가자미 | prawn 참새우(크기는 lobster와 shrimp 사이) | salmon 연어 *trout 송어 | salmon roe 훈제연어로제 | sardine 정어리 | scallop 가리비 | sea bass 농어 | sea urchin 성게 | swordfish 황새치 *tuna 참치

I'm sorry, but I ordered something different
죄송하지만 다른 걸 주문했는데요

I don't think I ordered this 이거 주문 안 했는데요

I ordered 3 cups of coffee. But we only got two
커피 3잔 주문했는데 2잔만 나왔어요

Which would you like to have, coffer or tea?
커피를 드시겠어요 아니면 차를 드시겠어요?

This glass is not very clean 이 잔이 깨끗하지 않은데요

Can I cancel my order, please? 주문 취소해도 돼요?

I have to leave soon. Could you please hurry up?
곧 나가야 하는데 서둘러줄래요?

Could you hurry with our orders? 음식 아직 멀었어요?

Will it take much longer? 시간이 많이 걸리나요?

Would you rush my order? 주문 좀 서둘러줄래요?

I think you can have it soon 곧 나옵니다

We'll bring your order right up 주문하신 것 바로 가져다 드릴게요

음식을 선택하기

06 **음식** 이 곳은 어떤 요리가 괜찮은 지 말씀해 주시겠어요?

I'd like to see a menu, please 메뉴 좀 갖다주세요

Could[May] I have a menu, please? 메뉴 좀 보여주세요

Can I see the menu again? 메뉴 좀 다시 보여주세요

Can I order now? 지금 주문해도 돼요?

Can I have only coffee? 커피만 마셔도 돼요?

Do you have a set menu? 세트메뉴 있어요?

Do you have a dessert menu? 디저트 메뉴 있어요?

What do you suggest[recommend]? 당신은 뭘 권하시겠어요?

What would you recommend[suggest] as an appetizer?
애피타이저로 뭘 추천해줄래요?

What would you recommend[suggest] for dessert?
디저트로 뭘 추천해줄래요?

Can you tell me what's good here?
이 곳은 어떤 요리가 괜찮은 지 말씀해 주시겠어요?

What do you think I should order? 뭘 주문해야 될까요?

What do you think is the best? 뭐가 가장 좋은 것 같아요?

What kind of wine do you have? 와인은 무슨 종류가 있어요?

May I see the wine list, please? 와인리스트 좀 볼 수 있을까요?

What kind of dressing do you have? 드레싱으론 뭐가 있어요?

What kind of salad do you have? 어떤 샐러드가 있나요?

What is the special of the day? 오늘의 스페셜은 뭔가요?

Can you tell me about the specials of the day?
오늘 스페셜이 뭐예요?

What is tonight's special? 오늘 스페셜이 뭐예요?

Look, I don't speak English well. Just let me have Today's special 저기요 영어가 달려서요. 그냥 오늘의 스페셜로 주세요

Do you have any local specialties? 이 지역 특산물이 있어요?

I can recommend the cheesecake. It's excellent
치즈스테이크가 좋아요

I'd recommend the nachos with hot peppers
후추를 곁들인 나초를 권해드릴게요

필수활용어구

vegetable 야채 | asparagus 아스파라거스 | bean 콩 | broccoli 브로콜리 | cabbage 양배추 | carrot 당근 | celery 셀러리 | corn 옥수수 | cucumber 오이 | eggplant 가지 | green pepper 피망 | kidney bean 강낭콩 | olive 올리브 | lettuce 상추, 양상추 | onion 양파 | parsley 파슬리 | pickels 절인야채 (특히 오이) | potato 감자 | pumpkin 호박 | spinach 시금치 | sweet potato 고구마 | tomato 토마토 | beverage 음료 | cream puff 슈크림빵 | parfait 아이스크림과 케익중간 | sherbet 셔벗(과즙 아이스크림) | souffle 아주 부드러운 케익 | tart 타트(과일 등을 얹은 작은 파이) | pudding 푸딩(밀가루에 달걀, 우유, 과일, 설탕, 향료를 넣고 구운 식후용 과자) | cereal 시리얼 *아침식사용 곡물 | confectionary 과자의, 사탕의 | croissant 크루아상(초승달 모양의 롤빵) | muffin 머핀(옥수수 가루 따위를 넣어서 살짝 구운 빵) | shortcake 네모난 과일 케이크 | whipped cream 거품 크림 | club sandwich 클럽샌드위치(찬 고기나 샐러드 등을 끼워 넣은 3겹 샌드위치) | roll 롤빵

I'd suggest the chicken wings to go with your beer
맥주엔 닭날개를 드세요

What comes with that? 함께 뭐가 나오나요?

Does it come with soup or salad and dessert?
수프나 샐러드, 디저트가 함께 나오나요?

Is coffee included with this meal?
식사에 커피가 포함되어 있나요?

What is that like? 그거 어떤 거예요?

What kind of dish is this? 이건 어떤 음식인가요?

I haven't made up my mind yet 아직 결정을 못했는데요

Does it contain any alcohol? 알코올이 들어있나요?

Do they contain any additives? 첨가물이 뭐 들어 있나요?

May I have another glass of water? 물 한 잔 더 주세요

Can I order wine by the glass? 잔으로 와인 주문돼요?

Please recommend a good wine for the dish?
음식에 맞는 좋은 와인 좀 추천해줘요

Can you please change my order? 주문 좀 바꿔줄래요?

Can you please take this away? 이것 좀 치워줄래요?

I'd like to have some more bread, please 빵 좀 더 주세요

Excuse me, I dropped my knife
죄송하지만 칼을 떨어트렸네요

Hamburger and Cola, take out, please
햄버거하고 콜라 포장해주세요

Small, medium or large size? 작은 거, 중간, 아니면 큰 걸로요?

Small hot dog and large Cola 작은 핫도그와 큰 콜라주세요

Is that all? 그게 전부인가요?

I'd like to have a light meal 가벼운 식사하려구요

How do I eat this? 이거 어떻게 먹어요?

No pickles with the hamburger, please
햄버거에 피클은 빼주세요

I want lots of ketchup 케첩을 많이 넣어주세요

No mustard, please 겨자는 넣지 마세요

07 음식 같은 걸로 주세요

I'll have the same 같은 걸로 주세요

Can I have the same as him? 저 사람과 같은 걸로 줄래요?

The same for me 나도 같은 걸로요

I'd like to have the same dish as the next table
옆 테이블과 같은 걸로 주세요

Make it two 같은 걸로 2개 주세요

I'll have that 그걸로 주세요

I'll take this one 이걸로 주세요

I'll take this and this 이거하고 이거 먹을게요

I'd like a steak 고기 먹을래요

I'd like some Italian food 이태리 음식 좀 주세요

I'd like a hamburger and an ice tea 햄버거하고 아이스티 주세요

I'd like to try the steak 고기를 먹어보죠

I'd like something to drink 마실 것 좀 주세요

I'd like some more wine 와인 좀 더 주세요

I'd like a cup of coffee, please 커피 한잔 주세요

I'd like another cup of coffee 커피 한잔 더 주세요

I'll have a chocolate muffin 초코렛 머핀으로 주세요

I'll have the chocolate mousse and my wife will have the cheesecake 전 초콜릿 무스, 아낸 치즈케익으로 줘요

Can I get a steak sandwich and a Coke?
고기샌드위치랑 콜라 한잔 줄래요?

Can you get me a glass of water, please?
물 한잔 갖다 줄래요?

May I have two hot dogs, please?
핫도그 두 개 주실래요?

I'd like my steak medium 고기는 미디엄으로 해주세요

Well-done, please 웰던으로 해줘요

No dessert, thank you. Just coffee, please

디저트는 됐구요, 그냥 커피주세요

Please give me a low calorie sugar, please 저칼로리 설탕주세요

음식 권하기

08 음식 원하는 거 아무거나 갖다 드세요

Help yourself 마음껏 드세요, 어서 갖다 드세요

Help yourself to some cheese and crackers
치즈하고 크랙커 갖다 드세요

Help yourself to anything (in the refrigerator)
(냉장고에 있는 거) 마음껏 드세요

Help yourself to whatever you like 원하는 거 아무거나 갖다 드세요

Enjoy your meal 맛있게 드세요

What's for dinner? 저녁식사 메뉴가 뭐야?

Is dinner ready? 저녁 됐어?

Today, we're having curry 오늘은 카레라이스야

Come and get it 자 와서 먹자, 자 밥 먹게 와라

Please feel free to have another 어서 더 들어요

Please take anything you like from the dessert tray
디저트 아무거나 다 갖다 드세요

Would you like some? 좀 드실래요?

Would you like another drink? 한 잔 더 할래요?

Do you want some more? 더 들래요?

Have some more 좀 더 드세요

Do you want a bite of this?
이거 좀 더 들어볼래요?

I've had enough 많이 먹었어요

필수활용어구

chef's specialty 주방장 특별요리 | pasta 파스타(달걀을 섞은 가루 반죽을 재료로 한 이탈리아 요리) | made-to-order food 주문(해 만든 요리) | cold cuts 가공육(얇게 저민 냉육과 치즈로 만든 요리) | filling (음식물의) 속, 내용물 | topping (음식물위에) 얹은 것 | whipping cream 거품이 일기에 알맞은 크림 | fat-free 지방을 뺀

I'm (getting) full 배가 불러요

I'm stuffed 배불러

I'm on a diet 다이어트 중이야

09 음식 음식이 어때?

How do you like the steak? 고기 맛이 어때?

How do you like the food? 음식이 어때?

How was the meal? 식사 어땠어요?

How's the food? 맛이 어때?

Does your soup taste all right? 스프 맛이 괜찮아?

Does it taste good? 맛이 좋아?

Is this delicious? 맛있어?

This looks great[good; delicious] 이거 맛있게 보인다

This smells great 냄새가 좋은데

This is so good 맛 좋다

It's good 맛 좋아

It's delicious 맛있어

That was good 맛 좋았어

It was delicious 맛있었어

This is the best steak I've eaten in a long time
이렇게 맛난 스테이크는 오랜만에 처음야

It doesn't taste good 맛이 안 좋아

필수활용어구

cuisine 조리법 | recipe 조리법 | baked (불에 대지 않고 열로) 구운 | boiled 삶은, 끓인 | broiled 구운 | casserole 냄비요리 | fried 튀긴 | grilled (가스나 숯불 위에서) 구운 | marinated 절인 | raw 날 것의 | roasted 불로 구운 | sauteed 뜨거운 불판에 빨리 익힌 | skewered 꼬치 | smoked 훈제 | stuffed 속을 넣은 | steamed 찐 | stewed 졸인 | well-done 잘 익힌 | rare 덜 익힌 | medium-rare 알맞게 덜 익힌 | medium 알맞게 익힌

This doesn't taste as good as it looks 보기처럼 맛있지 않아

This has a strong flavor 맛이 너무 강해

It's spicy/sweet 매워/ 달아

It's (too) salty 짜

It's too greasy 기름기가 너무 많아

It's too hot 너무 뜨거워

This sauce is so spicy. It's making my mouth burn
소스가 매워. 입이 탄다 타

My mouth is burning[on fire] 입이 타

This tastes strange[weird] 이건 맛이 넘 이상해

This yogurt tastes odd 이 요구르트는 맛이 이상해

This ham must be past its due date 이 햄은 유효기간이 지났을 거야

I hope you enjoyed your meal 식사 맛있었길 바래

We enjoyed it very much 아주 맛있게 먹었어

You're a good cook 너 참 요리 잘 한다

I'm afraid this steak is over done 고기가 너무 구워진 것 같아

술과 담배에 관해 표현들

10 **음식** 당신의 건강을 위하여!

Here's to you! 당신을 위해 건배!, 너한테 주는 선물이야!

Here's to your health! 당신의 건강을 위하여!

I'd like to propose a toast 축배를 듭시다

Let me propose a toast to Mr. Kim 미스터 김을 위해 건배할게요

Let's drink to Miss Park's future! 미스 박의 미래를 위해서 건배합시다!

Bottoms up! 위하여!

Cheers! 건배!

Say when 됐으면 말해

How about a drink? 술 한잔 어때?

I need a drink 술 한잔 해야겠어

Would you like to have a drink after work? 퇴근 후 한잔 할테야?

How much do you usually drink? 보통 술 얼마나 마셔?

He's a heavy drinker 걘 술 잘 마셔

I can drink a lot 술 많이 마실 수 있어

I have a hangover 술이 아직 안 깼나봐

I'm suffering from a hangover today 오늘 아직 숙취가 있어

I get drunk easily 난 쉽게 취해

I feel a little tipsy 아직 취기가 있어

I'm loaded [drunk] 술 취했어

Please don't drink too much 너무 과음하지마

I don't drink 난 술 안마셔

I prefer draft beer 생맥주가 좋아

I don't smoke anymore 더 이상 담배 안펴

I quit smoking 담배 끊었어

I stopped smoking 이제 담배 안펴

How many packs a day? 하루에 몇 갑이나 펴?

I'm a chain[heavy] smoker 난 줄담배 펴

Can I bum a smoke? 담배 한가치 줄래?

Do you serve alcohol? 알코올 팔아요?

What kind of beer would you like? 어떤 맥주를 드릴까요?

What do you have? 뭐가 있어요?

We have Budweiser and Heineken 버드와이저하고 하이네켄이 있어요

I'll have a Bud 버드로 주세요

Give me a cocktail, not so strong, please 세지 않은 칵테일 주세요

Let me buy you a drink 술 한잔 살게

Is that for here or to go? 여기서 드실 겁니까, 가지고 가실 겁니까?

식당에서 포장하기

11 음식 여기서 드실 겁니까, 가지고 가실 겁니까?

Will this be for here or to go? 여기서 드실거예요 아니면 포장예요?

For here or to go? 여기서요 아니면 포장요?

For here, please 여기서 먹을게요

Can I get it to go? 포장되나요?

I'd like it to go, please 포장으로 해줘요

(Do you want to) Eat here or take it out?
여기서 드실래요 아니면 포장인가요?

Will that be to go? 가져가실 건가요?

Take-out? 포장요?

Can we get take-out? 포장돼요?

Will you make it for takeout? 포장해주실래요?

Could I[we] have a doggie bag, please? 포장지 좀 줄래요?

Could you pack the rest of the meal for take-out?
남은 음식 가져가게 싸줄래요?

I'd like to take it with me. Can you pack it up, please?
가져갈게요. 포장해줄래요?

식당에서 지불하기

12 **지불** 내가 낼게

It's on me 내가 낼게

This one is on me 이번엔 내가 낼게

It's on the house 이건 서비스입니다

I'll pick up the tab[check] 내가 계산할게

Let me pick up the tab 내가 계산할게

Let me take care of the bill 내가 계산할게

This is my treat 내가 살게

I'll treat you 내가 대접하죠

This is my round 이건 내가 쏜다

It's my treat this time 이번은 내가 대접하는 거야

I'm buying 내가 살게

I'll pay for dinner 저녁은 내가 낼게

Where is the cashier? 계산대가 어디죠?

Does the price of this course include drink?
이 코스가격에 술도 포함된 건가요?

(I'd like the) Check, please 계산서 좀 주세요

I'd like to pay the bill, please 계산을 좀 하려구요

Could you bring me my bill? 계산서 갖다 줄래요?

What's the damage? 얼마죠?

What is this charge for? 이거 얼마입니까?

How much is the total? 총 얼마입니까?

I'll pay. What's the total? 내가 낼게요. 전부 얼마예요?

May I have a receipt, please? 영수증 주실래요?

Is tax included? 세금이 포함된 건가요?

Here is a little something for you 이건 얼마 안되지만 팁이에요

Please include the tip with my credit card 카드결재할 때 팁도 넣어요

How much should I leave on the table? 테이블에 얼마 남겨야 돼?

What kind of tip should I leave? 팁 몇 프로를 남겨둬야 돼?

We'd like[We want] to pay separately 각자 내려고요

Let's go halves 반반 내자

Let me share the bill 나도 반 낼게

Let's split the bill 나누어 내자

Let's go Dutch 자기가 먹은 건 자기가 내자

How much is my share? 내 몫은 얼마지?

How much is mine? 난 얼마야?

Can I pay with my credit card? 카드로 내도 돼요?

Can I use a credit card? 카드 돼요?

What kind of card can we use? 무슨 카드 돼요?

I'd like to pay in cash 현금으로 낼게요

Is the service charge included? 팁도 포함된 가격인가요?

I think the calculation is wrong 계산이 잘못 된 것 같아요

There's a mistake in the bill 계산서에 틀린 곳이 있네요

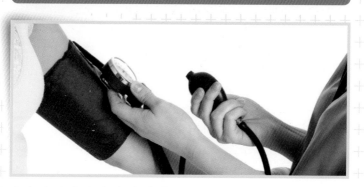

Chapter **06** 건강 | 운동

01 상담 오늘 기분 어때?

How do you feel? 오늘 기분 어때?

Are you (feeling) okay? 기분 괜찮아?

You don't look very well 오늘 안 좋아 보여

You look pale 창백해 보여

You look like you've lost weight lately
최근 너 살 빠진 것 같아

Are you all right? 괜찮아?

Are you well again? 다시 괜찮아졌어?

Are you back to normal? 다시 좋아 진거야?

Are you in good shape? 건강 좋아?

I'm in good shape[health] 건강이 좋아

My biggest problem is my pot belly 불쑥 나온 배가 나의 가장 큰 문제야

What's your secret for staying healthy? 건강을 유지하는 비결이 뭐야?

Have you completely recovered? 완전히 회복된거야?

I feel better 기분이 나아졌어

I don't feel any better 하나도 나아진 게 없어

I always stop eating before I feel full
난 항상 배가 부르기까지 먹지 않아

I keep early hours 일찍 일어나

I always get enough sleep 충분히 수면을 취해

You should quit smoking 넌 담배 끊는 게 나아

I gave up smoking for my health 건강 때문에 담배 끊었어

Do you get regular physical check-ups?
정기적으로 건강검진을 받아?

I get a dental check-up every six months
6개월마다 치과에서 정기검진 받아

I get a cancer check-up once a year 일년에 한번 암검사를 받아

Have you had your hepatitis shot yet? 아직 간염주사 안 맞았니?

Nothing can take the place of good health 건강만큼 중요한 게 없어

02 상담 어디가 아파요?

I'd like to see the doctor 진찰 좀 받고 싶은데요

You'd better go see a doctor 병원에 가봐야 돼

Please call a doctor 의사 좀 불러요

Could you send me a doctor? 의사 좀 보내줄래요?

Please take me to the hospital 병원으로 데려다 주세요

Please take me to the nearest hospital
가장 가까운 병원으로 데려다주세요

Can you find a doctor who speaks Korean?
한국말 하는 의사 좀 찾아주실래요?

Do you need a doctor? 의사가 필요하세요?

Can I buy medicine without prescription? 처방전없이 약 살 수 있어요?

Please call an ambulance 앰블런스 불러줘요

I want to know what's wrong with me 어디가 안 좋은지 알고 싶어요

I've come for a consultation about general health
전반적인 건강상태를 상담하러 왔어요

How is my overall health, doctor? 전반적인 건강상태가 어떤가요, 선생님?

I want to have my blood examined 혈압 좀 재주세요

Your blood pressure is stable now 혈압은 이제 정상입니다

I've never had any trouble with my health
건강엔 전혀 문제가 없었어요

Give me medicine for a cold, please 감기약 주세요

필수활용어구

hospital 종합병원 | clinic 진료소 | community hospital 지역병원 | hospice 안락원 | mental hospital 정신병원 | field hospital 야전병원 | emergency room 응급실 | sickroom 병실 | operating room 수술실 | examination room 진찰실 | delivery room 분만실 | recovery room 회복실 | outpatient 외래환자 | inpatient 입원환자 | case 환자 | contract the disease 병에 걸리다 | be hospitalized (be in the hospital) 입원하다

What's wrong? 어디가 아파요?

What's wrong with you? 어디가 아프세요?

What's your complaint? 어디가 아프세요?

What's the matter[trouble]? 어디가 아프세요?

Is (there) anything wrong? 어디 안 좋은데 있어요?

Where does it hurt? 어디가 아파요?

Where is the pain?/ Where do you have pain? 어디가 아프세요?

Where do you feel the pain most? 어느 부위가 가장 아파요?

What are your symptoms?/ What symptoms do you have? 증상이 어때요?

Let me check your temperature 체온 좀 재볼게요

Let me check your blood pressure 혈압 좀 재볼게요

Is there a history of heart disease in your family? 가족 중 심장병 앓은 분이 있나요?

How's your vision? 시력이 어떠세요?

Did you eat something unusual? 좀 색다른 거 드셨나요?

Do you still feel pain? 통증이 느껴지나요?

What kind of pain is it? 어떤 종류의 통증인가요?

Do you have pain anywhere else? 다른 데 아픈 곳이 있나요?

Do you have a high temperature? 열이 많이 나유?

Do you have a fever? 열이 있어요?

Do you have a cold? 감기 걸렸어요?

Do you have a severe headache? 두통이 심한가요?

Do you have a sore throat? 인후염이 있나요?

필수활용어구

stethoscope 청진기 | thermometer 체온계 | blood pressure machine 혈압계 | first visit 초진 | revisit 재진 | diagnosis 진단 | check-up 건강진단 | medical certificate 진단서 | medical history 병력 | family history 가족병 | injection 주사 | treatment 치료 | transfusion 수혈 | trauma 외상 | doctor's round 회진 | house call 왕진 | hygiene 위생 | oral medicine 내복약 | application 외용약 | tablet; pill 정제

Do you feel nauseous? 속이 울렁거리나요?

Do you have a diarrhea? 설사하세요?

Are you allergic to any kind of medication? 특정 약에 앨러지 있나요?

Does anyone in your family suffer from diabetes?
가족 중에 당뇨병 환자 있나요?

Do you suffer from insomnia? 불면증에 시달리나요?

Do you suffer from back pain? 등 통증에 시달립니까?

When was your last bowel movement?
마지막으로 변을 본 것이 언제지요?

How long have you had a problem with indigestion?
소화불량으로 얼마나 고생했나요?

Have you ever fractured your leg before?
전에 다리가 부러진 적 있습니까?

That's a nasty bruise. How did it happen?
타박상이 심하군요. 어쩌다 그랬어요?

Are you taking any medication? 치료는 받고 있나요

Are you taking any medicine regularly?
정기적으로 먹는 약 있어요?

I'm not taking any medicine 먹는 약 없어요

Have you had your wisdom teeth pulled out? 사랑니 뽑았어요?

How long have you had this pain? 이 통증이 시작한 지 얼마나 되었나요?

Since when has it hurt? 언제부터 아픈가요?

When did it start? 언제부터 그래요?

When did this trouble start? 이 통증이 언제 시작되었나요?

How long has it been bothering you? 얼마동안 고생하신 거예요?

How is your appetite? 식욕은 어때요?

Does it (still) hurt? (아직) 아픈가요?

Does it hurt much? 많이 아파요?

Does it hurt all the time? 계속 아파요?

Does it hurt when I touch it? 내가 만지면 아픈가요?

Do I have to come to the hospital every day?
매일 병원에 와야 하나요?

Should I be hospitalized? 입원해야 하나요?

How long will you be in the hospital for?
얼마나 입원해 있어야 하는 거야?

Will I be able to get well soon? 곧 좋아질까요?

How long does it take to get over this?
낫는데 시간이 얼마나 걸릴까요?

Do I need an operation?/ Will surgery be necessary?
수술해야 하나요?

Will surgery cure it? 수술하면 나을까요?

Is it all right to drink? 술을 마셔도 됩니까?

What foods should I avoid? 어떤 음식을 피해야 하나요?

What about my diet? 내 식이요법은 어떻게 하나요?

You'd better eat something that's easy to digest
소화가 잘 되는 것으로 드세요

I had shrimp last night 지난 밤에 새우를 먹었어요

Maybe the raw food for lunch was bad
아마도 점심으로 먹은 날 음식이 상했던 것 같아요

감기 등 몸이 안 좋아

03 통증 쉽게 피곤해져요

I'm not feeling very well 몸이 아주 안 좋아요

I don't feel well 몸이 좋지 않아요

It hurts here 여기가 아파요

I have a pain here 여기가 통증이 있어요

I get tired easily 쉽게 피곤해져요

I'm getting fat 살이 쪄

I've put on[gained] weight 살 쪘어

I tend to put on weight easily 난 살이 쉽게 찌는 스타일야

I feel sluggish 피곤해

I caught a cold 감기 걸렸어

I have a bad cold 감기가 심해

I've got the flu 유행성 감기에 걸렸어

I caught a cold from you 감기 너한테 옮았나봐

There's a bad cold going around 독감이 유행야

I have a runny nose 코가 흘러

My nose is running 코가 흘러

My nose won't stop running 코가 멈추지 않고 계속 흘러

I can't stop coughing 기침이 멈추지 않아요

I feel chilly 으실으실 추워

I don't have any appetite 식욕이 없어

I have only a small appetite 식욕이 별로 없어

머리, 코, 입, 눈 그리고 귀가 아파

04 통증 머리가 (조금, 아주) 아파

I have a slight[terrible] headache 머리가 조금 (아주) 아파

I always suffer from this headache 항상 이 두통으로 고생하고 있어

This part of my head particularly aches 머리의 이쪽 부분이 아파

My head hurts 머리가 아파

My head feels heavy 머리가 무거워

I have a migraine 편두통이 있어

I get a headache when I wear my glasses 안경을 쓰면 머리가 아파

I suffer from halitosis 난 입냄새가 나요

I'm afraid I have bad breath 내가 입냄새가 나는 것 같아요

It aches when I open my mouth 입을 벌릴 때 아파요

I have a swollen tongue 혀가 부었어요

My lips are[My mouth is] dry and rough 입[술]이 마르고 거칠어요

I have a toothache 치통이 있어

My tooth hurts 이가 아파

My tooth is killing me 이 아파 죽겠어

One of my teeth in the back hurts 어금니 중 하나가 아파요

I have two decayed teeth 충치가 2개 있어요

I have a cavity in one of my lower back teeth and it hurts
아래 어금니중 하나가 충치인데 아파요

It hurts so much I can't sleep at night 너무 아파서 밤에 잠을 못자요

When I chew on something, a sharp pain shoots through my jaw 뭔가 씹을 때 심한 통증이 턱을 관통해요

Even a slight touch to the tooth is intensely painful
이를 약간 대기만 해도 엄청 아파요

The tooth smarts when I eat something cold
뭔가 차가운 걸 먹을 때 이가 쑤셔요

When I drink something cold, there is a sharp pain
차가운 음료를 마실 때 통증이 심해요

The tooth hurts when food touches it 이가 음식이 닿으면 아파요

I can't chew my food well because of a toothache
치통 때문에 음식을 잘 못 씹어요

I have a loose tooth 이가 흔들려요

My teeth feel loose and I have difficulty in chewing
이가 흔들리는 것 같아 씹기 어려워요

The gums ache if I press them with my finger 손가락으로 누르면 잇몸이 아파요

The wisdom tooth aches 사랑니가 이파요

I want to have this tooth pulled out 이 이를 빼주세요

I want to have this cavity filled 이 충치를 치료해주세요

I want to have a false tooth put in 틀니를 넣어주세요

I have a sore throat/ My throat's sore 목이 아파요

I've got a really sore throat 목이 정말 아파요

My throat feels raw 목소리가 쑤셔요

I have an irritated throat 목에 염증이 있어요

My throat hurts when I swallow 삼킬 때 목이 아파요

My throat is swollen 목이 부었어요

I think my tonsils are swollen 편도선이 부었어요

I'm a little nearsighted 약간 근시(近視)예요

My eyes are sore 눈이 아파요

When I close my eyes, they hurt 눈을 감을 때 아파요

My eyes feel hot[itchy, tired] 눈이 충혈돼요[간지러워요, 피로해요]

My eyes feel irritated 눈에 염증이 있어요

When I look at close things, my eyes get tired
가까운 것을 볼 때 눈이 피로해져요

My vision is blurred 시력이 침침해졌어요

I'm afraid I have an ear infection 귀에 염증이 있어요

I have a ringing in my ears 귀가 멍멍해요

My ear hurts terribly when I touch it 귀를 만지면 엄청 아파요

At first it didn't hurt so much, but now there is a throbbing
pain 처음에는 별로 안 아팠는데 지금은 욱신거려요

The pain increases at night. It throbs so much I can't get
to sleep 밤에 통증이 심해져요. 욱신거려서 잠잘 수가 없어요

I'm a little hard of hearing these days 요즘 좀 난청이에요

It's difficult to catch what people say
사람들이 말하는 걸 알아 듣지 못하겠어요

I have a cold and sneeze a lot
감기가 걸려서 재채기가 심해요

Once I start sneezing, I can't stop
재채기를 하기 시작하면 멈출 수가 없어요

I have a running nose 콧물이 나요

My nose is running terribly and I have a headache
콧물이 심하게 나서 머리가 아파요

필수활용어구

specialist 전문의 | resident 레지던트 | intern 인턴 | family doctor 주치의 |
midwife 산파 | veterinarian 수의사 | therapist 심리치료사 | pharmacist 약제사
| surgery 외과 | surgeon 외과의 | internal medicine 내과 | physician 내과의
| neurology 신경과 | neurologist 신경과의 | psychiatry 정신과 | psychiatrist
정신과의 | eye doctor 안과의 | dentistry 치과 | dentist 치과의 | urology 비뇨
기과 | urologist 비뇨기과의

When I blow my nose, my ears squeak
코를 풀 때 귀가 삐꺽거려요

I have a nose bleed every morning 매일 아침 코피가 흘러요

My nose often bleeds 코에서 가끔 피가 나요

혈관, 심장, 배 등이 아플 때

05 통증 고혈압야

I have high[low] blood pressure 고[저]혈압야

I[My head] feel dizzy 어지러워

There is a sudden sharp pain in my chest
갑작스럽게 심한 가슴통증이 났어요

Doctor, my chest is killing me 의사 선생님, 가슴이 너무 아파요

I have a heavy feeling in my chest 가슴이 무겁게 느껴져요

I feel as if it is hard to breath 숨쉬기가 힘들게 느껴져요

I have heart disease 심장병이 있어요

I feel as if I have a convulsion in my heart 심장발작이 있는 것 같아요

I suffer from asthma 천식이예요

My fever has gone down 열이 내려갔어

I'm running a fever 열이 나

I think I have a fever 열이 있는 것 같아

I have a bit of a fever 열이 좀 있어

I have a high temperature 열이 높아

I have a stomachache 복통야

I'm troubled with chronic stomachaches 만성복통으로 아파

My stomach's upset 배탈났어

I have food poisoning 식중독야

I've got the runs 설사했어요

I have diarrhea 설사했어요

I have dull pain in the stomach 배가 뻐근해요

I have a squeezing pain in the stomach 배가 쥐어짜듯이 아파요

Sometimes, there is a sharp pain at the upper right-hand side of my stomach 때때로 오른 쪽 윗배 심한 통증이 있어요

It hurts all around my stomach. Especially when I cough and breathe deeply 배 주변 전체가 아파요. 특히 재채기를 하거나 숨을 깊게 쉴때 아파요

Whenever my stomach is empty, it begins to hurt 공복시마다 아프기 시작해요

My stomach aches after meals 식후에 배가 아파요

I don't feel well in my stomach 배가 좋지 않아요

I always feel uncomfortable in my stomach 배가 항상 좋지 않아요

My stomach hurts and I feel like vomiting 배가 아프고 토할 것 같아요

I have a pain in the upper abdomen when I'm hungry 배가 고프면 윗배가 아파요

I have a pain in my side 옆구리가 아파요

I have a pain in the lower abdomen 아랫배가 아파요

I feel pain from indigestion 소화불량예요

My stomach feels bloated and I have no appetite 복부가 팽창되어 있고 식욕이 없어요

I have gas in the stomach 복부에 가스가 찼어요

I always have the feeling of hunger 항상 배가 고파요

I have upset stomach 복통이예요

I have indigestion 소화불량예요

I feel like throwing up 토할 것 같아

I feel nauseated 토할 것 같아

I feel like vomiting and I have the hiccups 토할 것 같고 딸꾹질이 나요

쥐, 마비, 골절 등

06 통증 발목(손)이 삐었어요

I've got a really stiff neck 목이 너무 뻣뻣해서요

My neck is so stiff that I can't move
목이 너무 뻣뻣해서 움직이지 못하겠어요

My neck is so painful that I can't turn it
목이 너무 아파서 돌릴 수가 없어요

I strained my neck and can't move my head
목이 삐어서 머리를 움직이지 못하겠어요

I have a sharp pain if I try to turn my head
머리를 돌릴려고 하면 통증이 심해요

My neck snapped when I suddenly put on the brakes
급작스럽게 브레이크를 밟았을 때 머리가 젖혀졌어요

Lately when I get up, my shoulders hurt very much
최근 일어날 때 어깨가 무척 아파요

I have stiff shoulders/ My shoulders are stiff 어깨가 뻣뻣해요

I've got a pain in my side 옆구리에 통증이 있어.

I have a pain in my groin when I walk 걸을 때 사타구니 쪽이 아파요

I have severe pain in my back 등에 심한 통증이 있어요

My back hurts sometimes 등이 때때로 무척 아파요

My back itches 등이 간지러워요

I have a rash on my back 등에 뽀루지가 났어요

I suffer from back pain 요통이 있어요

When I was swinging my golf club, I suddenly felt a terrible pain and I haven't been able to move since 골프를 칠
때 갑작스러운 통증을 느꼈고 그 이후로는 움직이실 못하겠어요

When I try to straighten my back, the pain hits me
등을 펼려고 하면 통증이 와요

필수활용어구

long-sightedness 원시 *short-sightedness(근시) | bronchitis 기관지염 | insomnia 불면증 | Alzheimer`s disease 치매 | amnesia 건망증 | suffer from hallucinations 환각 | phobia 공포증 | megalomania 과대 망상증 | faint 실신하다 | character disorder 성격이상 | paralysis 마비 | sleepwalking 몽유병 | throw a fit 발작하다 | vomiting 구토 | chill 오한 | ulcer 궤양 | hepatitis 간염 | diarrhea[runs] 설사 | suffer from constipation 변비로 고생하다 | bowel movement 배변 | food poisoning 식중독 | gastritis 위염 | indigestion 소화불량 | heart disease 심장병 | heart attack 심장마비 | heart failure 심부전 | obesity 비만 | hemorrhoids 치질 | cast 깁스붕대 | prostate cancer 전립선 암

My legs have been cramping up 다리에 쥐가 났어요

I have a cramp in my thigh 허벅지에 쥐가 났어

I have cramps 쥐가 났어요

I sprained my ankle[finger] 발목(손)이 삐었어요

When I missed my step, I seem to have sprained my ankle
발을 헛디뎠을 때 발을 삔 것 같아요

I twisted my ankle 발목이 겹질러졌어요

I twisted my foot, and I'd like you to see if it's all right
발이 꼬였는데 괜찮은 지 알고 싶어요

I broke my leg[arm] 다리가[손이] 부러졌어

I fell down the steps and seem to have broken my leg
계단에서 넘어져서 다리가 부러진 것 같아요

My arm hurts so much I can't reach my back
팔이 아파서 뒤로 뻗을 수가 없어요

My joints ache 관절이 아파요

I sometimes have a pain in my knees 무릎이 때때로 아파요

I have a swollen foot 발이 부었어요

My legs are swollen 다리가 부었어요

I fractured my left leg while skiing
스키타다 왼쪽 다리에 골절상을 입었어요

기타 통증이나 병

07 통증 아파요

I'm a diabetic 당뇨예요

It's itchy 가려워요

It's bleeding 피가 나요

It hurts 아파요

Ouch! 얏!

Is somebody hurt? 누가 다쳤어요?

My hiccups won't stop 딸꾹질이 멈추질 않아요

I burned my hand 손이 데였어

I have blisters on my palm 손바닥에 물집이 있어요

I got a sunburn on the beach 해변에서 햇볕에 탔어요

I've got a cut here 여기 칼로 베었어요

I cut my hand with a knife 칼로 손을 베었어요

When I urinate, it hurts terribly 소변을 눌 때 무척 아파요

It's difficult to urinate 소변누기가 힘들어요

I have severe frostbite on my hands 두 손에 심한 동상을 입었어요

My tennis elbow began to ache again 팔꿈치 통증이 다시 시작했어요

My limbs feel numb and paralyzed 사지가 무감각하고 마비됐어요

The wound is swollen 상처가 부었어요

The wound is inflamed 상처가 염증을 일으켰어요

I have red specks on my face 얼굴에 붉은 반점이 있어요

I have rashes all over my body 온 몸에 뽀루지가 났어요

I have severe hives 심한 두드러기가 났어요

I'm allergic to fish 생선에 앨러지가 있어요

The itching is quite unbearable 가려움 증이 정말 못 참을 정도예요

I feel itchy all over my body 온 몸이 가려워요

I think I'm about to have a nervous breakdown
신경 쇠약에 걸릴 것 같아

Chapter **07** 쇼핑│구매

01 구매 몇 층에 의류가 있나요?

Tell me the closest shopping mall from here
여기서 가장 가까운 쇼핑몰을 알려주세요

Which floor has clothing items? 몇 층에 의류가 있나요?

Where can I get some shoes? 신발을 어디에서 살 수 있어요?

Which floor has foods? 음식은 몇 층에 있어요?

I'm looking for a discount shop 할인 점을 찾고 있어요

Can you recommend any shops for buying gifts?
선물을 살 상점을 추천해줄래요?

Where is the stationery section? 문구 쪽은 어디인가요?

Are there any flea markets? 벼룩시장이 있나요?

Could you please draw a map? 약도 좀 그려줄래요?

Is this the accessory floor? 여기가 액세서리 파는 층인가요?

Where's a duty free shop? 면세점은 어디 있나요?

Can I buy things duty free here? 여기서 면세로 살 수 있나요?

Can I buy it tax-free? 면세로 살 수 있나요?

02 구매 그냥 구경하고 있는 거예요

How may I help you? 어떻게 도와드릴까요?

How can I help[serve] you? 어떻게 도와드릴까요?

What can I do for you? 뭘 도와드릴까요?

Are you looking for anything special? 뭐 특별한 거 찾으시는 거 있나요?

I'm looking for a gift for my mother 어머니 드릴 선물 찾고 있어요

(No thanks,) I'm already being helped 이미 다른 분이 봐주고 계세요

I'm just looking (around) 그냥 구경하고 있는 거예요

(I'm) Just browsing 그냥 구경하는 거예요

When do you open? 언제 열어요?

When is closing time? 언제 닫아요?

Eighth, please 8층 부탁해요

The eighth floor, please 8층 부탁해요

Going down? Going up? 내려가세요? 올라가세요?

Where can I find ladies' wear? 여성복은 어디 있어요?

What're you looking for? 뭘 찾으세요?

Are you looking for anything in particular?
특별히 뭐 찾는 게 있습니까?

I'm looking for a jazz CD 재즈 CD를 찾는데요

I'm looking for a bag 가방을 찾는데요

I'd like a suit 옷을 사려고요

I want to buy a snowboard 스노보드를 사려고요

Do you have a shirt with a plainer pattern?
더 평범한 무늬의 셔츠 있어요?

Do you carry watch batteries? 시계 배터리 파세요?

I'm sorry, we don't carry that brand 미안해요, 그 브랜드는 취급 안 해요

We're having a big sale this week 이번 주에 큰 세일해요

This is a hot sale item nowadays 요즘 잘 나가는 품목이예요

Are there any nice gifts for kids? 아이들 줄 멋진 선물 뭐 있나요?

I'm looking for a gift for my kid 아이들 선물 찾고 있어요

살 물건 결정하기

03 구매 입어봐도 돼요?

May I try it on? 입어봐도 돼요?

May I wear this? 입어봐도 되나요?

I'd like to try this on 이거 입어보고 싶어요

What kind of style is now in fashion? 지금 유행중인 색깔은 뭔가요?

I'm looking for skirts which cost around 70 dollars
한 70달러 정도되는 치마를 찾고 있어요

Would you like to try it on? 입어보실래요?

Please show me this 이것 좀 보여주세요

Show me that ring, please 저 반지 좀 보여주세요

Show me another one, please 다른 것도 좀 보여주세요

Would you show me that one? 저것 좀 보여주실래요?

Do you have anything on sale? 세일 상품 뭐 있어요?

What brand do you prefer? 어느 브랜드를 좋아하세요?

Where is the fitting[dressing] room? 탈의실이 어디예요?

It's too small[big] for me 내게 너무 작[크]네요

It's a little bit tight 너무 쪼이네요

Could you please show me another jacket? 다른 쟈켓 보여줄래요?

Do you have them in any other colors? 이거 다른 색상들 있나요?

What is your size? 사이즈가 어떻게 돼요?

I don't know sizes in this country 여기 사이즈는 잘 모르겠는데요

Would you measure me? 제 치수 좀 재 주시겠어요?

Do you have this in my size? 이거 제 사이즈 있나요?

What size do you wear? 사이즈가 어떻게 돼요?

Would you have one in a smaller size? 좀 더 작은 사이즈 있어요?

Do you have this shirt in a smaller size? 이 셔츠 작은 사이즈 있어요?

This is too loose. Do you have a smaller one?
너무 헐렁해요. 더 작은 거 있어요?

It's too tight[loose, short, long] for me
내게 너무 쪼여요[헐렁해요, 짧아요, 길어요]

Do you have a bigger size? 더 큰 사이즈 있나요?

필수활용어구

department store 백화점 ｜ souvenir shop 기념품점 ｜ fitting room 탈의실 ｜
pure gold 순금 ｜ tax-free items 면세품 ｜ return 반품하다 ｜ refund 환불하다 ｜
shopping center 쇼핑센터 ｜ convenience store 편의점 ｜ ˈ stationery shop
문구점 ｜ antique shop 골동품점 ｜ barber shop 이발소 ｜ boutique (여성용 고급
유행복이나 액세서리를 파는) 가게, 상점

Can you make it in my size? 제 사이즈로 맞출 수 있어요?

Is there any other sizes? 다른 사이즈 있어요?

Do you have another type in this color? 이 색깔로 다른 타입 있나요?

Do you have this in black? 이거 검은 색 있나요?

Do you have any other designs? 다른 디자인 있어요?

How's this? 이건 어때요?

Does it look good on me? 내게 잘 어울려요?

The skirt matches this blouse, doesn't it?
이 치마가 이 블라우스랑 어울리죠 그렇죠?

This skirt and this blouse go together well
이 치마와 이 블라우스가 잘 어울려요

Can you help me choose a dress? 드레스를 고르는 거 도와드릴까요?

Do you have different colors? 다른 색 있어요?

Please show me the jacket in the display window
진열장에 있는 자켓 좀 보여주세요

Can I try some other clothes? 다른 색으로 입어볼 수 있나요?

Where is the fitting room? 탈의실이 어디인가요?

Could you alter this? 이거 수선돼요?

Are alterations free? 수선비는 공짜예요?

Can this be machine washed? 세탁기로 세탁해도 돼요?

Is this laundry washable? 세탁기로 세탁 가능해요?

What age is this good for? 어떤 나이에 어울리나요?

Which perfume is popular? 어떤 향수가 유행하나요?

Give me five of the same thing 같은 걸로 5개 주세요

Do you have the same as this? 이거랑 같은 거 있어요?

May I touch this? 이거 만져봐도 돼요?

What brand is this? 이거는 어디 브랜드인가요?

Where is this made? 이건 어디서 만들었나요?

Is this made in the USA? 이거 미국산인가요?

What is this made of? 이건 뭘로 만들었나요?

What material is this? 이거 재료는 무엇인가요?

Is this real leather? 이거 진짜 가죽예요?

Is this hand-made? 수공예 작품인가요?

I'll take three of them 저걸로 3개 주세요

Do you have better quality ones? 더 나은 제품이 있나요?

Thanks, but it's not what I want 감사하지만 제가 원하는 게 아니네요

This is nice 이거 좋은데요

This is better 이게 더 나아요

I like this better 이게 더 좋아요

I'll take[get] this one 이것으로 할게요

I'd like this one 이걸로 주세요

I'd like to buy this one 이거 살게요

It looks good on you 잘 어울리네요

Will that be all? 달리 더 필요한 것은 없으십니까?

Is that everything? 다 되셨습니까?

Will there be anything else? 더 필요한 건 없습니까?

값 흥정하기

04 결재 내가 얼마를 내면 되지?, 얼마죠?

How much do I owe you? 내가 얼마를 내면 되지?, 얼마죠?

What do I owe you? 얼마인가요?

What's the damage? 얼마예요?

How much? 얼마예요?

How much is the total? 전부 얼마예요?

What is the total? 총액이 얼마인가요?

What's the price of this? 이거 가격이 어떻게 돼요?

How much does it cost? 이거 가격이 얼마예요?

How much is this? 이거 얼마예요?

What's that in dollars? 달러로는 얼마예요?

It's twenty dollars, including tax 세금포함해서 20달러예요

I have only 30 dollars now 지금 단 30달러만 갖고 있어요

How much can you afford to spend? 예산은 얼마쯤 잡고 계시는데요?

What's your budget? 예산은 얼마로 잡고 계신데요?

How much would you like to spend? 얼마정도 쓰실려구요?

I'd like to get something for around 50 dollars
50달러 정도로 사려구요

I don't want to spend more than 30 dollars
30달러 내에서 쓰고 싶어요

I can't afford to buy it 그걸 살 여유가 없어

I can't afford it 살 여유가 없어

That's expensive! 무척 비싸구만!

How expensive! 엄청 비싸네!

That's too much! 너무 비싸다!

It's a bargain 싸다, 싸잖아

That's cheap! 야 싸다!

How cheap! 정말 싸다!

It's a real good buy at that price 그 가격이면 진짜 잘 사는 거야

Wow, that's a steal! 와, 거저네!

At 40 percent below market, this is a good buy
40% 할인가면 잘 산 거지요

Can[Would] you give me a discount? 좀 깎아 주실래요?

If it was a little cheaper, I could buy it 좀만 싸면 살텐데요

If you discount I'll buy 깎아주면 살게요

Can you give me a discount for paying cash?
현금내면 할인해줘요?

Can you make it cheaper? 좀 더 싸게 안돼요?

I'll take ten. So, would you give me a discount?
10개 살건데 깎아주실래요?

Can you make it a little cheaper? 좀 더 싸게 안돼요?

Sorry, we can't. This is our last price
죄송해요, 안돼요. 이게 마지막 가격입니다

That's over my budget. Could you give me a 20 dollars discount? 예산보다 비싸서 그런데 20달러 깎아줄래요?

Do you give discounts for cash? 현금이면 깎아주나요?

I'm sorry, I can't take a penny off 죄송하지만 한 푼도 못 깎아드려요

Take it or leave it 사시던지 아님 그냥 가세요

That's my final offer 내가 하는 마지막 제안예요

I got it at a bargain price 싼 가격에 그걸 샀어

Please show me less expensive one 좀 더 싼 걸로 보여주세요

Anything cheaper? 더 싼 거는 요?

My friend will also buy here 내 친구도 여기서 살 거예요

This is 5 dollars at another store 다른 가게에서는 5달러예요

I picked it up at a flea market for $5 벼룩시장에서 5달러에 샀어

I bought this on impulse 이거 충동구매했어

I got it for next to nothing 거의 거저에 샀어

I bought this for almost nothing 거의 거저에 산 거야

Can I make a down payment now and pay the rest later when I pick it up? 먼저 보증금내고 나중에 가져갈 때 나머지를 내도 되나요?

(Will that be) Cash or charge? 현금으로요 아니면 신용카드로요?

Would you like to pay by cash or charge?
현금으로 낼래요 아님 신용카드로 낼래요?

How would you like to pay for this? 어떻게 계산하실래요?

산 물건의 값을 치를 때

05 **결재** 현금으로요 아니면 신용카드로요?

Do you take checks? 수표 받나요?

Do you accept traveler's checks?
여행자수표 받아요?

Do you accept[take] Visa? 비자카드 받아요?

I'd like to pay for it by card. Do you take Visa?
카드로 결제할게요. 비자카드 되나요?

Can I use VISA? 비자카드 돼나요?

Can I pay in Korean won? 한국 원화로 낼 수 있어요?

Cash, please 현금으로요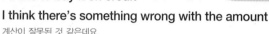

I'll charge it, please 현금으로요

I'll pay by check 수표로 낼게요

I'd like to buy it on credit 신용카드로 낼게요

I think there's something wrong with the amount
계산이 잘못된 것 같은데요

I'm afraid this isn't the correct change 잔돈이 안 맞는 것 같아요

I think your calculation is wrong 계산이 틀린 것 같아요

Can I have a receipt, please? 영수증을 받을 수 있을까요?

Here is your change and receipt 여기 잔돈과 영수증 요

Is it OK to sign here? 여기에 사인하면 돼?

Can I have these delivered to this address? 이 주소로 배달돼요?

Please deliver it to my home 이거 집으로 배달해줘요

Would you like these items delivered? 이 물건들을 배달해 드릴까요?

Do you send packages overseas? 해외로 배송하나요?

배송부탁하기

06 배송 해외로 배송하나요?

Please send it to this address by ship[air plane]
선편[항공편]으로 이 주소로 보내주세요

You can wrap these together
이것들 함께 포장해주세요

Could you please tie it with a ribbon? 리본 달아주실래요?

필수활용어구

I'd like to send this by air mail 항공우편으로 이걸 발송해주세요 | Do you have weight limits? 무게 제한이 있습니까? | I'd like to insure this package 이 짐에 보험을 들게요 | I'd like to send this parcel to Korea 이 짐들을 한국으로 보내주세요 | Where can I buy stamps? 우표를 어디서 사나요? | How much is the postage? 우표값이 얼마인가요? | Is there a post office near here? 근처에 우체국이 있나요? | Is anything fragile in it? 안에 깨지는 물건이 뭐 있나요? | Registered mail, please 등기우편으로 | Zip code 우편번호 | Sender 발송

Can you put a ribbon on it? 리본 달아줄래요?

Please wrap it 포장해주세요

Wrap as a gift, please 선물로 포장해주세요

07 **반품** 이거 반품할게요

I still haven't received the merchandise I ordered
주문한 거 아직 못 받았어요

I didn't receive the same merchandise I ordered
주문한 거랑 다른 게 왔어요

This is different from what I bought 구매한 거랑 다른 제품이 왔어요

The merchandise I received was damaged
주문한 물품이 손상이 됐어요

Here is a crack 여기 금이 갔어요

I haven't used it at all 전혀 쓰지 않았어요

This size doesn't fit me 사이즈가 맞질 않아요

It doesn't fit me 나한테 안 맞아요

This is broken 부러졌어요

Have you dropped it? 떨어트렸나요?

It was broken from the beginning 처음부터 망가져있었어요

Would you exchange it for me? 교환해줄래요?

I'd like to exchange this for something else 다른 걸로 교환해주세요

Please exchange it for a clean one 깨끗한 걸로 바꿔주세요

I'd like to return this 이거 반품할게요

Can I have[get] a refund? 환불되나요?

I'd like to get a refund, please 환불받고 싶어요

I'd like a refund, please 환불해 주세요

I'd like my money back, please 돈을 환불해주세요

I'd like to exchange this 이거 교환해주세요

Sorry, but exchange only, no refunds
죄송하지만 교환만 가능하고 환불은 안됩니다

Chapter **08** 비즈니스

Chapter **08** 비즈니스

01 회사 직업이 뭐예요?

What do you do for a living? 직업이 뭐예요?

What do you do? 무슨 일 하세요?

Who do you work for? 어디서 일해?

I work for Mr. Anderson 앤더슨 씨 회사에서 일해

보충설명 I work at[in]~ ···에서 일해

I have been working here for 3 years
여기서 일한지 3년 됐어

He got fired 걘 해고됐어

I'm being transferred 나 전근 가

I hear you've been promoted 승진했다며

You changed jobs? 직업을 바꿨어?

I recently changed jobs 최근에 직업을 바꿨어

I'm between jobs 백수야

I'm thinking of retiring soon 퇴직할 까 생각중야

I opted for early retirement last year
작년에 명예퇴직 신청했어

What are the (working) hours? 근무시간은?

Let's call it a day 퇴근합시다

Why don't we call it a day now? 오늘은 이제 그만 퇴근하자

Let's call it quits 퇴근합시다

Let's quit for today 오늘 그만 퇴근하죠

He's gone for the day 그 분은 퇴근했습니다

We're done for the day 그만 가자, 그만 하자

Are you working overtime tonight? 오늘 밤 야근해?

I'm working nights 난 밤근무야

I have the night shift this week 이번주 밤근무야

I'll be out of town all next week 다음 주 내내 출장갈거야

I'll be on the road most of next month
다음 달 대부분 출장중일거야

Can you take care of my work while I'm away?
나 없을 때 내 일 좀 맡아줄래?

I have to call in sick 아파서 결근한다고 전화해야겠어

일을 지시할 때

02 **업무** 내일까지 마무리해

Please get it done by tomorrow morning 내일 아침까지 마무리해

Can you have the report done by 6 o'clock?
6시까지 보고서 끝낼 수 있어?

Finish this report today! 오늘 이 보고서 끝내!

Do this right away 이거 지금 바로 해

Please do this 이거 해요

Would you please do this for me? 이것 좀 해줄래요?

Do this when you can 시간 될 때 해요

Please take care of this 이것 좀 처리하도록

Would you take a look at this paper? 이 서류 좀 한번 봐주실래요?

This is top priority 이게 최우선야

I want you to give this top priority 이거에 최우선을 두게

Please submit the document to me 이 문서를 내게 제출해요

Please hand the document in to me 이 문서를 내게 제출해요

This has to go out today 이건 오늘 나가야 돼

Who is handling this account? 이 건은 누가 맡고 있어?

Who's going to handle the paperwork? 이 서류작업은 누가 맡을 건가?

That can't wait 이건 급해

This can wait 그건 나중에 해도 돼

Can't that wait? 미루면 안돼?, 급한 거야?

You'd better work harder 더 열심히 일해라

Do your best! 최선을 다해!

Make sure they all know about it
걔들이 모두 알고 있도록 해

03 업무 일 시작합시다

Let's get down to business 자 일을 시작합시다

Let's get started 자 시작하자

Let's get started on the wedding plans
결혼식 계획을 실행하자

I gotta get started on my speech 연설을 시작하겠습니다

Let's roll 자 시작합시다

Let's get on with it 시작합시다

Get set[ready]! 준비해라!

Get ready for Christmas 크리스마스를 준비해

Get ready to run 뛸 준비해

All right, are you ready? 좋아, 준비됐어?

Ready? 좋아, 준비됐어?

I'll go 내가 할게

All set 준비 다 됐어요

I'm[We're] all set 난[우린] 준비 다 됐어

We're ready 준비됐어요

I'll get to work on it right now 지금 바로 시작할게요

Just get to work 바로 일 시작해

I'll get right on it 당장 그렇게 하겠습니다

First things first 중요한 것부터 먼저 하자

Work comes first 일이 우선이야

I'm working on it 지금 하고 있어

I'm on it 내가 처리 중이야

I'll look it over first thing in the morning
내일 아침 일찍 바로 검토할게

I'll do it immediately 당장 할게

04 업무 언제까지 해야 하는 거야?

When is this due? 마감일이 언제야?

When is the paper due? 이 서류 언제 마감야?

What's the due date? 마감일이 언제야?

It's due on the thirtieth 13일이 마감야

What's the deadline for this job? 이 일 마감이 언제야?

How much time do I have? 시간이 얼마나 있어?

The deadline is coming up 마감일이 다가오고 있어

The deadline's just a week away 마감일이 일주일 앞이야

We're behind schedule 일정보다 늦었어

The project is running a week behind schedule
그 프로젝트가 예정보다 일주일 늦고 있어

The schedule is just too demanding 일정이 너무 빡빡해

This is a tight schedule 일정이 빡빡하네

We're about two days ahead of schedule
일정보다 한 이틀 앞서가고 있어

When will it be ready? 언제 준비될까?

When does this have to be finished by?
이거 언제까지 끝내야 돼?

Is the report ready? 보고서 준비됐어?

Are the papers ready? 서류들 준비됐어?

Have you finished the report? 보고서 끝냈어?

What happened to the project? 그 프로젝트는 어떻게 됐어?

What happened to the documents I left here?
내가 여기 둔 문서는 어떻게 됐어?

We're still at it 아직도 하고 있어

There are no problems so far 지금까지는 아무 문제없어

Right now, things look pretty good 지금 상황은 꽤 좋아보여

It's moving right along 잘 되어 가고 있어

It's still in the planning stage 아직 기획단계예요

Nothing has been done about that project
그 프로젝트는 아직 된 게 없어

This paperwork is really a pain 이 서류작업은 정말 골칫거리야

We're finally getting somewhere 마침내 좀 진전했네요

We should start pushing them 걔들을 다그치기 시작해야 겠어

That can't be done overnight 밤새 그렇게 한다는 건 불가능해요

05 업무 최선을 다 했어요

I did all I could do 난 할 수 있는 최선을 다 했어요

That's all I can do 이게 내가 할 수 있는 최선야

We're putting every effort into it 모든 노력을 기울이고 있어요

I have to work late today 오늘 야근해야 돼

I have to work overtime today 오늘 야근해야 돼

He's a hard worker 걘 일 열심히 하는 사람야

I'm a workaholic 난 일밖에 모르는 사람야

Let's see what happens 어떻게 되나 보자고

I'll be sure to double-check everything from now on
지금부터 철저히 확인할게요

I'll try not to let you down 실망하지 않도록 할게요

06 업무 다했어?

You done? 다했어?

Are you done with this? 이거 끝냈니?

Are you done with your meal? 밥 다 먹었니?

When will you be done with your work? 언제까지면 일이 끝날 것 같아?

I'm done with this 이거 다 끝냈다

I'm (all) done with my work 이 일 (거의) 다 끝냈어

All done! 다 끝냈어!

It's done 끝냈어

I'm not done 못 끝냈어

I'm finished working 일 끝냈어

It's 90 percent finished 90% 정도 끝냈어

We're almost there 거의 다 됐어, 거의 끝났어

We're almost finished 거의 다 마쳤어

We'd like to wrap this up today 이거 오늘 끝내자고

Let's finish it up 이거 끝내자

07 업무 생각 좀 해보고요

I'd like to think it over 생각 좀 해볼게요

Let me think it over a little longer 좀 더 생각 좀 해볼게요

It's under review 검토 중이야

I'll give you an answer after giving it some thought
생각 좀 해보고 답줄게

I'll give you an answer after I've talked with my manager
상사와 논의후 답줄게

I don't have the authority to do that 그렇게 할 권한이 없어요

I don't have the authority to decide on this matter
이 건에 대한 결정권이 없어요

I can't do something like that without discussing it with my superiors 상사와 토의없이 그런 걸 할 수는 없어요

I have to talk it over with the boss
사장과 그 문제를 이야기해봐야 돼

Let me check with my superiors 상사분들과 확인해볼게요

You'd better check with the boss 사장에게 확인해봐요

You'd better run it by the boss 사장과 상의해봐요

We're waiting for a decision from the people upstairs
윗분들 결정 기다리고 있어

The boss refuses to give it his OK 사장이 승낙하지 않고 있어

I can't say for sure right now 지금 당장 확실히 말씀 못 드려요

It requires a detailed analysis 세부적인 분석이 필요해요

Do you need an answer right now? 지금 당장 답변이 필요해요?

I'll give you a firm answer by Friday 금요일까지 확실한 대답을 줄게요

Thank you for your quick decision 빠른 결정을 해줘 감사해요

I'm going with it 난 그것으로 할게요

It's now or never 지금 아니면 안돼

The sooner, the better 빠를수록 좋아

It's all or nothing 모 아니면 도야

08 업무 누가 책임자야?

Who is in charge? 누가 책임자야?

I'm in charge of the project 내가 이 일의 책임자입니다

Who calls the shots? 누가 결정권자야?

I'm calling the shots 내가 결정해

That's[It's] your call 네가 결정할 문제야, 네 뜻에 따르게

You decide 네가 결정해

You must decide 네가 결정해야 해

It's up to you 네가 결정할 일이야

It's your choice 네가 선택하는 거야

The choice is up to you 선택은 너한테 달렸어

You're the boss 분부만 내리십시오, 맘대로 하세요

You're the doctor 네 조언에 따르게

09 업무 좀 쉬자

Let's take a break 좀 쉽시다
Let's break for coffee 쉬면서 커피 한잔 합시다
I need some rest 좀 쉬어야겠어
I need a day off 하루 쉬어야 되겠어
He has a day off 그 사람은 오늘 하루 쉬어요
I need to take a day off 하루 좀 쉬어야겠어
How about going out for a drink tonight? 오늘 밤 한잔하러 나가자?
Let's go have a drink together tonight 오늘 밤 함께 한잔 하자
Let's have a drink 한잔 하자

10 업무 할 일이 무척 많아

I've got so much to do 할 일이 많아
I have so much to do 할 일이 많아
I have many things to do 할 일이 많아
I have a lot to do 할 일이 많아
There's a lot of work piled up on my desk 내 책상에 할 일이 쌓여있어
I'm tied up all day 하루 온종일 꼼짝달싹 못하고 있다
I'm tied up with something urgent 급한 일로 꼼짝달싹 못해
I'm tied up at the moment 지금 바빠서 꼼짝도 못해
I'm not available 바쁘다, 시간이 안돼
I'm swamped (with work) 나 (일이) 엄청 바빠
I had a pretty hectic day 정신없이 바빴어
I'm busy with a client 손님 때문에 바빠요
I kept myself busy 그동안 바빴어
I don't have time to breathe 숨쉴 시간도 없어
I don't (even) have time to catch my breath 숨쉴 겨를이 없어

My hands are full right now 지금 무척 바빠

I've got my hands full with the work I'm doing now
지금 일로 무척 바빠

I'm totally burned out 완전히 뻗었어

I'm tired[worn] out 녹초가 됐어

I'm stressed out 스트레스로 피곤해

I'm exhausted 지쳤어

I'm so beat 지쳤다

I'm burned out 난 완전히 기운이 소진됐어

I'm wiped out 완전히 뻗었어

능력이 안되서 못한다고 말하기

11 업무 나 이건 못해

I can't do this 나 이건 못해

I'm not very good at promoting myself 나 자신을 홍보하는데 서툴러

I'm bad at accounting 회계에 약해

I'm hopeless with machines 난 기계치야

I'm allergic to things like computers 컴퓨터 같은 거에 앨러지가 있어

I don't know the first thing about computers 컴퓨터의 컴자도 몰라

It's far beyond my ability 내 능력 밖이야

I'll never get through this 난 절대 못해낼 거야

I don't feel up to it 내 능력으론 안돼

It's not up to that yet 아직 그정도는 안돼요

I can't handle all this work on my own
나 혼자 이 일을 다 처리할 수 없어

I'm afraid it's more than I can manage
내가 할 수 있는 것 이상인 것 같아

I don't stand a chance 난 가능성이 없어

He doesn't have what it takes, does he? 걔는 자질이 없어, 그지?

I got cold feet 나 자신없어

That's easy for you to say 그렇게 말하긴 쉽지

That's easier said than done 행동보단 말이 쉽지

능력이 돼서 할 수 있다고 자신감있게 말하기

12 **업무** 내가 할 수 있어

I can do that[it, this] 내가 할 수 있어

I can do it better 내가 더 잘 할 수 있어

Let me take care of it 나한테 맡겨

I'll take over now 이제 내가 책임지고 할게요

You can count on me 나한테 맡겨

I'm counting on you 난 널 믿고 있어

Leave it to me 나한테 맡겨, 내가 할게

He's very good at arithmetic 걘 계산에 능해

He's good with numbers[computers] 걘 숫자[컴퓨터]에 강해

He's familiar with all phases of this business
걘 이 사업의 전 단계를 잘 알아

Let me handle it[this] 내가 처리하죠

All in all, I feel he's the best choice
종합해 볼 때 걔가 최고의 선택인 것 같아

He's the man you want 쟤는 네가 찾던 사람야

She's cut out for this job 쟨 이 일에 타고 났어

Can you manage? 할 수 있겠어?

It's much easier than you think 네가 생각하는 거보다 훨씬 쉬워

It's a cinch 거저 먹기야(= It's a piece of cake)

잘 나가고 있다고 말해보기

13 **업무** 해냈어

I made it! 해냈어!

He made it big 걔는 크게 해냈어

You made it! 너 해냈구나!

I did it! 해냈어!

You did it! 해냈구나!

You win 내가 졌어

I won 내가 이겼어

You're a loser 넌 패자야, 멍청이야

You got me beat 나보다 낫네

You've got me 나도 몰라.

She is on a roll 그 여자 한창 잘나가고 있어

Now there you have me 그건 정확한 지적이야, 내가 졌어, 모르겠어

I've got to hand it to you! 너 정말 대단하구나, 나 너한테 두손 들었다

It works! 제대로 되네!, 효과가 있네!

It worked! 된다!

I'm making (some) money 돈을 좀 벌고 있어

I'm making money hand over fist 돈을 왕창 벌고 있어

I made a killing 떼돈 벌었어

Show me the money 돈을 벌어다 줘

Money talks 돈으로 안되는 일 없지

I'm broke 빈털터리야

I have no money 돈이 없어

I don't have much money on me now 지금 수중에 돈이 많이 없어

I'm out of money[cash] 현금이 없어

I'm a little short of money now 지금 현금이 좀 부족해

회의일정 정하기

14 회의 회의 일정이 변경됐어요

회의 일정이 변경됐어요.

There's been a change in the meeting schedule.

· Everyone must attend the morning meeting tomorrow at 5:00 a.m.
  모두 내일 아침 5시의 오전 회의에 참석하도록 하세요.

오늘 오후에 있을 회의에 참석해주세요.

I need you to attend my meeting this afternoon

· It looks like it's going to be a long meeting, doesn't it?
회의가 길어질 것 같아네요, 그렇지 않아요?

회의는 차후 통보시까지 연기되었습니다.

The meeting has been put off until further notice.

· Is the conference room available?
회의실 쓸 수 있어요?

회의를 다음달까지 연기해도 되겠습니까?

Do you mind if we postpone our meeting until next month?

· There's been a change in the meeting schedule. It was postponed.
회의일정이 변경되었어요, 연기되었습니다.

전부 다 준비됐나요?

Is everything all set up?

· Can I please have a copy of the schedule?
일정표를 한 부 얻을 수 있을까요?

오늘 오후에 있을 회의시간 좀 확인해 주세요. 시간 변경은 없겠죠, 그렇죠?

I need you to double-check the time of the meeting this afternoon. There hasn't been any change in the time, has there?

회의를 시작하기

15 회의 여러분 주목해 주십시오

여러분 주목해 주십시오.

May I have your attention, please?

· Please take your seat, as we are about to begin the meeting
모두 자리에 앉아 주십시오, 곧 회의를 시작하겠습니다

· Now that everyone is finally here, let's get this meeting started
이제 모두 모였으니, 회의를 시작하겠습니다

우선, 갑작스런 소집에도 불구하고 오늘 이렇게 참석해 주셔서 감사합니다.

First of all, I would like to thank you for coming today on such short notice.

회장님의 개회사로 회의를 시작하겠습니다.

We would like to begin with some opening remarks from our CEO.

....

회의를 시작하기 전에, 오하이오의 자매사(社)에서 오신 맥케이씨를 소개하겠습니다.

Before we get started, I'd like to introduce Mr. Mackay from our sister company in Ohio.

....

오늘 회의에는 영업을 담당하는 스미스 씨와 품질 관리 전문가인 클라크 씨가 함께 하겠습니다.

At our meeting today, we have Mr. Smith, who is in charge of sales. Also, we have Ms. Clark, who is a quality control specialist.

....

카터씨, 지난번 회의록을 낭독해 주시겠습니까?

Mr. Carter, would you please read the minutes from the last meeting?

· Before we start, let's briefly review the last meeting's notes
  시작하기 전에 간단히 지난번 회의록을 검토해 봅시다

┌─────────────────────────┐
┆ 회의목적을 언명하기 ┆
└─────────────────────────┘

16 회의 이번 회의의 목적은…

이번 회의의 목적은 첫째 3사분기의 이윤을 검토하기 위함이며, 둘째로 4사분기의 새 전략에 관해 의논하기 위해서입니다.

Our goal for this meeting is, first, to go over our third quarter's profit, and secondly, to discuss new strategies for the fourth quarter.

· The goal for this meeting is to~   이번 회의의 목적은…

....

이미 알고 계시겠지만, 우리의 주식이 이번 분기 말까지 한 번 더 분할될 것입니다.

As you probably know, our stock is going to split once again before the end of the quarter.

· As you (probably) know,~ 아시다시피,…

현재, 상황이 위급합니다, 따라서 우리는 앞으로 48시간 이내에 결정을 내려야 합니다.
The situation is now critical, so we will need to make a decision in the next 48 hours.
· The situation is now~ 현재상황은…

이번 회의는 첫째 우리 경영진에 대해 떠도는 소문에 관해 얘기하고, 둘째로 회사 재정 상태가 어렵다는 소문을 종식시키기 위해 소집되었습니다.
I've called this meeting first, to discuss the rumors about our manager, and secondly, to put an end to the speculation that the company is in financial trouble.
· I've called this meeting to~ 이번 회의를 소집한 것은…

아시다시피, 우리가 이번 회의를 갖는 것은 내년도 우리 회사의 비즈니스 전략을 토의하기 위함입니다.
As you probably know, we are holding this meeting to discuss our company's business strategy for next year.
· We're holding this meeting to discuss~
　이번 회의는 …을 논의하기 위해서입니다

회의의 본론으로 들어가 토론하기

17 **회의** 본 안건을 시작하죠

오늘 우리가 집중적으로 다뤄야 할 본 안건으로 들어갑시다.
Let's get started on the main issues that we're going to focus on today.
· Let's get started on the main issues (that)~
　…한 본 안건을 시작합시다

본론으로 들어가 이제 토론하죠.
Let's get down to the business that we are all here to discuss.
· Let's get down to the business (that)~ …한 본론으로 들어가죠

첫번째 안건은 채용절차 개선 문제입니다.

The first thing on the agenda is revising our hiring procedures.

· The first thing on the agenda is the issue involving a reorganization of our staff
첫번째 안건은 사원 재편성에 관한 문제입니다

· The first thing on the agenda is~ 첫번째 안건은…

....

이 문제는 이제 그만 마무리하고 다음 주제로 넘어가죠.

I think it's time to close up this argument and go on to our next topic.

· Shall we go on to the next item on the agenda? 다음 안건으로 넘어갈까요?

....

블랙 씨에서 먼저 시작해 주시겠어요?

Mr. Black, would you like to begin?

· A, would you like to begin? A씨, 시작해주시겠어요?

....

그린 씨께서 사내 안전에 관한 토론을 먼저 시작해 주시겠어요?

Mr. Green, would you like to begin the discussion on safety in the workplace?

· A, would you like to open[begin] the discussion on~
A씨, …관한 토론을 시작해주시겠어요?

· Who would like to begin the discussion today? 누가 오늘 토론을 시작하시겠어요?

· Who's next? 누가 할 차례죠?

┌─────────────────────────────┐
  상대방의 의견을 물어보기
└─────────────────────────────┘

18 **회의** …에 대해 어떻게 생각하십니까

쓰레기 매립지에 대한 새 제안에 대해 어떻게 생각하십니까?

What do you think about the new proposal for the landfill site?

· What do you think about~ ?   …에 관해 어떻게 생각하십니까?

....

우리의 뮤츄얼펀드에 투자액이 증가하고 있는 현상에 대해 어떻게 생각하세요?

What are your views on the increasing amount of money

being invested in our mutual fund?

· What are your views on~ ? ···대해 어떻게 생각하시나요?

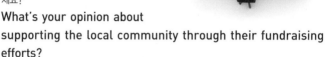

모금행사 운동을 통해 지역사회를 후원하는 문제에 대해서 어떻게 생각하세요?
What's your opinion about supporting the local community through their fundraising efforts?

· What's your opinion about~ ? ···관해 어떤 의견을 갖고 계신가요?

지난 달 매출 감소에 대해 어떤 의견이라도 있으십니까?
Do you have any concerns about the decrease in sales that has been occurring this past month?

· Do you have any concerns about~ ? ···에 대해 어떤 의견이라도 있습니까?

최종표결에 들어가기 전에 이 상황에 대해 의견을 제시하실 분 계십니까?
Has anybody any comments to make before we take a final vote on the situation?

· Has anybody any comments to make~ ? 의견을 제시할 분 계십니까?
· Does anyone have any comments or considerations ~ ? ···할 문제나 의견이 있는 사람 있나요?

내일 아침에 있을 인수건에 대해 어떻게 생각하십니까?
What are your feelings about the takeover that is scheduled to occur tomorrow morning?

· What are your feelings about~? ···에 관해 어떻게 생각하십니까?

┌─ 내 의견을 피력하기 ──────────────┐

19 **회의** 개인적으로 ···하다고 생각됩니다

개인적으로 매우 힘든 프로젝트라고 생각됩니다.
Personally, I believe that it would be a very difficult project.

· (Personally), I think[believe] that~ (개인적으로) ···라고 생각합니다

계속 밀고 나가면, 매출이 증가하리라고 확신
합니다.

**I really believe that if we persist,
there will be an increase in
sales.**

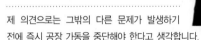
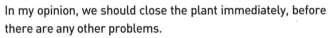

· I really believe that~ …을 확신합니다

제 의견으로는 그밖의 다른 문제가 발생하기
전에 즉시 공장 가동을 중단해야 한다고 생각합니다.

**In my opinion, we should close the plant immediately, before
there are any other problems.**

· In my opinion,~ 제 의견으로는 　　As I see it,~ 제가 보기에

그 보고서는 무작위 표본 조사는 아닌 것 같습니다만.

It seems to me that the report is not a random sample study.

· It seems to me that~ …인 것 같습니다
· It seems to me that we might be making the right decision 올바른 결정을 내리는
　것 같아요

이 일에 보다 적합한 사람을 찾을 수 없다고 확신합니다.

**I'm sure that you won't be able to find a better person for the
job.**

· I'm sure that~ …을 확신합니다

몇 달 새 시장경기가 반전되리라 확신합니다.

**I'm convinced that the market will turn around in a few
months.**

· I'm convinced that~ …을 확신합니다

틀림없이 그가 우리의 요구에 응하여 거래를 맺게 될 것입니다.

**I feel quite sure that he will return our calls and sign a deal
with us.**

· I feel quite sure that~ 틀림없이 …라고 생각합니다

20 회의 …을 강력히 제안하는 바입니다

시제품(試製品)은 좀더 테스트를 거쳐야 한다고 강력히 제안하는 바입니다.

We strongly recommend that the prototype undergo more testing.

· We strongly recommend that~ …을 강력히 제안합니다

비록 그게 일시적인 해고라는 대가를 치르더라도 우린 계획대로 밀고 나가야 합니다.

We must stick to our plan, which may mean some temporary layoffs.

· We must~ …을 해야 합니다

시장이 달아있을 때 부동산을 매각하자고 건의하는 바입니다.

My recommendation is that we sell the property while the market is hot.

· My suggestion [recommendation] is that~ …을 제안합니다

지난 주 제 동료 한사람이 알려준 건의사항이 하나 있습니다.

I have a suggestion that was given to me by a colleague last week.

· I have a suggestion that ~ …을 제안합니다

유일한 해결책은 논쟁을 멈추고 그들에게 5%의 급여인상을 해주는 것입니다.

The only solution is to give in and give them the five-percent raise.

· The only solution is to~ 유일한 해결책은…

가능한 한 빨리 대안을 제시하는 수밖에 다른 방도가 없습니다.

The only other alternative is to submit a counteroffer as soon as possible.

· The only other alternative is to~ 유일한 대안은….

몇 명이나 건의된 계획을 마음에 들어하는지 알아봅시다.
Let's get an idea of how many people like the proposed plan.

· How about~ ? …은 어떨까요?   Why don't we~? …을 합시다

21 회의 …하는 데 찬성입니다

월요일 아침 일찍 그 계약에 관해 총투표를 하자는 데
찬성입니다.
I'm for having a general vote on the contract first thing Monday morning.

· I'm for~ …에 찬성합니다

네, 그건 사실입니다만, 지금으로부터 2년 후면 이
상황이 어떻게 될까요?
Yes, that may be true, but what will the situation be like two years from now?

· That may be true, but~ 그건 사실이지만…
· Well, you have a point there, but~ 음, 당신 말에도 일리는 있습니다만…

무슨 말씀인지 잘 알겠습니다만, 다른 사람들도 그렇게 생각하지는 않을 겁니다.
I can see your point, but I don't think the others feel the same way about it.

· I can see your point, but~ 무슨 말씀인지 알겠지만…

말도 안됩니다. 현재 우리에겐 재정지원이 없잖습니까.
That's out of the question, we don't have the financial backing.

· That's out of the question,~ 말도 안됩니다…

우리에게 협력사가 없다면 그 의견에 전적으로 반대입니다.
I'm absolutely against the idea, unless we have a partner.

· I'm (absolutely) against~ 전적으로 …반대합니다

그 제안에 반대합니다. 왜냐하면, 첫째 시행착오를 거칠 여유가 없고, 둘째 그것은 성장을 고려하지 않았습니다.

I'm against the proposal, because firstly, there is no room for error, and secondly, it doesn't allow for growth.

· I'm against~ , because firstly, S+V ~ and secondly, S+V ~ 첫째는 … 둘째는 …라는 이유로 반대합니다

결론을 끌어내기

22 **회의** …하는데 동의하십니까?

협상을 계속해야 한다는데 동의하십니까?

Do we agree that we should proceed with the negotiations?

· Do we agree that~ ? …에 동의하십니까?

··

더이상의 반대의견이 없으시면 투표에 들어가겠습니다.

If there are no more objections then we should vote on the matter.

· If there are no more objections (then) we should~

더이상 반대의견이 없으면, …을 하겠습니다

··

모든 분들이 다 찬성하신다면 이제 이 문제를 처리할 위원회를 조직해야겠습니다.

If everyone's in favor, we should create a committee to deal with the issue.

· If everyone's in favor[agreement] (then) we should~

모두 찬성한다면 …을 하겠습니다

··

지금까지 우리가 토론한 것을 정리해 봅시다.

Let's summarize what we have done up until now.

· Let's summarize~ …을 정리해보죠

··

이로써 우리는 사람들에게 정보를 제공하기 위한 일련의 모임을 개최해야 한다는데 동의했습니다.

To summarize, we agreed that we should hold a series of meetings to inform the public.

· To summarize[conclude], we agreed[decided] that~ 요약하자면, …에 동의했습니다

최종결론엔 이르지 못했지만 내일이면 협상을 마무리할 수 있을 것입니다.
We haven't made a final decision, but we expect to finish negotiations tomorrow.

· We haven't made a final decision, but~ 최종결론엔 이르지 못했지만,

01 숫자영어 87.5 점을 받았어

I got a score of 87.5(eighty-seven point five) percent
87.5점 받았어

I usually wear size 9 1/2(nine and a half)
보통 9와 2분의 1사이즈를 신어

I saved five times as much as I did last year
작년보다 5배나 저축했어

I think it's about 4.5[four point five] meters long
4.5 미터쯤 될 거예요

He was born in 1985 1985년에 태어났어

In the early '90s(nineties) 90년대 초반이에요

What're you planning to do on the 31st of December?
12/31일에 뭐 할 거야?

She's in her early twenties 그녀는 20대 초반야.

Here we are, sir. That'll be $4.50
다 왔습니다, 손님. 4달러 50센트입니다

It's area code four, one, six, two, two, five, double oh, four,
one 지역번호 416에 225-0041야

It's 010-741-8529 010-741-8529입니다

It's Jero_[underline]t@aol.com
제로 언더라인 티 앳 에이오엘 닷컴야

What time is it now? 지금 몇시야?

Do you have the time? 몇시야?

What time have you got? 몇시야?

It's five twenty-four 5시 24분

It's ten to two 10시 2분야

It's five after[past] one 1시 5분야

The clock is five minutes slow[behind] 시계가 5분 늦어

The clock is five minutes fast 시계가 5분 빨리가

It's 37°(thirty-seven degrees) celsius and sunny 37도고 화창해

02 숫자영어 맨체스터가 3대 1로 이겼어

Manchester United won five to three
맨체스터 유나이티드가 3대 1로 이겼어

Can you believe Chicago White Sox crushed the Yankees by a score of five to zero? 시카고 화이트삭스가 양키스를 5대 0으로 묵사발 냈다는 것이 믿기지 않아

We're winning by two goals 우리가 두골차로 이기고 있어

Colorado is leading by two points 콜로라도가 2점차로 이기고 있어

The Red Sox lost five to four 보스톤이 5대 4로 졌어

They won by four points 4점차로 이겼어

The Jets beat the Flames seven to five 젯츠가 플레임즈를 7:5로 이겼어

Giants by five 자이언츠가 5점차로 이겼어

They were ahead at halftime 그들이 전반전에 이기고 있었어

3-2[three two] with 15 minutes to go 15분 남겨놓고 3대 2로 이기고 있어

It ended in a one-one draw 1:1로 끝났어

Their players didn't try hard enough, and they lost
열심히 안뛰더니 지더라고

She just couldn't turn it around 다시 뒤집지를 못했어

Ji-yai Shin is five strokes behind the leader
신지애가 선두와 5타 뒤져

Michelle had an impressive round of golf today
미셸이 오늘 골프를 인상적으로 쳤어

03 데이트 그 사람 내 타입이네

He's really my type 걘 딱 내 타입이야

You're my type 넌 내 타입야

He is Mr. Right 걘 내 이상형이야

The right woman is just waiting for you 네 연분이 널 기다리고 있다구

You're the right girl for me 넌 내 이상형야

What type of man[woman] do you like? 어떤 남자[여자]를 좋아해?

May I ask you out? 데이트 신청해도 돼요?

Would you go on a date with me? 나와 데이트 할래요?

Are you asking me out? 데이트 신청하는 거야?

Are you asking me for a date? 데이트 하자고 하는 거야?

Are you asking me out on a date? 데이트 신청하는 거야?

He's going out with Jane 그 사람은 제인하고 사귀는 중이야

Are you seeing someone? 누구 사귀는 사람 있어?

Are you dating anyone now? 지금 사귀는 사람 있어?

Are you going steady with someone? 애인 있어?

I'm seeing her 난 그녀하고 사귀고 있어

I'm not seeing anybody 난 지금 사귀는 사람 없어

I'm just flirting 좀 추근거린 것뿐이야, 작업 좀 들어간 것뿐인데

Are you coming on to me? 지금 날 유혹하는 거예요?

Are you trying to seduce me? 날 유혹하는 거야?

Are you hitting on me? 지금 날 꼬시는 거야?

He made a move on me 그 사람 내게 추근대던데

He made a pass at me 그 남자가 나한테 수작을 걸었어

상대방에게 좋다고 사랑한다고 말할 때

04 **사랑** 난 너한테 빠져있어

I'm crazy about you 난 너한테 빠져있어

I'm nuts[mad] about you 널 미친듯이 좋아해

I've got a crush on you 난 네가 맘에 들어

I think he has a crush on you 걔가 널 무척 좋아하는 것 같아

I'm so into you 나 너한테 푹 빠져 있어

I have (strong) feelings for her 나 쟤한테 마음있어

You've had feelings for me? 너 나한테 마음있지?

He has[got] a thing for her 걘 그 여자를 맘에 두고 있어

What do you see in her? 그 여자 뭐가 좋아?, 어디가 좋은 거야?

What do you see in this guy? 이 사람 어디가 좋은 거야?

They really hit it off 쟤네들은 바로 좋아하더라고

I (really) hit it off with her[him] 난 걔랑 정말 금세 좋아졌어

We have chemistry 우린 잘 통해

You turn me on 넌 내 맘에 쏙 들어, 넌 날 흥분시켜

I fell in love with Dick 딕하고 사랑에 빠졌어

I'm deeply in love with Jessica 제시카와 깊은 사랑에 빠졌어

I can't live without you 너 없이는 못살아

I don't want to live without you 너없인 살고 싶지 않아

Life isn't worth living without you 너없는 삶은 살가치가 없어

You mean everything to me 난 너밖에 없어

I can't stop myself from loving you 널 사랑하지 않고는 못배겨

I'm happy to have been part of your life 네 삶의 일부가 되어서 기뻐

You make me happy 네가 있어 행복해

You belong to me 넌 내 소유야

You're mine 넌 내꺼야

I'm [all] yours 난 네꺼야

It was meant to be 운명이었어, 하늘이 정해준거야

You're the one for me 넌 내 짝이야

I'm dying to see her 걔 보고 싶어 죽겠어

I've never felt like this before 이런 기분 처음이야

좀 더 구체적으로 사랑하기

05 **사랑** 그 사람과 사랑을 나누었어

He made love to me 그 사람과 사랑을 나눴어

It was just a one night thing 하룻밤 잔 것뿐이야

I want to have a fling 번개 좀 해야겠어

How about a quickie? 가볍게 한번 어때?

I want to make out with my girlfriend 애인하고 애무하고 싶어

I want to have sex with you 너하고 섹스하고 싶어

I want to get laid 섹스하고파

They're doing it 쟤네들 그거 한다

He got lucky with Julie 걔가 줄리랑 잤대

06 결혼과 이혼 나랑 결혼해줄래?

Will you marry me? 나랑 결혼해줄래?

Will you be my wife[husband]? 내 아내[남편]이 되어줄래요?

I want to share the rest of my life with you
나의 여생을 당신과 보내고 싶어

She wants to start a family 걔는 가정을 꾸미고 싶어해

She is not marriage material 그 여자는 결혼상대는 아냐

He is not boyfriend material 그 사람은 애인감이 아냐

How's your married life? 결혼생활 어때?

We're a well-matched couple 우린 잘 어울리는 커플야

I'm pregnant 나 임신했어

I'm going to have a baby 애를 가질거야

I'm expecting 임신중야

What did she have? 남자야 여자야?

I'm going to break up with you 우리 그만 만나자

We're on a break 잠시 떨어져 있는거야

I'm over you 너랑은 끝났어

I'm through with you 너랑 이제 끝이야

I dumped him 내가 걔 찼어

We fight a lot 우린 싸움을 많이 해

My wife's cheating on me 아내가 바람을 폈어

My wife's a two-timer 아내가 바람둥이야

I had an affair with my secretary 내가 비서와 바람을 폈어

We're living separately now 우린 현재 별거하고 있어

I'm separated from my wife 아내와 별거하고 있어

I wish I had never met you 널 안 만났더라면 좋았을 텐데

I regret meeting you 널 만난 걸 후회해

I wish you were never a part of my life
너를 만나지 않았더라면 좋았을 텐데

숫자로 말하는 영어 ||||||||||||||||||||||

1. 월일(month, date) 말하기
   • 「month + date의 서수」 ex. November 25th
   • 「the + date의 서수 + of + month」 ex. the 25th of November
     ex. June 15th = June fifteenth 혹은 the fifteenth of June

2. 년도 말하기 4자리를 두개씩 끊어읽는 것이 일반적이다
     ex. 1999 : nineteen ninety-nine   ex. 2000 : two thousand
     ex. 2005 : two thousand five   ex. 2012 : two thousand twelve

3. 나이말하기 20대: in one's twenties 30대: in one's thirties
     ex. 20대 초(중,후)반 : in one's early (mid, late) twenties

4. 돈말하기
     ex. $9.23: nine twenty-three | nine dollars and twenty-three cents
     ex. $11.03: eleven oh three | eleven dollars and three cents
     ex. $3,000: three thousand dollars | three grand

5. 전화번호 카드번호 읽듯이 숫자 하나하나를 각각 기수로 읽어주면 된다
     ex. 867-0023 : eight, six, seven, double oh, two, three
     ex. 010-9876-5100 oh, one, oh, nine, eight, seven, six, five, one hundred

6. 스포츠 경기 결과
     ex. The LA Dodgers beat the New York Yankees by a score of 10 to 3
     ex. The Bears defeated the Raiders (by a score of) 42 to 7
     ex. The Blue Jays won 5 to 3
     ex. The Mets were defeated by the Yankees in overtime by a score of
       1 to 0 (one to zero, one to nothing)
     ex. The Giants lost the game by a score of 3 to 2
     ex. The game ended in a tie
     ex. We're winning by three goals
     ex. We are down 2 to 3
     ex. The Bulls are leading by eight points

SMART ENGLISH | SECTION

Basic English

02

기본영어회화

Chapter 01 | 만남 | 약속

01 인사 "잘 지냈어?"

How (are) you doing? 안녕?, 잘 지냈어?

How are you? 잘 지내?(만났을 때), 괜찮어?(상대방에게 괜찮냐고 물어볼 때)

How's it going? 잘 지내?

How's it going today? 오늘 어때?

How's everything going? 다 잘돼 가?

What's new? 뭐 새로운 일 있어?

What's new with you? 그러는 넌 별일 없어?

[보충설명] What's new?라고 묻는 상대방의 인사에 답하는 전형적인 인사.

What's up? 어때?

What's happening? 어떻게 지내?, 잘 지내니?

What's going on? 무슨 일이야?

What's going on in there[here]? 거기[여기] 무슨 일 있어?

What's going on with him? 그 사람 무슨 일 있어?

(You) Doing okay? 잘지내?, 괜찮어?

(Is) Everything okay? 잘 지내지?, 일은 다 잘 되지?

(Have) (you) Been okay? 그동안 잘 지냈어?

How're you getting along? 어떻게 지내?

How's the[your] family? 가족들은 다 잘 지내?

How's the wife[your kid]? 부인[애들]은 잘 지내?

How's business? 일은 어때?

02 인사 오랜만야?, 이게 누구야?

How (have) you been? 어떻게 지냈어?, 잘 지냈어?

What have you been up to? 뭐하고 지냈어?, 별일 없어?

What have you been doing? 뭐하고 지냈어?

Long time no see 오랜만이야

It's been a long time 오랜만이야

I haven't seen you for a long time[for ages] 오랜만이야

What're you doing here? 여긴 어쩐 일이야?

Fancy meeting you here 이런 데서 다 만나다니

Look who's here! 아니 이게 누구야!

I didn't expect to see you here 여기서 널 만날 줄 생각도 못했어

I never thought I'd see you here 여기서 널 만날 줄 생각도 못했어

Are you here on business? 여기 비즈니스로 온거야?

What's the story? 어떻게 지내?

How's life[the world] treating you? 사는 건 어때?

Nice weather, huh? 날씨 좋으네 그지?

그밖의 인사표현

03 인사 오늘 어땠어?

How was your day? 오늘 어땠어?

How are you feeling? 기분 어때?

Where're you headed? 어디 가?

Where're you going? 어디 가?

Where're you off to? 어디 가?

What're you doing? 뭐해?

Where have you been? 어디 갔었어?

I ran into her 그 여자와 우연히 마주쳤어

I keep bumping into you 우리 자꾸 마주치네요

특별한 날에 하는 인사법

04 인사 생일 축하해!

Happy birthday! 생일 축하해!

Happy New Year! 새해 복많이 받아!

Happy New Year to you, too! 너도 새해 복많이 받아!

(You) Have a Merry Christmas! 메리 크리스마스!

I wish you a Merry Christmas! 성탄절 즐겁게 보내!

Happy holidays! 휴일 잘 보내!

Happy Valentine's Day! 발렌타인 잘 보내!

Happy Thanksgiving! 추석 잘 보내!

Happy Chusok! 추석 잘 지내!

뭔가 심상치 않을 때

05 인사 무슨 일이야?

What's wrong (with you)? 무슨 일이야?, 뭐 잘못됐어?

What's the problem? 무슨 일인데?

What's the matter with you? 무슨 일이야?, 도대체 왜그래?

What happened? 무슨 일이야?, 어떻게 된 거야?

What happened to[with] you? 너 무슨 일이야?, 왜 그래?

What's with you? 뭐 땜에 그래?

What's with your hair? 머리가 왜 그래?

What's with her[him, the guys]? 쟤(들) 왜 저래?

What's gotten into you? 뭣 때문에 이러는 거야?

What's gotten into your head? 무슨 생각으로 그래?

What's cooking? 무슨 일이야?

What's eating you? 뭐가 문제야?, 무슨 걱정거리라도 있어?

What gives? 무슨 일 있어?

Why the long face? 왜 그래?, 무슨 기분 안좋은 일 있어?

What's bothering you? 뭐가 잘못됐어?

What's on your mind? 왜 그래?, 문제가 뭔대?

Do you have something on your mind? 왜 그래?

What are you up to? 뭐해?, 뭘 할거야?

I know what you're up to 네 속셈 다 알아

상대방이 좋아 보일 때

06 **인사** 너 좋아 보인다

Look at you 얘 좀 봐라!, (어머) 얘 좀 봐!

보충설명 상대방이 멋진 차림을 하였거나 혹은 바람직한 행동을 했을 경우 혹은 어처구니 없는 행동을 한 상대방을 향해 비난하면서도 쓰인다.

You look good[great]! 너 멋져 보인다!
You haven't changed at all 너 하나도 안 변했네
You haven't changed much 너 별로 안 변했어
You've really changed 너 정말 많이 변했다
You've grown up 너 많이 컸다
Are you gaining weight? 살쪘어?
Are you getting fatter? 뚱뚱해졌어?
Are you losing weight? 살 빠졌어?

상대방이 안 좋아 보일 때

07 **인사** 너 안 좋아 보여

You don't look good today 오늘 너 안 좋아 보여
You look serious 너 심각해 보여
You seem nervous 너 초조해 보여
Something's wrong with you today 너 오늘 좀 이상해
You look depressed 너 매우 지쳐보여
You look sad, today 너 오늘 슬퍼보여
You look exhausted 너 지쳐보인다
You look very tired 너 매우 피곤해 보여
You need a break 너 좀 쉬어야 돼

08 인사 잘 지내고 있어

I'm doing OK 잘 지내고 있어

I'm fine. How about you? 잘 지내. 넌 어때?

I'm cool 잘 지내

Not bad 그리 나쁘지 않아

Pretty good 잘 지내

(It) Couldn't be better 최고야, 아주 좋아

Things have never been better 최고야

(Things) Could be better 별로야, 그냥 그래

> 보충설명 Could be better는 '더 좋을 수도 있는데 그렇지 않다'라는 의미로 다소 부정적인 표현인 반면 다음의 Could be worse는 '더 나쁠 수도 있는데 그렇지 않다'라는 의미로 다소 긍정적인 표현임.

Could be worse 그럭저럭 잘 지내지

I couldn't ask for more 최고야, 더 이상 바랄 게 없어

(I) Can't complain 잘 지내

(I have) Nothing to complain about 잘 지내

No complaints 잘 지내

Not (too) much 별일 없어, 그냥 그럭저럭

Nothing much 별로 특별한 건 없어, 별일 아냐

So so 그저 그래

Nothing special 별일 아냐, 별일 없어

Nothing in particular 별일 아냐

Same as always 맨날 똑같지 뭐

Same as usual 늘 그렇지 뭐

Same old story[stuff] 늘 그렇지 뭐

Not very well 안 좋아

Not good 안 좋아

Not so great 좋지 않아

09 인사 데이빗이라고 합니다

Hello, my name is David 안녕하세요, 데이빗이라고 합니다

I'd like to introduce myself 제 소개를 하겠습니다

I'd like you to meet a friend of mine 내 친구 한 명 소개할게

I want you to meet Sam 샘하고 인사해

Paul, meet Jane 폴, 제인이야

Mina, this is Peter...Peter, Mina 미나, 이쪽이 피터야… 피터, 이쪽은 미나야

Mr.Kim, this is Mr.Johnson, my boss 미스터 김, 이분은 사장님인 존슨 씨야

Mary, have you met Dan? 메리야, 댄 만나본 적 있니?

Tom, Laura is the girl I was telling you about
탐, 얘가 내가 말하던 로라야

I've heard so much[a lot] about you 네 얘기 많이 들었어

Just call me John 그냥 존이라고 불러

You can call me by my first name 이름으로 불러

Who's this? 이 사람 누구야?

Do you know each other? 둘이 아는 사이니?

Have you two met before? 너희 둘 전에 만난 적 있어?

Don't I know you from somewhere? 어디서 만난 적 있지 않나요?

We've never met before 우린 초면야

I don't think we've met before 초면인 것 같은데요

May I have your name, please? 이름 좀 알려줄래요?

10 인사 만나서 반가워요

Nice to meet you 만나서 반가워요

(It's) Nice to see you 만나서 반가워요, 만나서 반가웠어요

It's great seeing you again 다시 만나 반가워

I'm happy to see you 만나서 반가워

I'm glad[pleased] to meet you 만나서 반가워요

(It's, It was) Good to see you 만나서 반가워, 만나서 반가웠어

Good to see you again 다시 만나니 반가워

Good to see you too 나도 만나서 반가워

(It was) Nice meeting you 만나서 반가웠어

Nice talking to you 만나서 반가웠어

잠시 자리를 비울 때

11 인사 금방 돌아올게

I'll be back 다녀 올게, 금방 올게

(I'll) Be right back 바로 올게

(I'll) Be back soon 금방 돌아올게

(I'll) Be back in a sec 곧 돌아올게

(I'll) Be back in just a minute 금세 돌아올게

She'll be back any minute 그 여자는 곧 돌아올거예요

I'll be right with you 잠시만, 곧 돌아올게

I'll be with you in a sec[minute] 곧 돌아올게

Can[Could] you excuse us? 실례 좀 해도 될까요?, 자리 좀 비켜주시겠어요?

Could[May] I be excused? 이만 일어나도 될까요?, 실례 좀 해도 되겠어요?

그만 가봐야 된다고 일어서기(1)

12 인사 이제 그만 가봐야 겠어

I have (got) to go 이제 가봐야겠어, 이제 (전화를) 끊어야겠어

I'd better go now 이젠 가야겠어

I have to go to + 장소 …에 가야 해

보충설명 I have to go to 다음에 동사가 오면 「…하러 가야 돼」라는 의미가 된다.

Example I have to go to a wedding. 결혼식에 가야돼

Example I'm really sorry but I have to go to work. 미안하지만 일하러가야 돼요.

I have to leave 출발해야겠어

Let's leave 가자, 출발하자

I must be going 그만 가봐야 될 것 같아

I think I'd better be going 그만 가봐야 될 것 같아

It's getting late and I'd better be going 늦어서 가봐야 돼

It's time we should be going 그만 일어납시다

I should get going 서둘러 가봐야겠어

I'd better get going 가보는 게 좋겠어

I've got to get going 가야겠어

Let's get going 이젠 어서 가자

I('ve) got to get moving 가봐야겠어

You'd better get moving 너 그만 가봐야지

(It's) Time for me to go 갈 시간이야, 일어서야겠어

Time to move 갈 시간이야

Let's hit the road 출발하자고

그만 가봐야 된다고 일어서기(2)

13 인사 그만 일어서야 겠어

I'm going to take off 그만 일어서야겠어

I must be off 이제 가봐야겠어

(I'd) Better be off 가봐야겠어

I'd better be going 가봐야겠어

I am off (now) 나 간다

I'm off to Jeff's 제프네 집에 가려구

I'm off to see your dad 너희 아빠 만나러 갈래 (be off to + 동사)

I've got to run 서둘러 가봐야겠어

(I've) Got to fly 난 이만 사라져야겠어

I'm out of here 나 갈게

I'm not here 나 여기 없는 거야

I'm gone 나 간다

I'm getting out of here 나 간다, 지금 나 갈건데

Let's get out of here 나가자, 여기서 빠져 나가자

I'm leaving. Bye! 나 간다. 안녕!

Are you leaving so soon? 벌써 가려구?, 왜 이렇게 빨리 가?

I don't want to wear out my welcome
넘 번거롭게 하는게 아닌지 모르겠네

I wish I could stay longer 더 남아 있으면 좋을 텐데

You're excused 그러세요, 괜찮다, 그만 나가 보거라

You're dismissed 가도 좋아, 해산

Class dismissed 수업 끝났습니다

> 나중에 다시 보자고 하면서 헤어지기

14 인사 나중에 보자

See you later 나중에 봐

(I'll) See you guys later 얘들아 나중에 봐

I'll try to see you later 나중에 봐

(I'll) Be seeing you 또 보자

See you soon 또 보자

See you around 또 보자

See you in the morning[tomorrow] 아침에[내일] 보자

I'll see you then 그럼 그때 보자

Catch you later 나중에 보자

I'll catch up with you in the gym 체육관에서 보자

I'll catch up with you later 나중에 보자

I'll try to catch you some other time 언제 한번 보도록 하자

Goodbye for now 그만 여기서 작별하죠

Bye for now 그만 여기서 헤어지자

Goodbye until next time 다시 만날 때까지 잘 있어

Bye Jane! 제인아 잘가!

Bye-bye! 안녕!

Don't work too hard 너무 무리하지 말구

Take care! 조심하고!

Take care of yourself 몸조심해

Be careful 조심해

Ciao! 잘 가!

Sayonara! 잘 가!

Hasta la vista! 잘 가!, 또 보자!

15 인사 오늘 잘 지내

Have a nice day 오늘 잘 지내

Have a nice weekend 주말 잘 보내

Have a nice trip! 여행 멋지게 보내고!

Have fun! 재미있게 보내!

Enjoy yourself! 즐겁게 지내!

Good luck 행운을 빌어

Good luck with that! 행운이 있기를!

(The) Best of luck (to someone)! 잘 되기를 빌게!

I wish you success! 성공하길 빌어!

Good luck, go get them 행운을 빌어, 가서 잡으라고

Good luck (to you), you'll need it 행운을 빌어, 행운이 필요할거야

My fingers are crossed 행운을 빌어요

I'll keep my fingers crossed (for you)! 행운을 빌어줄게!

Lucky me 나한테 다행이구만

Lucky bastard! 그놈의 자식 운도 좋구만!

Wish me luck! 행운을 빌어줘

16 인사 너를 보고 싶을 거야

I'm going to miss you 보고 싶을 거야

I will (really) miss you 네가 그리울 거야

We're all going to miss you 우리 모두 널 보고 싶을 거야

I'm already missing you 벌써 그리워지려고 해

I hope I can come back again 다시 오기를 바래

I hope to see you again (sometime) (조만간에) 다시 한번 보자

Could I see you again? 다시 한번 볼 수 있어?

Don't stay away so long 자주 좀 와

Give me a call sometime 한번 전화해

Call me later 나중에 전화해

I wish I could go with you 너랑 같이 가면 좋을텐데

Let's get[keep] in touch! 연락하고 지내자!

Don't forget to e-mail me 잊지말고 메일 보내

Don't forget to write 잊지말고 편지 써

Drop me a line 나한테 편지 좀 써

Give my best to your folks 가족들에게 안부 전해줘

All the best to everyone 모두에게 안부 전해줘

Please give my regards to your family 가족에게 안부 전해줘

Say hello[hi] to your wife 부인에게 안부 전해 주게나

집이나 파티에 초대하기

17 초대 우리 집에 들려

Come over to my place[house] 우리 집에 들려

Please come to John's farewell party this Friday
금요일 존 송별회에 와

Please attend our office party 회사 회식에 참석해요

Drop by for a drink 언제 한번 놀러 와 한잔 하자고

If you're ever in Seoul, do drop by 서울에 오게 되면 들리라고

Drop by sometime 언제 한번 들려

You're invited to Bob's bachelor party 밥의 총각파티에 참석했으면 해

We cordially invite you to attend the wedding
결혼식에 참석해줬으면 해요

Hope you can make it 너도 올 수 있으면 좋겠어

Hope you can come 네가 올 수 있기를 바래

I'm sorry I can't make it 미안하지만 못가

When can I come over? 내가 언제 갈까?

When can I stop by? 내가 언제 들를까?

When can you come over? 언제 올 수 있어?

방문하거나 방문한 사람에게 누구냐고 물어볼 때

18 방문 아무도 안계세요?

Hello, is anyone there? 여보세요?, 아무도 안계세요?

Is anyone here? 누구 안 계세요?

(Hello) Anybody home? 누구 집에 없어요?, 안 계세요?

I'd like to see Mr.James 제임스 씨를 만나뵈려고요

I came[am] here to see Mr. Smith 스미스 씨를 만나뵈러 왔어요

Who is it? 누구세요?, 누구야?

Who's there? 누구세요?

Who was it? 누군데? 누구였어?

Would you get that? 문 좀 열어줄래?, 전화 좀 받아줄래?

Could you answer it for me? 대신 좀 열어[받아]줄래?

I'll get it 내가 받을게

Let me 내가 받을게

I'm home 나 왔어

Come on in 어서 들어와

Please come in 어서 들어와

Welcome home 어서 와

Welcome! 어서 왜!

Welcome to our Christmas party 크리스마스 파티에 오신 걸 환영합니다

Welcome aboard 함께 일하게 된 걸 환영해, 귀국[귀향]을 축하해

Won't you come in? 들어오지 않을래?

It's nice to be here 저도 여기 오게 돼서 기뻐요

It's great to be here 여기 오게 돼 무척 기뻐요

19 손님맞이 와줘서 고마워

I'm glad you could come 네가 와줘서 기뻐

How nice of you to come 와줘서 고마워

Thank you for coming 와줘서 고마워

Thank you[Thanks] for inviting me 초대해줘서 고마워

I really like your apartment 너희 아파트 정말 좋다

Can I park my car here? 여기 주차해도 돼?

Is parking okay here? 여기 주차해도 괜찮아?

Is it all right to park my car here? 차 여기다 주차해도 돼?

Have[Take] a seat 앉아

Please sit down 앉으세요

Make yourself at home 편히계세요

Please feel free to make yourself at home 집처럼 편히하세요

Please make yourself comfortable 편히하세요

Make yourself a drink and relax 술 한 잔 따라 마시며 편히 쉬어

May I use your rest room? 화장실 좀 써도 될까요?

May I use your bathroom[toilet]? 화장실 좀 써도 될까요?

Where's the bathroom? 화장실이 어디예요?

How can I get to the bathroom? 화장실 어떻게 가죠?

20 약속 시간 있어?

(You) Got a minute? 시간돼?

Do you have (some) time? 시간 있어요?

Are you available on Thursday morning? 목요일 오전에 시간 돼?

Are you available after the meeting for lunch?
회의 후에 점심 가능해?

Are you available? 시간돼?

Will you be free to + 동사 ? ···할 시간이 돼?

Example Will you be free to go to the movies on the weekend? 주말에 영화보러 갈 수 있어?

Are you free in the afternoon? 오후에 시간 있어?

Do you have time to + 동사 ? ···할 시간이 있어요?

Example Do you have time to talk for a bit? 잠깐 얘기할 시간이 있나요?

Example Do you have time to see me on the weekend?
주말에 만날 수 있을까?

Let's get together (sometime) (조만간) 한번 보자

Why don't we get together on Wednesday?
수요일에 만날까요?

Let's meet to talk about it 만나서 그 얘기해보자

I'd like to meet with you after work if you're not too busy
바쁘지 않으면 퇴근후 봤으면 해

I wonder if we could get together on the 15th
15일에 만날 수 있을까

Shall we get together on Thursday after five?
목요일 5시이후에 볼래요?

Are you doing anything this afternoon? 오후에 뭐 계획있어?

Okay, let me check my schedule 일정을 한번 확인해 보죠

I'd like to set up an appointment for Monday
월요일로 약속정하고 싶어요

Can you make time to discuss our purchases?
시간내서 구매품 의논할 수 있어?

┌─────────────────────┐
│ 언제 어디서 만날지 정할 때 │
└─────────────────────┘

21 **약속** 내일 오전이 어때?

How about + 구체적인 장소/시간 ? ···가 어때?

Example How about tomorrow morning? 내일 오전이 어때?

Example How about Friday in my office? 금요일날 내 사무실에서 어때?

About what time? 몇시에?

Would this afternoon be all right with you? 오늘 오후 괜찮겠어요?

Is + 시간 + all right? …가 괜찮아?

When can you make it? 몇시에 도착할 수 있겠니?

make it은 'to arrive in time' 이란 의미로 「약속 시간에 닿다」라는 의미.

Can you make it? 올 수 있어?

Can you make it at 7? 7시에 올 수 있겠니?

When and where can I meet you? 언제 어디서 만날까?

What time is[would be] good for you? 몇시가 좋겠어?

When is good for you? 언제가 좋아?

What time would you like to meet? 몇시에 만날래?

When is the most convenient time for you?
언제가 가장 편리한 시간야?

Does this afternoon work for you? 오후에 괜찮으세요?

That works for me 나도 그때가 괜찮아요.

You decide when 언제 만날지 네가 결정해

You decide where 어디서 만날지 네가 결정해

That'll be fine. See you then 그게 좋겠군요. 그때 봐요

Whenever you're free 네가 시간나면 아무때나

Whenever 아무 때나

When you have time 네가 시간될 때

Anytime is fine 아무 때나 좋아

22 약속 다음으로 미루자

I'll take a rain check 이번에는 다음으로 미룰게

Do you mind if I take a rain check? 다음으로 미뤄도 될까?

Maybe some other time 다음을 기약하지

We'll try again some other time 나중에 기약하자

I have no time available this week 이번 주엔 시간낼 수가 없어

I have no time to see you in the afternoon 오후에 만날 시간이 없어

I'm afraid I have another appointment 미안하지만 선약이 있어

I have another appointment at that time
그 시간에는 선약이 있는데요

That's a bad day for me 그날은 안되는데

Sorry, I won't be able to make it this weekend
미안 주말 약속 못 지켜

I won't be able to make it to the presentation 발표회에 못가

I won't be able to make it 못갈 것 같아

Could we change it to Monday? 월요일로 바꿀 수 있어?

I'd rather make it later if that's okay
괜찮다면 날짜를 더 미루는 게 낫겠어요

I'm afraid I have to cancel tomorrow's appointment
내일 약속 취소해야 돼

I'll be there 갈게

I'll be right there 곧 갈게, 지금 가

I'm going to be there 갈게, 갈거야

You bet I'll be there 꼭 갈게

She's going to be here 걔는 여기 올거야

I'm going to make it to the wedding
결혼식에 갈 예정이야

I'm going 나 가

I'm not going 나 안가

약속시간에 늦거나 못온다고 말하기

23 **약속** 좀 늦을 것 같아

I'm sorry but I'm going to be a little late 미안하지만 좀 늦을 것 같아

I might be about thirty minutes late 한 30분 정도 늦을 것 같아

I'm sorry I'm late 늦어서 미안해

Something's come up 일이 좀 생겼어

Something unexpected came up 갑자기 일이 생겨서요

What time do you think you will show up? 몇시에 올 수 있을 것 같아?

I'll be there soon 곧 갈게

I'll try and get there as soon as I can 가능한 한 빨리 가도록 할게

I'm sorry I kept you waiting so long 너무 오래 기다리게 해서 미안해요

I'm sorry to have kept you waiting for so long
넘 오래 기다리게 해서 미안

How long have you been waiting? 얼마동안 기다린거야?

Please excuse me for being late 늦어서 미안해

I apologize for being so late 늦어서 죄송해요

What took you so long? 뭣 때문에 이렇게 오래 걸렸어?

I don't know what's keeping her 걔가 뭣 때문에 늦는지 모르겠어

I lost track of time 시간이 어떻게 되는 지 몰랐어

I got held up at work 일에 잡혀서 말야

Everyone's waiting for us 다들 우리를 기다리고 있어

You kept me waiting for an hour 한 시간 동안 널 기다렸어

You're always late for everything 매사에 항상 늦는구만

Chapter **02** **감사** | **격려**

thank와 appreciate를 이용해 고맙다고 말하기

01 감사 고마워

Thank you very[so] much 고마워

Thanks a lot 고마워

Thank you for the lovely present 선물 고마워

보충설명 Thank you for + 명사 …에 대해 고마워

Thanks a lot for the great meal! 맛있는 식사 고마워!

Thank you very much for your help
도와줘서 정말 고마워

Thank you for your time 시간내줘서 고마워

Thank you for the compliment 칭찬해줘서 고마워

Thank you for your concern 걱정해줘서 고마워

Thank you for all you've done 여러모로 고마워

Thank you for the help 도와줘서 고마워

Thank you for giving me another chance
기회를 한 번 더 줘서 고마워

보충설명 Thank you for ~ ing …해줘서 고마워

Thank you for telling me 말해줘서 고마워

Thank you for letting me know 알려줘서 고마워

Thanks for saying so 그렇게 말해줘서 고마워

Thank you anyway 어쨌든 고마워

Thanks anyway, though 어쨌든 고마워

Thank you in advance 고맙구만

I really appreciate this 정말 고마워

I appreciate it 고마워

I appreciate your help 도와줘서 감사해요

I appreciate the support 도와줘서 감사해요

I appreciate your kindness
친절을 베푸셔서 감사해요

02 감사 정말 친절하시군요

That's very kind of you 정말 친절하군요

How kind of you to say so 그렇게 말씀해주시니 정말 친절하네요

It's[That's] very nice of you 정말 친절하네요

It's very thoughtful of you 사려가 깊으시군요

That's so sweet 고맙기도 해라

보충설명 주로 여성들이 쓰는 말로 주어를 바꿔 This is so sweet, It's so sweet라고 해도 된다.

You're so sweet 정말 고마워

You're so generous 맘씨가 참 좋으네

You're such a kind person 정말 친절하네요

You've got such a good heart 넌 무척 자상한 얘야

I'm really grateful to you 정말 감사드려요

I don't know how to thank you 고마워서 어쩌죠

I have no words to thank you 뭐라고 감사해야 할지 모르겠어

I can't thank you enough 뭐라 감사하다고 해야 할지

I don't know what to say 뭐라고 말해야 할지

You shouldn't have done this 이러지 않아도 되는데

I'm flattered 그렇게 말해주면 고맙지, 과찬의 말씀을

I'm honored 영광인데요

It was a great help 큰 도움이 됐습니다

You were a great help 정말 많은 도움이 되었어요

You've been very helpful 넌 참 도움이 많이 됐어

You've been a big[great] help 넌 큰 도움이 되었어

I owe it to my colleagues 제 동료 덕이에요

I owe you a favor 신세를 졌구만

I owe you one 신세가 많구나

You saved my life 네 덕택에 살았네

How nice! 고마워라!

She's very supportive 그 여자는 도움이 많이 되고 있어

He's been incredibly supportive of me

그 남자는 날 정말 많이 도와주고 있어

God bless you! 이렇게 고마울 수가!

보충설명 God bless you!는 고맙다는 인사 뿐만 아니라 상대방이 재채기를 할 때 "신의 가호가 있기를"
이라는 의미로 쓰이기도 하는데 이는 재채기를 할 때 혼이 달아난다는 미신 때문에 생긴 표현

상대방이 감사하다고 할 때 괜찮다고 말하기

03 감사 뭘요, 별 말씀을 요

You're welcome 천만에요

보충설명 강조하려면 You're very welcome, You're quite welcome,

Not at all 뭘요

Don't mention it 신경쓰지 마요

(It's) My pleasure 도움이 됐다니 내가 기쁘네요

The pleasure is mine 제가 좋아서 한 일인데요

No problem 뭘 그런걸

No sweat 뭘 별것도 아닌데

Never mind 마음쓰지마

(Please) Think nothing of it 마음쓰지 마

It was nothing 별거 아닌데

Don't worry about it 별거 아닌데

I'm glad you think so 그렇게 생각한다니 고마워

I'm glad I could help 내가 도움이 되서 기뻐

I'm sure you would have done the same (in my position)

너도 (내입장이면) 나처럼 했을거야

상대방에게 잘했다고 칭찬이나 축하를 할 때(1)

04 칭찬/축하 아주 잘했어

(That's) Great! 잘됐다!

Excellent! 아주 좋아!

Fantastic! 끝내주네!

Wonderful! 멋져!

You did a good[nice] job! 아주 잘했어!

Good for you 잘됐네, 잘했어

Good for me 나한테 잘된 일야

Lucky for you 잘됐어

You deserve it 넌 충분히 그럴만해

You more than deserve it 너 정도면 충분히 그럴 자격이 되고도 남아

Nice going! 참 잘했어!

Well done 잘했어

Top notch! 최고야, 훌륭해!

There is nothing like that! 저 만한 게 없지!

보충설명 문맥에 따라서는 단순히 "그와 같은 건 없다"라는 의미로도 쓰인다.

Nice move 좋았어, 잘했어

Nice try (하지만) 잘했어

보충설명 목적을 달성하지 못했지만 그래도 잘했다고 상대방이 한 시도를 칭찬할 때 쓰는 표현.

You can't beat that 짱이야, 완벽해

Can't top that 끝내준다

Congratulations! 축하해!

Congratulations on your marriage! 결혼 축하해!

Congratulations on your promotion! 승진축하해!

상대방에게 잘했다고 칭찬이나 축하를 할 때(2)

05 칭찬/축하 잘하고 있어

You're doing fine! 잘하고 있어!

Way to go! 잘한다 잘해!

I am happy for you 네가 잘돼서 나도 기쁘다

That's the spirit! 바로 그거야

That's the stuff 바로 그거야, 잘했어

That's the ticket 바로 그거야, 안성맞춤이야, 진심이야

It's not that bad 괜찮은데

Good boy 잘했어

That was very smart 아주 현명했네

I envy you 부럽네

I knew I could count on you 넌 믿음직해

I have confidence in you 난 널 신뢰해

I'm depending on you 난 널 의지하고 있어

You were great! 너 대단했어!

I'm impressed 인상적이야

Everyone was really impressed 사람들이 모두 정말 감동했어

Give me five 손바닥 부딪히자

It gets two thumbs up 최고야

Attaboy! 야 잘했다!

한번 해보라고, 할 수 있다고 격려를 할 때

06 격려 한번 해봐

Give it a try! 한번 해봐!

Just try it! 한번 해봐!

Try it! 해봐!

Try again! 다시 해봐!

Let's give it a try 한번 해보자

Why don't you try it? 해보지 그래?, 한번 해봐

Go for it 한번 시도해봐

Let's go for it 한번 시도해보자

Give it a shot 한번 해봐

Let's give it a shot 한번 해보자

Let me have a shot at it 내가 한번 해볼게

It can't[won't] hurt to try 한번 해본다고 해서 나쁠 건 없지

It wouldn't hurt 해본다고 나쁠 건 없어

It doesn't hurt to ask 물어본다고 손해볼 것 없어, 그냥 한번 물어본 거예요

You've got nothing to lose 밑져야 본전인데 뭐

Nothing to lose 밑질 거 없지

I will try my luck (되든 안되든) 한번 해봐야겠어

Get started 시작해봐

You can do it 넌 할 수 있어

If you try, you can do it 노력하면 넌 할 수 있어

Get it together! 잘해봐!

보충설명 get it together의 의미는 'to be organized and successful in your life, job etc.' 이다.

You can do anything if you really want to
네가 진정 원한다면 뭐든 다 할 수 있어

계속하라고 북돋아 줄 때

07 격려 계속 해

Keep going! 계속 해!

Keep going like this 지금처럼 계속해

Get going 계속해

Let's keep going 자 계속하자

Keep talking 계속 이야기해봐

Keep (on) trying 계속 정진해, 멈추지 말고 계속 노력해

Carry on 계속해

Go on (어서) 계속해

Get on with it 제대로 계속해봐

Keep it up 계속 열심히 해

Keep at it 열심히 해

Keep up the good work 계속 열심히 해, 계속 잘 하렴

Do your best! 최선을 다해!

There's a chance 기회가 있어

There's a possibility 가능성이 있어

Try harder next time! 다음 번엔 더 열심히 해!

08 격려 아직 포기하지마!

Don't give up (yet)! (아직) 포기하지마!
Never give up! 절대 포기하지 마
Don't quit trying 포기하지 마
Don't give up too easily 너무 쉽게 포기하지마
You (always) give up too easily 넌 (늘) 너무 쉽게 포기하더라
Cheer up! 기운 내!, 힘내!
Get your act together 기운 차려
Pull yourself together 기운 내, 똑바로 잘해
Hang in there 끝까지 버텨
Stick with it 포기하지마, 계속해
Never say die! 기운내!, 약한 소리하지마!
Keep your chin up 힘 좀 내
Be positive 긍정적으로 생각해
Look on[at] the bright side 밝은 면을 보라고
You go back out there 다시 뛰어야지
You gotta get back in the game 다시 뛰어야지, 다시 한번 싸워야지
It's not impossible 불가능한 일은 아니지
Don't lose your nerve 자신없어 하지마
Don't chicken out 겁먹고 물러서지 마
Don't be a chicken[coward] 겁먹지 말라고

09 미안 미안해

I'm (terribly) sorry (정말) 미안해
I'm so sorry! 정말 미안해!
Oh, sorry 어, 미안
Oops, so sorry 아이구, 미안해라

I'm sorry about that 미안해

I'm sorry about the other day 요전날 미안했어.

(I'm) Sorry for the inconvenience 불편하게 해서 미안해

> 보충설명 미안하게 된 원인을 말하려면 I'm sorry for 담에 명사 혹은 동사의 ing를 붙이면 된다.

I'm sorry to trouble you 귀찮게 해서 미안해

I'm sorry if I caused any trouble 말썽피웠다면 미안해

> 보충설명 I'm sorry 다음에 (that) 절 혹은 if 절 등을 붙여 미안한 내용을 말해도 된다.

I'm sorry it slipped my mind 깜박해서 미안해

I'm sorry I couldn't come 오지 못해서 미안해

You can't believe how sorry I am 내가 얼마나 미안한지 모를거야

I can't tell you how sorry I am 얼마나 미안한지 말로 할 수도 없어

Excuse me 미안해

> 보충설명 역시 미안해하는 내용은 Excuse me for 이하에 말하면 된다.

I just want to apologize for that 내 사과할게요

I don't know how to apologize to you 뭐라 사과해야 할지 모르겠네요

I have no words to apologize to you 뭐라 사과해야 할지 모르겠어요

Please accept my sincere apologies 진심어린 사과를 드립니다

I accept your apology 용서했어요

Please forgive me 용서해줘

> 나의 잘못이라고 솔직히 말하기

10 미안 내 잘못이야

It was my mistake 내 잘못이야

My mistake 내 잘못이야

Oops. My mistake 아이고, 내 실수

I made a mistake 내가 실수했어

It was a simple mistake 단순한 실수였어

It was a big[huge] mistake 크나큰 실수였어

It is my fault 내 잘못이야

That's my fault 내 잘못이야

I am sorry!

This is all[totally] my fault 모두 내 잘못야

I did it wrong 내가 잘못했어

It was careless of me to do so 내가 그렇게 한 건 부주의한 거였어

I went too far 너무 지나쳤어

I screwed up! 완전히 망했네!

I blew it (기회 등을) 망쳤다, 날려버렸다

I guess I dropped the ball 큰 실수를 한 것 같아

I was way off (base) 내가 완전히 잘못 짚었네, 내 생각[행동]이 틀렸네

잘못해놓고 스스로 후회와 변명을 해보기

11 미안 그러지 말았어야 했는데

I shouldn't have done that 그러지 말았어야 했는데

I shouldn't have said that 그렇게 말하는 게 아니었는데

I should have asked him 걔한테 물어봤어야 하는데

I feel so guilty 정말 미안해 죽겠어

How silly[clumsy; stupid] of me! 내가 참 멍청하기도 하지!

I regret doing that 그렇게 안하는 건데

I wish I was dead (잘못을 저지르고 미안해서) 미안해 죽겠어

I wish it had never happened 그러지 않았더라면 좋았을텐데

Please don't be offended 기분 상하지마

I was too nervous 내가 너무 긴장했었어

I didn't mean any harm 해를 끼칠려고 한 건 아니야

I didn't mean to cause you any trouble 너를 곤란케 하려는 건 아니었어

I was only trying to be funny 난 단지 웃자고 한 거였는데

I didn't do it on purpose 일부러 그런 건 아니야

I did it just for kicks 그냥 재미삼아 해본 건데

No damage 손해본 건 없어

No harm (done) 잘못된 거 없어

What's the harm? 손해볼 게 뭐야?

12 미안 다신 그런 일 없을 거야

I won't let it happen again 다신 그런 일 없을 거야

I'll see it doesn't happen again 다신 그러지 않도록 조심할게요

I'll try to be more careful 더 조심하도록 노력할게

It won't happen again 이런 일 다시는 없을 거야

It'll never happen again 다시는 이런 일 없을 거야

(I swear) I won't do it again, I promise 다신 안 그러겠다고 맹세할게, 믿어줘

I take the blame 내가 책임질게

I have no excuses 변명의 여지가 없어

I want to try to make it up to you 내가 다 보상해줄게

I[We] will make it up to you 내[우리]가 다 보상할게

I'll try to make it up to you 보상하도록 할게

13 위로 다 그런거지 뭐

That's (just) the way it is[goes] 다 그런 거지 뭐, 어쩔 수 없는 일이야

That's the way the cookie crumbles 사는 게 다 그런거지

That's the way the ball bounces 사는 게 다 그런거야

That's life 사는 게 그렇지

Such is life! 그런 게 인생이야!

That happens[happened] 그럴 수도 있지, 그런 일도 있기 마련이지

It happens 그럴 수도 있지 뭐

It happens to everybody[lots of people] 누구에게나 그럴 수 있어

Those[These] things happen 그런 일도 생기기 마련이야

Shit happens (살다보면) 재수없는 일도 생기는 법이야

It could happen 그럴 수도 있겠지

It could happen to anyone 누구나 그럴 수 있어

I don't blame you 그럴 만도 해, 네가 어쩔 수 없었잖아

Don't blame yourself 너무 자책하지마

It's not your fault 네 잘못이 아니야

Everyone makes mistakes now and then 누구나 때때로 실수하는거야

It's a common mistake 그건 누구나 하는 실수인데

You have to expect a lot of ups and downs
좋을 때도 있고 안 좋을 때도 있는거야

It could[might] have been worse 그나마 다행이야

Win a few, lose a few 얻는 게 있으면 잃는 것도 있어

That was a close call 하마터면 큰일날 뻔했네, 위험천만이었어

별일아니니 걱정하지 말라고 위로하기

14 위로 걱정마

Don't worry 걱정마, 미안해할 것 없어

Don't worry about it 걱정마, 잘 될 거야

Not to worry 걱정 안해도 돼

You don't have to worry 걱정하지 마

There's nothing to worry about 걱정할 것 하나도 없어

There's no need to worry about it 걱정할 필요없어

That's all right 괜찮아

It's all right 괜찮아

It's[That's] okay 괜찮아

No problem 문제 없어

Never mind 신경쓰지 마, 맘에 두지마

That's[It's] no big deal 별거 아냐

No big deal 별거 아냐

What's the big deal? 별거 아니네?, 무슨 큰 일이라도 있는 거야?

It was nothing 별거 아닌데

This is nothing 별거 아니야

Don't take it too seriously 너무 심각하게 받아들이지 마

Don't be sorry 미안해 하지마

You don't have to say you're sorry 미안해 할 필요없어

Don't sweat it! (별일 아니니) 걱정하지 마라

15 **위로** 그냥 잊어버려

Let it go 그냥 잊어버려, 그냥 놔둬

Would you let it go? 잊어버려요

Forget (about) it! 잊어버려, 됐어

Don't give it a second thought 걱정하지 마

Don't give it another thought 잊어버려

Don't think about it anymore 더 이상 그것에 대해 생각하지마

Don't be so hard on yourself 너무 자책하지마

Don't let it bother you 너무 신경 쓰지마!

Don't let A get you down A 때문에 괴로워하지마

Don't feel so bad about it 너무 속상해하지마

You must be very upset (about~) (…에 대해서) 정말 화나겠어

You must be so upset 정말 화나겠구만

Stop torturing yourself 자학하지마

Stop beating yourself up! 그만 자책해라!

Let's let bygones be bygones 지나간 일은 잊자고

It's no use crying over split milk 엎지른 물을 다시 담을 수 없어

16 **위로** 안됐구나

I'm sorry to hear that 안됐네

I'm sorry about that 안됐어

That's too bad 저런, 안됐네, 이를 어쩌나

What a pity! 그것 참 안됐구나!

That's a pity! 참 안됐네!

What a shame! 안됐구나!

I know just how you feel 어떤 심정인지 알겠어

I know the feeling 그 심정 내 알지

That hurts 그거 안됐네, 마음이 아프겠구나

You poor thing 안됐구나

Oh, poor thing! 가엾은 거!

Ah, poor Jim! 아, 가엾은 짐!

It must be tough for you 참 어려웠겠구나

Tough luck 참 운도 없네

That's unfortunate 운이 없구만

How awful 참 안됐다

My heart goes out to you 진심으로 위로의 마음을 전합니다

You have all my sympathy 진심으로 유감의 말씀을 드립니다

I really sympathize with you 진심으로 위로의 말을 전합니다

┌───┐
╎ 다 잘 될거라고 위로하기   ╎
└───┘

17 **위로** 다 잘될 거야

Everything's going to be all right 다 잘 될거야

Everything will be fine 모든 게 잘 될거야

She's going to be all right 걘 괜찮을 거야

It's going to be all right 그건 괜찮을 거야

It's going to be okay 잘 될거야, 괜찮을거야

Things will work out all right 잘 해결될거야

It's going to get better 더 잘 될거야

You're going to be great 넌 잘 될거다

It's all for the best 앞으로 나아질거야

You never know 그야 모르잖아, 그야 알 수 없지

보충설명 You never know 주어+동사 …일지 누가 알아

You can never tell! 단정할 순 없지!

Your time will come 좋은 때가 올거야

Chapter 03 충고 | 불만

01 충고 진정해

Take it easy 좀 쉬어가면서 해, 진정해, 잘 지내

Calm down 진정해

Calm down and think carefully 진정하고 잘 생각해봐

Cool down[off] 진정해

Be[Keep] cool 진정해라

Cool it 진정해, 침착해

Don't get[be] mad! 열받지 말라고!

Don't get worked up 흥분하지마

Don't get so uptight 그렇게 화내지말고

Don't be upset! 화내지 말고!

Go get some rest 가서 좀 쉬어

Just relax! 긴장풀고 천천히 해!

02 충고 조심해

Watch out 조심해

Watch out for him! 걔 조심해!

Watch it! 조심해

Watch your step! 조심해!

보충설명 Watch your step은 넘어지지 않도록 조심하라는 의미 뿐만 아니라 상대방에게 말이나 행동거지를 조심하라고 할 때도 쓰인다. 또한 Watch your back은 뒤(배신 등)를 조심하라는 표현.

Look out! 조심해!, 정신 차리라고!

(You) Be careful! 조심해!

Be careful of him 걔를 조심해

Heads up! 위험하니까 잘 보라구!

Behind you! 조심해!

03 충고 천천히해라 혹은 서둘러라

Easy does it 천천히 해, 조심조심, 진정해

Easy, easy, easy! 천천히 조심조심!

Take your time 천천히 해

Hold your horses 서두르지마, 진정해

What's the[your] rush? 왜 이리 급해?

What's the hurry? 왜 그렇게 서둘러?

There's[I'm] no hurry 서두를 것 없어, 급할 것 없어

There's no need to rush 서두를 필요없어

You don't need to hurry 서두르지 않아도 돼

No rush[hurry] 급할 거 없어

Slow down 천천히 해

Haste makes waste 서두르면 일을 망친다

We still have a long way to go 아직 가야할 길이 많아

Hurry up! 서둘러!

Step on it! 빨리 해, (자동차 엑셀레이터를) 더 밟아

I haven't got all day 여기서 이럴 시간 없어, 빨리 서둘러

Don't push (me)! 몰아 붙이지마!, 독촉하지마!

Get a move on it! 서둘러!

I'd better get a move on it 빨리 서둘러야겠어

Come on! 어서!, 그러지마!, 제발!, 자 덤벼!

04 충고 정신차려라

Get a life! 정신차례!

Get real! 정신 좀 차리라구!

Don't even think about it 꿈도 꾸지마, 절대 안되니까 헛된 생각하지마

Don't you dare do that! 그럴 꿈도 꾸지마!

Act your age! 나이값 좀 해!

You have to grow up 철 좀 들어라

You can't have everything 너무 욕심내지마

Real life isn't that easy 사는 게 그렇게 쉽지는 않아

You wish! 행여나!

In your dreams! 꿈 깨셔!

Dream on! 꿈 한번 야무지네!

Stop goofing off! 그만 좀 빈둥거려라!

행동에 앞서 신중히 꼼꼼히 생각해보라고 말하기

05 충고 한 번 더 생각해봐

Think twice before you do it 실행하기에 앞서 한번 더 생각해봐

Think it over carefully before you decide 결정에 앞서 신중히 생각해

You shouldn't be so quick to judge! 그렇게 섣불리 판단해선 안돼!

You can't be too careful 아무리 조심해도 지나치지 않아

(It's) Better safe than sorry 뒤늦게 후회하느니 조심해야지

Don't jump to conclusions! 섣부르게 판단하지마!

Let's not jump the gun 경솔하게 속단하지마

Don't count your chickens before they're hatched
김치국부터 마시지 마

Don't judge a book by its cover 겉만 보고 속을 판단하지 마

Never judge something by its looks 뭐든 외양만 갖고 판단하면 안돼

Don't fall for it (속아) 넘어가지 마, 사랑에 빠지면 안돼

Don't trust it 믿지마

Don't be so impatient 너무 조급해하지마

He's better than you think 걔는 네가 생각하는 거 이상야

You'll be sorry 넌 후회하게 될거야

You'll regret it 넌 후회하게 될거야

You (just) wait and see 두고보라고

We'll see 좀 보자고, 두고 봐야지

You'll see 곧 알게 될 거야, 두고 보면 알아

Let's wait and see how things go 일이 어떻게 돼가는지 지켜보자

말을 신중히 가려서 하라고 충고할 때

06 충고 말 조심해

Watch your tongue! 말 조심해!

Watch your language[mouth] 말 조심해

Hold your tongue! 제발 그 입 좀 다물어!

Bite your tongue 입 조심해, 말이 씨가 되는 수가 있어

You've got a big mouth 너 참 입이 싸구나

Big mouth! 입 한번 엄청 싸네!

Shut up! 닥쳐!

Shut your face! 입다물어

You talk too much 말이 너무 많네

시간낭비하지 말라고 충고하기

07 충고 시간 낭비하지마

Don't waste your time 시간 낭비하지마

Don't waste my time
남의 귀한 시간 축내지마, 괜히 시간낭비 시키지 말라고

You're (just) wasting my time 시간낭비야, 내 시간 낭비마

It's a waste of time 시간낭비야

What a waste of time and money! 시간과 돈 낭비야!

I don't like wasting my time 시간낭비하고 싶지 않아

It isn't worth it 그럴만한 가치가 없어, 그렇게 중요한 것도 아닌데

It isn't worth the trouble 괜히 번거롭기만 할거야

08 충고 제대로 해라

Do it right 제대로 해

Let's just do it right 제대로나 하자

We can do it right! 우린 제대로 잘 할 수 있어!

Use your head! 머리를 좀 쓰라구!, 생각이라는 걸 좀 해라!

Where's your head at? 머리는 어디다 둔거야?

You heard me 명심해

You'll get the hang[knack] of it 금방 손에 익을거야, 요령이 금방 붙을거야

(There's) Nothing to it 아주 쉬워, 해보면 아무것도 아냐

You have to get used to it 적응해야지

I'm getting used to it 난 적응하고 있어

Don't leave things half done 일을 하다 말면 안돼

You should finish what you start 시작한 건 끝내야지

09 충고 다신 그러지마

Don't let it happen again 다신 그러지 마

Please be sure it doesn't happen again 다신 그러지 않도록 해

Not again! 어휴 또야!, 어떻게 또 그럴 수 있어!

Please don't do that 제발 그러지마

Don't do that anymore 더는 그러지마

Don't ever do that again 두번 다시 그러지 마

You can't do that! 그러면 안되지!

We can't do that 우리가 그러면 안되지

Here we go again 또 시작이군

There you go again 또 시작이군

Haven't you learned your lesson yet?
아직 따끔한 맛을 못봤어?

Don't make such stupid mistakes again!
다신 그런 어리석은 실수하지마래!

10 충고 그렇게 말하면 안되지

You shouldn't + 동사~ …해서는 안돼
Example You shouldn't say things like that 그렇게 말하면 안되지

You must not + 동사~ …해서는 안돼
Example You must not hit your children 때론. 애들을 치면 안돼지

You'd better not + 동사~ …하지 않는 게 좋아
Example You'd better not go outside. It's too cold 나가지 마. 밖은 너무 추워

You're not supposed to + 동사~ 너는 …해서는 안돼
Example You're not supposed to do that 그러면 안되는데
Example I'm not supposed to be here 난 여기 있으면 안되는데

You don't want to + 동사~ …하지 마라
Example You don't want to use that computer
그 컴퓨터는 사용하지 않는 게 좋아

You don't have to + 동사~ …안해도 돼
Example You don't have to walk me home 집까지 안 데려다 줘도 되는데

You should know better than~ …하지 않을 정도는 돼야지
Example You should know better than to tell him a secret
너 그 사람한테 비밀을 말하면 안되는 줄은 알았을 것 아냐

Don't + 동사 …하지 마라
Example Don't touch me 만지지마
Example Don't cut in line 끼어들지마

Don't be + 형용사 …하지 마라
Example Don't be selfish 이기적이지 마라
Example Don't be jealous 질투하지 마라

If I were you, I wouldn't + 동사~ 너라면 난 …하지 않을 텐데
Example If I were you, I wouldn't let him know until tomorrow
내가 너라면, 내일이나 걔한테 말할텐데

I wouldn't if I were you 내가 너라면 그렇게 하지 않겠어

11 충고 스스로 해라

Do it yourself 스스로 해라

Do as[what] I said! 내가 말한대로 해!

Do what I told you to do! 내가 지시한 대로 하라고!

Be + 형용사 …해라
Example **Be good to others** 다른 사람들에게 잘 대해
Example **Be strong!** 건강하라고!

Be + 명사 …가 돼라
Example **Be a good boy** 착한 애가 돼라
Example **Be a man!** 남자답게 행동해라

You should do it this way 넌 이런 식으로 그걸 해야 돼

This is the way you should do it 이런 방식으로 그걸 해야 돼

This is the first thing to do 가장 먼저 해야 되는 건 이거야

You should do this first 이걸 먼저 해야 돼

Let me give you a piece of advice 내가 네게 충고 좀 할게

I'm telling you this from experience 내 경험상으로 말하는 건데

What you need is a little more effort 조금만 더 노력하면 돼

Better than nothing 아무 것도 안 하는 것보단 낫지

It's your responsibility 너의 책임야

It's your duty 너의 의무야

That's the name of the game 그게 가장 중요한 거야

That's the most important thing 그게 가장 중요한 거야

12 충고 잠깐, 그만둬!

Wait a minute, please! 잠깐만요!

Just[wait] a moment 잠깐만

Hold on (a second)! 잠깐

Hold it! 잠깐, 그대로 있어!

Stop that[it]! 그만해!

Just drop it! 당장 그만둬!

Don't move! 움직이지마!

Don't make a move! 움직이지마!

Freeze! 꼼짝마!

Stop saying that! 닥치라고!, 그만 좀 얘기해!

Cut it out! 그만둬!, 닥쳐!

Knock it off 조용히 해

Come off it! 집어쳐!, 건방떨지마!

Cut the crap 바보 같은 소리마, 쓸데 없는 이야기 좀 그만둬

Listen to yourself 멍청한 소리 그만해

상대방에게 실망이나 불만이 있을 때

13 불만 실망시키지마

Don't disappoint me 실망시키지마

This is disappointing 실망스럽구만

What a disappointment! 참 실망스럽네!

Don't let me down 기대를 저버리지 마

You let me down 너한테 실망했어

I'm ashamed of you 부끄러운 일이야, 부끄러워 혼났어

You should be ashamed (of yourself) 창피한 줄 알아

Aren't you ashamed of yourself? 창피한 줄도 몰라?

Shame on you 부끄러운 줄 알아야지, 창피한 일이야

For shame 창피한 일이야

I was frustrated with you 너 때문에 맥이 풀렸어

I'm bummed out 실망이야

I don't like it 마음에 안들어

I'm not happy with it 마음에 안들어

Do you have a problem with me?
나한테 뭐 불만있는 거야?

Does anybody have a problem with that?
누구 문제 있는 사람 있어?

Do you have a problem with that? 그게 뭐 문제있어?

정도를 넘어서는 상대방에게 짜증내기

14 불만 정말 너무 하는구만

That's (just) too much! 해도 해도 너무해!, 그럴 필요는 없는데!

That's asking too much 너무 많이 요구하는 구만

You're going too far 너무하는군

You go too far 너 오바야

You have gone too far 네가 너무했어, 심했다

What do you want from me? 나보고 어쩌라는 거야?

He went overboard 그 사람이 좀 너무했어

Don't go overboard 과식[과음]하지마

How can you say that? 어떻게 그렇게 말할 수 있나?

How could you say such a thing? 네가 어떻게 그런 말을 할 수 있니?

How could you not tell us? 어떻게 우리에게 말하지 않을 수 있지?

How could you do that? 어쩌면 그럴 수가 있어?

How could you do this to me[us]? 내[우리]한테 어떻게 이럴 수 있니?

How dare you + 동사~ ? 어떻게 …할 수가 있어?

Example How dare you insult me! 감히 날 모욕하다니!

상대방에게 맘대로 하라고 말하기

15 불만 네 맘대로 해라

You wouldn't dare (to do something)! 어쩜 감히 이럴 수가!

You're pushing your luck 운을 과신하는 구만, 화를 부르는 구만

Have[Do] it your way 네 맘대로 해, 좋을 대로 해

He gets his way 갠 제멋대로야

Suit yourself! 네 멋대로 해!, 맘대로 해!

Do what you want 원하는 대로 해

Do whatever you want 뭐든 원하는 대로 해

Do as you please 맘대로 해

Do as you like 좋을 대로 해

날 놀리지 말라고 경고하기

16 싸움 날 뭘로 보는 거야?

What do you take me for? 날 뭘로 보는 거야?

Who do you think you're talking to?
너 나한테 그렇게 말하면 재미없어 ·

Who do you think you're kidding?
설마 나더러 그 말을 믿으라는 건 아니지

You're pulling my leg 나 놀리는 거지, 농담이지

Are you pulling my leg? 나 놀리는 거니?

Don't pull my leg 놀리지 마

Do I look like I was born yesterday? 내가 그렇게 어리숙해보여?

I wasn't born yesterday! 누굴 햇병아리로 보내!

How dumb do you think I am? 내가 바본 줄 아니?, 누굴 바보로 아는 거니?

Why are you picking on me? 왜 날 괴롭히는 거야?

I'm not stupid 난 바보가 아냐

Are you trying to make a fool of me? 나를 놀리려고 하는 거야?

You're telling me that 주어+동사~? …라고 말하는 거야?

보충설명 말투나 상황에 따라 상대방의 말을 확인하거나 혹은 시비를 걸 때 사용한다.

Example You're telling me that you can't finish it? 그걸 끝내지 못한다는 거야?

Stop kidding[joking] 농담하지마

Don't make fun of me! 나 놀리지 마

You're making fun of me?
너 지금 나 놀리냐?

Don't tease me! 놀리지 마!

You're teasing me
나 놀리는 거지

17 싸움 꺼지라고!

Get out of here! 꺼져!, 웃기지 마!

Get out of my face! 내 눈 앞에서 안보이게 사라져!

Get out of my way 비켜라, 방해하지 마라

Go away! 꺼져!

Get lost! (그만 좀 괴롭히고) 꺼져!

(You) Back off! 비키시지!

You stay out of it! 좀 비켜라!

Keep[Stay] out of my way 가로.막지 좀 마

Stay away from me! 꺼져!

(You) Just watch! 넌 보고만 있어!

Don't mess with me 나 건드리지마

I don't want to get in the way 방해되고 싶지 않아

18 싸움 점잖게 행동해

Behave yourself 버릇없이 굴면 안돼(아이들에게), 점잖게 행동해

Where are your manners? 매너가 그게 뭐야, 매너가 없구나

Remember your manners 버릇없이 굴지 말구, 예의를 지켜야지

Mind your manners! 방정맞게 굴지마!

Be sure to mind your manners! 예의바르게 굴도록 해!

Mind your P's and Q's! 품행[말]을 조심해라

Don't be rude! 무례하게 굴지마!

Watch your step 말(혹은 행동거지) 조심해

Your behavior is out of place 네 행동은 무례한 짓이야

Be on your best behavior 점잖게 행동해라

You have a bad attitude 너 태도가 안 좋구나

I don't like your attitude 너 태도가 맘에 안 들어

Manners count, even between close friends
친할수록 예의를 지켜야지

Use good etiquette 예의바르게 행동해

19 싸움 너 미쳤어?

You crazy? 너 미쳤어?

Are you insane[nuts]? 너 돌았니?

You're driving me crazy 너 때문에 미치겠다

You've driving me up the wall 너 때문에 미치겠다

What do you think you're doing? 이게 무슨 짓이야, 너 정신 나갔어?

Are you out of your mind? 너 제 정신이야?

You're out of your mind! 너 미쳤구만!

He's out to lunch 걔 요즘 얼이 빠져있어

You are not yourself 제정신이 아니네

I'm not myself 나 지금 제 정신이 아냐

Is he all there? 걔 미쳤어?

He's not all there 쟨 정신나갔나봐

There's nobody home! 정신 어디다 두고 있는거야!

The lights are on but nobody's home 어쩜 그렇게 맹하고 느려터졌니

Anybody home? 집에 아무도 없어요?, 정신있니 없니?

I'm losing my mind 내가 제 정신이 아니야

You seem spaced out 너 정신이 나간 것 같구나

20 싸움 이건 말도 안돼

It doesn't make any sense 무슨 소리야, 말도 안돼

It makes no sense 그건 말도 안돼

Does that make any sense? 그게 말이 돼?

Don't be ridiculous 바보같이 굴지 마

Don't be silly[foolish] 바보같이 굴지마

This is ridiculous 이건 말도 안돼

This is crazy[nuts] 이건 말도 안되는 짓이야, 말도 안돼

Don't make me laugh! 웃기지 좀 마, 웃음 밖에 안 나온다!

Don't lie to me 거짓말하지마

Don't tell me lies 거짓말하지마

That's a lie! 거짓말야!

Liar! 거짓말쟁이!

Don't say stupid things 바보 같은 말 하지마

Don't play dumb! 순진한 척하지마!

Don't give me that! 그런 말 마, 정말 시치미떼기야!

변명하는 상대방에게 일침하기

21 싸움 그런 말 하지마

That's no excuse 그건 변명거리가 안돼

No more excuses! 변명은 그만해!

Don't make any excuses! 변명 좀 그만해!

I've heard enough of your excuses 네 변명은 이젠 지겨워

That's not a good excuse 그럴 듯한 변명도 아니네

I don't want to hear any excuses 어떤 변명도 듣고 싶지 않아

That doesn't excuse your behavior
그렇다고 너의 행동을 용인할 수가 없어

That hardly explains your actions
그건 너의 행동에 대한 변명이 안돼

Tell me another 거짓말마, 말이 되는 소리를 해라

Spare me! 집어치워!, 그만둬!

No ifs, ands or buts! 군말 말고 시키는 대로 해!

Now what? 그래서 뭐?

22 싸움 남의 일에 신경쓰지마

It's none of your business 남의 일에 신경쓰지마, 참견마

Mind your own business! 상관 말라구!

I'll thank you to mind your own business
신경꺼주면 고맙겠어

That's really my business 그건 내일이니 신경꺼

Keep[Get] your nose out of my business 내 일에 참견마

Stay out of this! 상관마!, 참견마!

보충설명 Stay out of this!는 개인적인 문제이니까 "참견하지 마라"라는 의미이며 Stay away (from me)!는 "내 면전에서 꺼지라"라고 말하는 경고성 문구이다.

Don't get involved 상관마

Who asked you? 누가 너한테 물었어?

Who cares what you think? 누가 너한테 물어봤어?, 맘대로 생각해라

Butt out! 참견말고 꺼져!, 가서 네 일이나 잘해!

It's not your concern 상관마

It's personal 개인적인 거야

23 싸움 들켰다

You caught me 들켰다

He caught me smoking
담배피우다 그 사람한테 들켰어

You screwed me! 날 속였군!

You did a number on me 내가 당했구만

I'm so busted 딱 걸렸어

Gotcha! 잡았다!, 속았지!, 당했지!, 알았어!

I'm fucking with you 널 놀리는 거야

She gave it to me 나 걔한테 혼쭐이 났어

24 싸움 당해싸다

You asked for it 자업자득이지, 네가 자초한 일이잖아, 그런 일을 당해도 싸다

You'll pay for that! 당해도 싸네!, 꼴 좋군!

You had it coming! 네가 자초한 거야!

(It) Serves you right! 넌 그런 일 당해도 싸, 꼴 좋다!

That'll teach her! 그래도 싸지, 당연한 대가야

Well, that'll teach you a lesson 그래, 이제 좀 정신차리겠지

You'll never get away with it 넌 그걸 피할 수 없어

Well, you got what you deserved 당해 싸다

You've brought this on yourself 네가 초래한 거야

There's no reason to complain 당연한 결과지

25 싸움 나한테 왜 이래

You can't do this to me 나한테 이러면 안되지, 이러지마

Why are you doing this to me? 내게 왜 이러는 거야?

What have you done to me? 내게 무슨 짓을 한거야?

Don't tell me what to do! 나에게 이래라 저래라 하지마!

Don't call me names! 욕하지 마!

Don't blame me 나한테 뭐라고 하지마

Don't insult me 날 모욕하지마

Don't say it's my fault 내 잘못이라고 하지마

I didn't do anything wrong! 난 잘못한 것 하나도 없어!

You're to blame 네가 잘못이다

You can't talk to me like that 내게 그렇게 말하면 안돼

Don't look at me like that 그런 식으로 날 보지마

Don't talk back to me! 내게 말대꾸하지마!

Take it back 취소해

I don't want to cause problems 문제 일으키고 싶지 않아

Why are you trying to make me feel bad?
왜 날 기분 나쁘게 만드는 거야?

한심한 상대방을 대놓고 무시하기

26 싸움 넌 몰라

You don't know the first thing about it 아무것도 모르면서, 쥐뿔도 모르면서

You don't know the half of it 별로 알지도 못하면서

You have no idea 넌 모를거야

You have no idea what this means to me!
이게 내게 얼마나 중요한 건지 넌 몰라!

You have no idea how much I need this
이게 내게 얼마나 필요한지 넌 몰라

You have no idea how much this hurts
이게 얼마나 아픈지 넌 모를 거야

What do you know about + 명사? …에 대해 네가 뭘 알아?
Example What do you know about love? 네가 사랑이 뭔지 알기나 해?

You never learn 넌 구제불능이야

잘난 척하는 상대방 한번에 기죽이기

27 싸움 잘난 척 마라

Who do you think you are? 네가 도대체 뭐가 그리도 잘났는데?

Don't be a smart-ass 건방지게 굴지마

Don't be smart with me! · 잘난 체 하지마!

You think you're so smart[big] 네가 그렇게 똑똑한 줄 알아

You are nothing special 당신 대단한 거 없어

Look who's talking 사돈 남말하네

You're one to talk 사돈 남 말하시네

Very funny! 그래 우습기도 하겠다!

Take your own advice 너나 잘해

Don't be bossy 삐기지 마

28 싸움 어디 한번 해보자고!

Bring it on! 한번 덤벼봐, 어디 한번 해보자구!

Gang up on me! 다 덤벼봐!

Bite me 배 째라!, 어쩌라구!

보충설명 주로 10대들이 쓰는 무례한 표현으로 성인들 사이에서는 농담조로 쓰인다.

Make my day! 할테면 해봐라!

Go ahead, make my day! 덤벼봐, 한번 해보자구!

He's a dead man 쟨 이제 죽었다

It's your funeral 그 날로 넌 끝이야

So sue me 그럼 고소해 봐

We've got to get even 되갚아 줘야 돼

I want to get even with him 앙갚음 하겠어

I lost my temper 내가 열받았어

I've run out of patience 더 이상 못참아

Stop fighting! 그만 싸워!

Did you make up? 화해했니?

Let's make up 화해하자

Can't you patch things up? 화해가 안돼?

Chapter **04** **기쁨** | **슬픔**

01 기쁨 정말 신난다

I'm so happy 정말 기뻐

I'm so excited[thrilled] 정말 신내[짜릿해]

I'm glad to hear that 그것 참 잘됐다, 좋은 소식이라 기쁘다

That's great to hear 참 잘됐어

I'm glad that 주어+동사 …해서 너무 기뻐

Example I'm glad you like it 네가 좋다니 기뻐

I feel great[good] 기분 아주 좋아

I feel terrific 기분 끝내줘

I feel a lot better now 기분이 좀 나아져

You made me happy 너 때문에 행복해

It makes me feel better 그 때문에 기분이 좋아졌어

That makes me feel so good 그게 기분을 좋게 해줘

I'm in a good mood today 오늘 기분이 좋아

It was really fun 정말 재밌었어

I had a good time 즐거웠어

I got lucky 운이 좋았어

I was just lucky 그냥 운이 좋았어

It was just luck 운이 좋았던 거야

I've never been this happy 이처럼 행복한 적이 없어

I couldn't be happier 정말이지 아주 행복해

This is the happiest moment in my life 내 인생에서 가장 행복한 순간야

I'm relieved to hear that 그 이야기를 들으니 맘이 놓여

What a relief! 참 다행이야!

02 슬픔 그럴 기분이 아니야

I'm not in the mood 그럴 기분이 아냐

I'm in a bad mood 기분이 안좋아

I'm under the weather 몸이 찌뿌둥해

I'm feeling a little sick 몸상태가 좀 안좋네

I don't feel like doing anything 아무 것도 하기 싫어

I feel sad 슬퍼

I'm sad[unhappy] 슬퍼[행복하지 않아]

I'm depressed 지쳤어

It's really frustrating 정말 맥빠지게 해

> 보충설명 embarrass, frustrate, depress, interest 등은 모두 타동사로 ~ing을 붙여 embarrassing 하게 되면 「…을 당황케하는」이라는 의미이고 반면 embarrassed하면 「…에 의해 당황한」이라 는 뜻이 된다.

It's depressing 지치게 해

I've got the blues today 오늘 울적해

He looks gloomy today 걔 오늘 우울해보여

I miss you 그립다

That's just my luck 내가 그렇지 뭐

Tough break! 재수 옴 붙었군!

I feel so used 기분 참 더럽네

┌ 난처하고 곤란한 상황에서 ┐

03 **곤란/당황** 어떻게 해야 할 지 모르겠어

I don't know what to do 어떻게 해야 할 지 모르겠어

I don't know what to say 뭐라 해야할 지 모르겠어

I don't know what else to do 달리 어떻게 해야 할 지 모르겠어

What should I do? 어떻게 해야 하지?

What am I supposed to do? 내가 어떻게 해야 되지?

What am I going to do? 어떻게 하지?

What am I going to say? 뭐라고 말하지?

I'm so humiliated 쪽 팔려, 창피해 죽겠어

This is a slap in the face 창피해서 원, 치욕스러워라

That's so embarrassing! 정말 황당하다!

How embarrassing! 정말 당혹해라!

You embarrass me 너 때문에 창피하다

I'm so embarrassed 당황했어

I got screwed 망신 당했어, 수모를 당했어

We're in trouble 곤란한 상황야

I'm ashamed of myself 창피해

I'm ashamed that I did that 내가 한 일로 창피해

It's a big problem 문제가 커

It's a really serious problem 정말 곤란한 문제야

It's a pain in the neck[ass] 골칫거리야

That's the hard part 그게 어려운 부분야

오늘 하루가 좋거나 안좋을 때

04 오늘일진 정말 오늘 일진 안좋네

This is not my day 정말 일진 안좋네

This is not your[his] day 오늘은 네가[걔가] 되는 게 없는 날이다

Today wasn't my day 오늘 정말 일진 안좋았어

Today is my lucky day 오늘 일진 좋네

What a lucky day! 정말 운 좋은 날이네!

This must be my lucky day! 오늘은 내가 운이 좋을거야!

It's your lucky day 너 재수 좋은 날이야

I had a bad day 진짜 재수없는 날이야

I'm having a really bad day 정말 오늘 안좋네

I had a rough day 힘든 하루였어

Rough day for you? 힘든 하루였지?

It has been a long day 힘든 하루였어

I'm not feeling up to par today
오늘은 좀 평소와 달라, 컨디션이 좀 안좋아

It hasn't been your day 되는 일이 아무 것도 없는 날이야

Boy, what a day! 야, 정말 짜증나는 날이야!

05 짜증 이제 그만!

That's enough! 이제 그만!, 됐어 그만해!

That's enough for now 이젠 됐어

I've had enough of you 이제 너한테 질렸어

I've had enough of it! 이제 지겨워 죽겠다!

Enough is enough! 이젠 충분해!

I'm sick of this 진절머리가 나

I'm fed up with it! 진절머리나!

It's boring 지루해, 따분해

I've had it[enough]! 지겹다!, 넌더리나!

I've had it with you guys 너희들한테 질려버렸다

보충설명 have it with somebody[something] 「...라면 질렸다」라는 숙어.

I've had it up to here with you 너라면 이제 치가 떨려, 너한테 질려버렸어

I've had it up to here 아주 지긋지긋해

I can't take it anymore 더 이상 못 견디겠어요

I can't stand this 이건 못참겠어

I can't stand your friends 네 친구들은 정말 지겨워

I can't stand losing 지고는 못살아

That's the last straw 해도해도 너무 하는군, 더 이상 못참겠어

06 짜증 나 좀 내버려둬

Leave me alone 나 좀 내버려둬, 귀찮게 좀 하지마

Leave me in peace 나 좀 가만히 내버려둬

Give me a break 좀 봐줘요, 그만 좀 해라

Give it a rest! 그만 좀 하지 그래!

Stop bothering me 나 좀 가만히 놔둬

Don't bother me 귀찮게 하지 좀 마

Stop picking on me 못살게 굴지 좀 마

Please stop bugging me 나 좀 귀찮게 하지마

Stop pestering me 그만 좀 괴롭혀

Get your hands off of me! 내 몸에서 손떼!

Get off my back 귀찮게 굴지 말고 나 좀 내버려둬

Get off my case 귀찮게 하지 좀 마

Go easy on me 좀 봐줘

> 보충설명 go easy on something하게 되면 「...을 적당히 하다」라는 의미의 표현으로 예로 Go easy on the whisky하면 "위스키 좀 적당히 마셔"라는 뜻.

Have a heart 한번만 봐줘, 온정을 베풀라구

Don't be so hard on me 나한테 그렇게 심하게 하지마, 그렇게 빡빡하게 굴지마

Don't give me a hard time 나 힘들게 하지마

Cut me some slack 좀 봐줘요, 여유를 좀 줘, 너무 몰아세우지 마

I can cut him some slack 걔를 좀 봐줄 수도 있지

짜증나 열받은 경우에

07 짜증 열받아!

I'm pissed off! 열받아!, 진절머리나!

She made me mad 걔 때문에 화나

I'm mad[angry; upset] 화나, 열받아

He got worked up 걔 열 받았어, 걔 대단했어

You're a pain in the neck[ass] 너 참 성가시네

You're getting on my nerves 신경거슬리게 하네

You're bothering me 너 때문에 귀찮아

That burns me (up)! 정말 열받네!

It's really getting to me 진짜 짜증나게 하네

She really gets to me 걔때문에 열받아(= She really makes me mad)

This makes me sick 역겨워

That's disgusting 정떨어진다

That's gross 역겨워

It sucks! 밥맛이야!, 젠장할!

That[This] sucks! 빌어먹을!

You suck! 재수없어!

This vacation sucks 이번 휴가는 엉망진창이야

It stinks 젠장, 영 아니야

That marriage stinks 저 결혼은 영 아니야

믿을 수 없는 일을 겪거나 충격받았을 때

08 놀람/감탄 믿을 수가 없어!, 설마!

I can't believe it! 설마!, 말도 안돼!, 그럴 리가!,이럴 수가!

I can't believe you did that 네가 그랬다는 게 믿기지 않아

I don't believe this! 이건 말도 안돼!

I don't believe it! 그럴 리가!

Unbelievable! 믿을 수가 없어!

Incredible! 믿기지 않아!

Awesome! 끝내주네!, 대단하네!

I'm surprised[shocked] 놀랐어[충격야]

What a surprise[shock]! 놀라워라!

You surprised[scared] me 너 때문에 놀랬어

Isn't it amazing? 대단하지 않아?, 정말 놀랍지 않아?

That's amazing! 거 대단하다!

Isn't that great? 대단하지 않니?

How about that! 거 근사한데!, 그거 좋은데!

Imagine that! 어 정말야?, 놀라워라!

How do you do that? 어쩜 그렇게 잘하니?, 어떻게 해낸 거야?

What a coincidence! 이런 우연이!

What a small world! 세상 참 좁네!

It's a small world 세상 참 좁네요

You don't say! 설마!, 아무려면!, 정말!, 뻔한 거 아냐!

Don't tell me! 설마!

I never heard of such a thing 말도 안돼

What do you know! 놀랍군!, 네가 뭘 안다고!

Fancy that! 설매, 도저히 믿기지 않는다!

I'm speechless 할말이 없어, 말이 안나와

Would you believe 주어+동사? …가 믿겨져?

Example Would you believe he gave me a car? 내게 차를 줬는데 놀랍지 않아?

Would you believe it? 그게 정말이야?

It was the last thing I expected 생각도 못했어

어떻게 이런 일이 있을 수 있나 탄식하기

09 놀람/감탄 어떻게 이럴 수가 있니!

How could this[that] happen? 어떻게 이럴 수가 있니?

How can this be happening? 어떻게 이런 일이 일어나는 거지?

How could this happen to me?! 나한테 어떻게 이런 일이 생긴단 말야?!

It never happened 이런 적 한번도 없었어

That never happened to me 이런 경험 처음이야

That has never happened before 난생 처음 겪는 일이야

Can you believe this is already happening? 벌써 이렇게 됐어?

I guess I just can't believe any of this is happening
이런 일이 생기다니 믿을 수가 없는걸

How is that possible? 어떻게 그럴 수가 있지?

That can't be good[smart] 그럴 리 없어, 안 좋을텐데

It can't be 이럴 수가

It can't be true 그럴 리가 없어

Something's wrong 뭔가 잘못된거야

That's (so) weird 거 (정말) 이상하네

This feels (very) weird 이상한 것 같아

That's funny 거참 이상하네, 거참 신기하다

Chapter **05** 부탁 | 제안

01 부탁 좀 도와줄래?

Can[Would] you give me a hand? 좀 도와줄래?

Could[Would] you do me a favor? 부탁 좀 들어줄래요?

Can[May] I ask you a favor? 좀 도와 줄래요?

Can[May] I ask you something?
뭐 좀 부탁해도 돼?, 뭐 좀 물어봐도 돼?

I'd like to ask you something
뭐 좀 부탁할게[물어볼게]

Let me ask you something 뭐 좀 부탁할게[물어볼게]

Can you help me? 나 좀 도와줄래?

Would you please help me? 좀 도와줄래요?

I need to ask for your help 네 도움이 필요해

I need to ask you for some help 네게 도움 좀 청해야 겠어

Would you help me + 동사[with+명사]? …하는 걸 좀 도와줄래요?
Example Would you help me set up the computer?
컴퓨터를 설치하는 거 도와줄래요?

Would you + 동사~? …해줄래요?
Example Would you lend me your phone? 전화기 좀 빌려줄테야?

I'd like you to + 동사 네가 …을 해주었으면 좋겠어
Example I'd like you to come to my party 파티에 왔으면 좋겠어

I want you to + 동사 네가 …을 해줘
Example I want you to be my friend again 다시 나랑 친구하자

I'd appreciate it if you would + 동사~ …해주면 고맙겠어요
Example I'd appreciate it if you could bring an appetizer
전채요리를 가져다 주면 감사하겠어요

I would be pleased if you + 동사 …해주면 좋겠어요
Example I'd be pleased if you could join us for dinner
저녁식사를 함께 했으면 좋겠네요

Consider it done 그렇게 하지

No strings (attached) 아무런 조건없이

02 부탁 뭘 도와줄까?

What can I do for you? 뭘 도와줄까?

Is there anything I can do for you?
뭐 도와줄 것 없어?

Do you want any help? 좀 도와줄까?

Need any help? 도와줘?

Do you need some help? 뭐 좀 도와줄까?

Can I give you a hand? 도와줄까?

Do you need a hand? 도와줄까?

If there's anything you need, don't hesitate to ask
필요한 거 있으면 바로 말해

If you need any help, just call 뭐 도움이 필요하면 전화해

If you need me, you know where I am
도움이 필요하면 바로 불러

You know where to find me 내 연락처는 알고 있지

Feel free to ask 뭐든 물어봐, 맘껏 물어봐

I'd be happy to help you 기꺼이 도와줄게요

I'd be glad to do it 기꺼이 그렇게 할게요

With pleasure 기꺼이

I'll do anything for you 뭐든지 해줄게

Anything for you 널 위해선 뭐든지

What are friends for? 친구 좋다는 게 뭐야?

Sure. What is it? 그래. 뭔대?

Sure. How can I help? 그래. 어떻게 도와줄까?

Sure, what can I do? 그래, 내가 어떻게 해줄까?

Have you had any problems? 뭐 문제있어?

Is there a problem? 문제가 있는 거야?

What seems to be the problem? 문제가 뭔인 것 같아?

03 허가 들어가도 돼?

Is it okay to come in? 들어가도 돼?

Is it okay[all right] to[if]~ ~? …해도 괜찮아?
Example Is it okay if I go out now? 지금 가도 돼?

Would[Do] you mind ~ing[if]~? …해 줄래요?, …해도 돼요?
Example Would[Do] you mind if I smoke here? 여기서 담배펴도 돼요?
Example Would[Do] you mind if I go now? 지금 가도 될까요?

I was wondering if you[I] could ~? …할 수 있을지 모르겠네요?
Example I was wondering if I could get a ride home with you
집까지 같이 타고 가도 돼?

I'm sorry to trouble you, but could I borrow a pen?
미안하지만, 펜 좀 빌려줄래요?

Let's leave now, if that's all right with you 네가 괜찮다면 지금 나가자

if you don't mind 네가 괜찮다면

if it's okay with you 당신이 좋다면, 괜찮다면

04 제안 뭐 좀 갖다 줄까?

Can I get you something? 뭐 좀 사다줄까?, 뭐 좀 갖다줄까?

Can I get you anything? 내가 뭐 사다줄[갖다줄] 거라도 있어?

Can I get you some coffee? 커피 좀 갖다줄까?

Can I get you another glass of wine?
와인 한 잔 더 갖다드릴까요?

What can I get for you? 뭘 갖다 줄까?

I('ve) got something for you 네게 줄 게 있어

I got this for you 이거 너 줄거야

Here's something for you 이거 너 줄려고

This is for you 널 위해 준비했어, 이건 네 거야

05 제안 …해라[하자]

Why don't you + 동사? …해라

Example Why don't you ask for her number? 전화번호를 물어봐

Why don't we +동사? …을 하자

Example Why don't we head over to the mall and do some shopping?

쇼핑센터가서 쇼핑하자

You should + 동사 …해라

Example You should get her a present 걔한테 선물해줘라

Let's + 동사 …하자

Example Let's go to the coffee shop around the corner

모퉁이 커피숍으로 갑시다

How about + ~ing[명사; 주어+동사]? …하는 게 어때?

보충설명 How about 다음에는 동사의 ~ing형이나 명사만 오는 것이 아니라 '주어+동사' 의 절의 형태로도 많이 쓰인다.

Example How about we have one more beer? 맥주 한 잔 더 하는 게 어때?

Shall we ~? …할까요?

Example Shall we say around seven? 7시로 할까요?

Would you like[care] to + 동사 ? …할래?

Example Would you like to begin after a short break?

잠시 쉬었다가 시작할래?

Would you like me to + 동사 ~? 내가 …해줄까?

Example Would you like me to read them to everyone?

사람들에게 읽어줄까요?

Do you want to + 동사~? …할래

Example Do you want to come over to my place tonight?

오늘 밤 우리 집에 올래?

Do you want me to + 동사~ ? 내가 …할까?

Example Do you want me to give you a ride to the airport?

내가 공항까지 태워다 줄까?

How would you like to + 동사~? …하는 게 어때?

Example How would you like to get together? Say next Monday?

만나는 게 어때? 담주 월요일로?

If I were in your situation[shoes], I would + 동사~

너의 입장이라면 …할텐데

보충설명 If I were you, I would+동사 '내가 너라면 난 …할텐데,' If it were me, I would+동사
'나라면 난 …할텐데'도 많이 쓰이는 형태.

Example I wouldn't surf the Internet during business hours if I were you
나라면 근무시간 중에는 인터넷을 하지 않겠어

It would be smart to + 동사 …하는 게 좋을 걸

Example It'd be smart to work hard to get promoted
승진하려면 열심히 일하는 게 현명해

I have an idea 내게 생각이 있어

I have come up with an idea 좋은 생각이 하나 떠올랐어

I have a good idea 내게 좋은 생각이 있어

I suggest 주어+동사 …을 해봐, …을 제안할게

Example I suggest that you present a speech at the next conference
다음 회의에서 네가 발표해라

I want to make a suggestion 제안 하나 할 게

Won't you join us? 우리랑 함께 할래?

We might as well + 동사 …하는 게 나아

Example We might as well go home now 지금 집에 가는 게 나아

Chapter **06** 의사소통

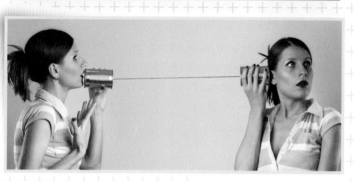

01 대화 잠깐 얘기 좀 할까?

Can I talk to you for a second? 잠깐 얘기 좀 할까?

Can I talk to you for a minute? 잠깐 얘기 좀 할까?

Can I tell you something? 말씀 좀 드려도 될까요?

Can we talk? 얘기 좀 할까?

Can we have a talk? 얘기 좀 할까?

Can[May] I have a word (with you)? 잠깐 얘기 좀 할까?

I want to talk to you (about that) 얘기 좀 하자고

I gotta talk to you 할 얘기가 있어

We need to talk (about that) 우리 얘기 좀 하자

We have to talk 얘기 좀 하자

Let's talk 같이 이야기해보자

We'll talk later 나중에 이야기 하죠

Let's talk about it[you] 그 문제[너]에 대해 얘기해보자

Can I (just) ask you a question? 질문 하나 해도 될까?

Let me ask you a question 뭐 하나 물어보자

I have a question for you 질문 있는데요

Let me ask you something 뭐 좀 물어볼게, 뭐 좀 부탁할게

Let me ask you one thing 뭐 하나 물어보자

Let me get back to you (on that)
나중에 이야기합시다, 생각해보고 다시 말해줄게

I'll get back to you (on that) 나중에 이야기하자고

02 대화 이것 좀 봐

Look at this 이것 좀 봐

Look here 이것 봐

Well 어, 저기

So 그래서

Look 저기

Anyway 어쨌든, 좌우간

By the way 참, 그런데, 참고로, 덧붙여서

You know 저 말야

As you know 너도 알다시피

Let me (just) say 말하자면, 글쎄

Let me see 그러니까 (내 생각엔), 저기

보충설명 뒤에 명사나 절이 나오면 「…보자」, 「생각해보자」라는 의미가 된다.

As I mentioned before 내가 전에 말했듯이

As I said before 전에 말했다시피

How should I put it? 뭐랄까?

Put it another way 달리 표현하자면

How can I say this? 글쎄, 이걸 어떻게 말하죠?

말하려는 내용을 강조하려고 먼저 꺼내는 말

03 **대화** 그거 알아?

You know what? 그거 알아?, 근데 말야?

Guess what? 저기 말야?, 그거 알아?

I'll tell you what 이럼 어때, 이러면 어떨까, 있잖아

Tell you what 있지

Let me tell you something 내 생각은 말야, 내 말해두는데

I have to tell you (something) 말할게 있는데, (솔직히) 할 말이 있어

I have to[gotta] tell you this 이 말은 해야겠는데요

(Do) You know something? 그거 알아?

(Do you) (want to) Know something? 궁금하지 않아?

I'm telling you 정말이야, 잘 들어

I'm telling you 주어+동사 정말이지…

Example I'm telling you that you'll regret it. 정말이지 너 후회하게 될거야.

You won't believe this 이거 믿지 못할 걸

You're not gonna believe this 넌 못 믿을 걸, 믿기지 않을거야

You'll never guess what I heard 내가 들은 얘기는 넌 짐작도 못할거야

Do you know about this? 이거 아니?

Have you heard? 얘기 들었어?

Did you hear? 너 얘기 들었니?

Last but not least 끝으로 중요한 말씀을 더 드리자면

꺼내기 어려운 이야기를 할 때

04 | 대화 어떻게 말해야 할지 모르겠지만

I'm sorry I didn't tell you this before, but~
전에 말하지 않아 미안하지만…

Example Sorry I didn't tell you this before but I'm no longer at my job
미리 말 안해 미안하지만, 난 실직했어

I don't know how to tell you this, but~
어떻게 이걸 말해야 할지 모르겠지만…

Example I don't know how to tell you this, but I think your wife's cheating
on you 뭐라 얘기해야 할지 모르겠지만 네 아내 바람피고 있어.

I'm afraid to say this, but~ 이런 말 하기 좀 미안하지만…
Example I'm afraid to say this, but you're not going to get a raise
말하기 좀 그렇지만 너 임금동결야

I've never told you this, but~ 전에 말한 적이 없지만…
Example I've never told you this, but I'm not good at numbers 전에 말한 적
없지만 숫자에 약해

I don't know if I've told you this, but~
내가 이걸 말했는지 모르겠지만…

Example I don't know if I've told you this, but I'm rich
이걸 말했는지 모르겠지만, 나 부자야

If (my) memory serves me correctly[right] 내 기억이 맞다면

That reminds me 그리고 보니 생각나네

That rings a bell 얼핏 기억이 나네요

Rumor has it (that) 주어+동사 …라는 소문을 들었어
Example Rumor has it that you'll be transferred to New York
소문듣자니 뉴욕으로 전근간다며

A little bird told me 소문으로 들었어

I heard through the grapevine that~ …라는 것을 풍문으로 들었다

Example I heard through the grapevine that you're going to get married
네가 결혼할거라는 소문을 들었어

I got wind of it 그 얘기를 들었어, 그런 얘기가 있더라

I'm probably out of line here 이렇게 말해도 좋을지 모르겠지만

I have a confession to make 고백할 게 하나 있어

상대방이 말을 하도록 유도하는 표현들

05 대화 말 좀 해봐

Tell me something 말 좀 해봐

Tell me what you're thinking 네 생각이 뭔지 말해봐

So, tell me 자, 말해봐

Let's have it 어서 말해봐, 내게 줘

Just try me 나한테 한번 (얘기)해봐, 기회를 한번 줘봐

Like what? 예를 들면?

Such as? 예를 들면?

What else is new? 뭐 더 새로운 소식은 없어?

Anything else? 다른 건 없니?

You were saying? 당신 말은?, 그래서?

Please go on 계속해봐

하려는 말이 기억이 나지 않을 때

06 대화 깜박 잊었어

It completely slipped my mind 깜박 잊었어

It's on the tip of my tongue 혀 끝에서 뱅뱅 도는데

I was somewhere else 잠시 딴 생각했어요

I totally forgot 까맣게 잊어버렸어

I just forgot 그냥 잊었어

Where was I? 내가 무슨 얘길 했더라?, 내가 어디까지 이야기했더라?

Where were we? 우리 어디까지 얘기했지?

What was I saying? 내가 무슨 말하고 있었지?

The cat got your tongue? 왜 말이 없어?

상대방말을 잘 듣지 못해 다시 말해달라고 할 때

07 이해 뭐라고?

Excuse me? 뭐라고?

Excuse me, I didn't hear 미안하지만 잘 못들어서

I can't hear you (well) (잘) 못들었어

I'm sorry? 예?, 뭐라고?

Come again? 뭐라구요?

Say it again? 뭐라구요?, 다시 한번 말해줄래요?

Say it once more, please 한 번 더 말해주세요

Pardon me? 죄송하지만 뭐라고 하셨어요?

Pardon? 뭐라고요?

I beg your pardon? 뭐라고 하셨죠?

What was that again? 뭐라고 했어요?

What did you say? 뭐라고 했는데?, 뭐라고?

Say what? 뭐라고? 다시 말해줄래?

Says who? 누가 그래?, 누가 어쨌다구?

Would you speak slower, please? 조금 천천히 말씀해줄래요?

Could[Would] you please repeat that? 다시 한번 말해줄래요?

Tell her what? 그녀에게 뭐라고 하라고?

You're what? 뭐하고 있다고?, 뭐라고?

You did what? 네가 뭐 어쨌다구?

You did it when? 언제 그랬다구?

Who did what? 누가 무엇을 했다고?

You did? 그랬어?

You do? 아 그래?

You are? 그래?

You were? 그랬어?

You have? 그래?

08 이해 그게 무슨 말이야?

What do you mean? 그게 무슨 말이야?

What does it mean? 그게 무슨 뜻이야?

I'm not sure what you mean 무슨 말인지 모르겠어

What do you mean by that? 그게 무슨 말이야?

What do you mean 주어+ 동사? …라는 게 무슨 의미죠?

Example What do you mean you quit? You can't quit!
그만둔다는 게 무슨 말야? 안돼!

What's your[the] point? 요점이 뭔가?, 하고 싶은 말이 뭔가?

What are you driving at? 말하려는 게 뭐야?

What are you getting at? 뭘 말하려는 거야?

I don't know what you're getting at 무슨 말 하려는건지 모르겠어

What are you talking about? 무슨 소리야?

I'm not sure what you're talking about
네가 무슨 얘기를 하는지 잘 모르겠어

What's the bottom line? 요점이 뭐야?

What's the catch? 속셈이 뭐야? 무슨 꿍꿍이야?

What are you trying to say? 무슨 말을 하려는 거야?

I don't get it[that] 모르겠어, 이해가 안돼

I didn't quite get that 잘 이해가 안돼

I can't get it right 제대로 이해 못하겠어

I didn't catch that 그 말을 못 알아들었어요

I didn't catch what you just said 네 말이 무슨 뜻인지 모르겠어

You lost me 못 알아듣겠는데

보충설명 You lost me (back) at ~ …부터는 무슨 얘긴지 모르겠어

I can't follow you 무슨 말인지 모르겠어

I can't see your point 무슨 말하는지 모르겠어

That's not clear 분명하지가 않아

상대방의 말을 이해했다고 말할 때

09 이해 무슨 의미인지 알아

I know what you mean 무슨 의미인지 알아

I know what you're saying 무슨 말인지 알아

That's what I'm saying 내 말이 그 말이야

I got it 알았어

I get the idea 알겠어

I get the picture 알겠어

You got it 맞아, 바로 그거야, 알았어

I get your point 무슨 말인지 알아들었어, 알겠어요

I (can) see your point 네 말을 알겠어

I can see that 알겠어, 알고 있어요

So I figured it out 그래서 (연유를) 알게 되었지

Say no more 더 말 안해도 돼, 알았어 무슨 말인지

We're talking the same language 이제 얘기가 된다

You're speaking my language 이제 얘기가 되는 구만

We're not speaking the same language 말이 안 통하는군

Now you're talking 그래 바로 그거야, 그렇지!

Bingo 바로 그거야

You took the words right out of my mouth
내가 하고 싶은 말이야

You're getting it! 이제 알아듣는 구만!

Am I getting warm? (정답 등에) 가까워지고 있는 거야?

Not even close 어림도 없어

You came close! (퀴즈 등) 거의 다 맞췄어!

10 이해 일리가 있어

That makes sense 일리가 있어

That does make sense 그건 정말 일리가 있는 말이야

That figures 그럴 줄 알았어, 그럼 그렇지

That explains it 그럼 설명이 되네, 아 그래서 이런 거구나

No wonder 당연하지

It all adds up 앞뒤가 들어 맞아

I knew it 그럴 줄 알았어

It is just as I imagined 내 생각했던 대로야

It's just like I dreamed 내가 생각했던 거와 똑같아

See? I told you 거봐? 내가 뭐랬어

See? I told you so 거봐? 내가 그랬잖아

See? I'm right 거봐? 내가 맞잖아

See? Didn't I tell you so? 거봐? 내가 그러지 않았어?

I said that, didn't I? 내가 그랬지, 안그래?

You see that? 봤지?, 내 말이 맞지?

That's why 주어+동사 그래서 …하는 거야
Example That's why I decided to quit 그래서 내가 그만 두려고 하는 거야

That's because 주어+동사 그건 …때문이야
Example That's because I didn't want you to come! 네가 오길 원치 않으니까!

11 이해 이해가 됐어?, 알았어?

You got it? 알았어?

You got that? 알아 들었어?

You got that, right? 제대로 알아 들었어?

(Do) You know what I mean? 무슨 말인지 알겠어?

(Do) You know what I'm saying? 무슨 얘기인지 알겠어?

(Do) You understand what I'm saying? 내 말 이해돼요?

See what I'm saying? 무슨 말인지 알지?

You know what I'm talking about? 내 말이 무슨 말인지 알아?

Are you with me? 내 말 이해 돼?, 내 편이 돼줄테야?

Are you following me? 알아듣고 있지?

Do you follow me? 내 말 아시겠죠?

Do I make myself clear? 내 말이 무슨 말인지 알겠어?

Am I making myself understood? 제 말이 잘 전달되었는지 모르겠어요

I didn't make myself clear 제 말 뜻을 이해하지 못하셨군요

Am I getting through on this? 이 문제에 관해서는 내 말을 잘 알겠지?

(Do) You get the picture? 너 이해했어?

Get the message? 알아들었어?

Understood? 알았어?

Do you understand? 이해했어?

Is that clear? 분명히 알겠어?

Do you read me? 내 말 들려?, 무슨 말인지 알겠어?

(Do you) See? 알겠어?

상대방을 이해시키기 위해 들어보라고 말할 때

12 이해 내 말 좀 들어봐

(You) Listen to me! 내 말 좀 들어봐!

Are you listening to me? 듣고 있어?

You don't seem to be listening
안 듣는 것 같은데

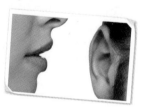

You're just not listening 딴 짓하고 있네

Hear me out 내 말 끝까지 들어봐

I'm talking to you! 내가 하는 말 좀 잘 들어봐!

Stay with me 끝까지 들어봐

That's not the end of the story 얘기가 끝난 게 아냐

How many times do I have to tell you?

도대체 몇번을 말해야 알겠어?

If I've told you once, I've told you a thousand times
한 번만 더 얘기하면 천번 째다

I'm listening 듣고 있어, 어서 말해

I'm not listening to you 난 네 말 안 듣는다고

They're not listening to me 걔네들이 내 말 들으려고 하지도 않아

I am all ears 귀 쫑긋 세우고 들을게

She was all ears 그 여자는 열심히 경청했다

비밀을 이야기 할 때

13 이해 우리끼리 이야기인데

This is just between you and me 이건 우리끼리 이야기야

It's a secret 비밀야

This is for your eyes only
이건 너만 알고 있어야 돼

Keep your mouth shut(~)
(…에 대해) 누구한테도 말하면 안돼

Mum's the word 입 꼭 다물고 있어

Don't tell anyone my secret! 아무한테도 말하지마!

Could you keep a secret? 비밀로 해주실래요?

Your secret's safe with me 비밀 지켜드릴게요

My lips are sealed 입다물고 있을게요

I won't say a word 한 마디도 안 할게

I'll take it to my grave 그 얘기 무덤까지 가지고 가마

I won't breathe a word (of it) 입도 뻥긋 안 할게

It was a slip of the tongue 내가 실언했네

I spoke out of turn 말이 잘못 나왔어, 내가 잘못 말했어

I let the cat out of the bag 비밀이 들통났어

I didn't say anything 난 아무 말도 안했어

That's an open secret now 지금은 다 공공연한 비밀인데

14 오해 고의로 그런 건 아냐

I didn't mean it 고의로 그런 건 아냐

I didn't mean any harm 마음 상하게 할 생각은 없었어

I really didn't mean any offense 기분상하게 할려는 건 아니었는데

I didn't mean to offend you 기분 상하게 할 의도는 아니었어

That's not what I mean 실은 그런 뜻이 아냐

That's not what I said 내 말은 그런 게 아냐

I'm sorry, I meant to + 동사~ 미안하지만 …할 생각이었어

Example I'm sorry, I meant to say thank you 미안하지만 네게 고맙다고 말할 생각이었어

Don't get me wrong 오해하지마

You've got it all wrong 잘못 알고 있는거야

There're no hard[ill] feelings (on my part)

악의는 아냐, 기분 나쁘게 생각하지마

No offense 악의는 없었어, 기분 나빠하지마

Don't take it personally 기분 나쁘게 받아들이지마

Don't take this wrong 잘못 받아들이지마

15 오해 …란 말야?

Do you mean~? …란 말야?

Example Do you mean you won't be coming over for dinner?

저녁 먹으러 못 온다고?

You mean,~ 네 말은…

Example You mean you're not going to come over? 못 온다는 말이지?

Let me make sure~ 확실히 하자면 …란 말이지

Example Let me make sure I understand. You don't love her?

제대로 알아들었는지 확인해볼게. 아내를 사랑하지 않는다고?

Let me get this straight 이건 분명히 해두자, 얘기를 정리해보자고

We need to get this straight 이건 분명히 해둬야 돼

Let's just get one thing straight 이거 하나는 분명히 해두죠

That isn't the way I heard it 내가 들은 이야기랑 다르네

You're just saying that 그냥 해보는 소리지, 괜한 소리지

You're just saying 주어+동사 그냥 …라고 하는 거지
Example You're just saying that because you're my biggest fan
나의 열렬한 팬이니까 그러는거지

Would you please be more specific?
좀 더 구체적으로 말씀해줄래요?

Are you saying that~? …라는 거지?
Example Are you saying that it's a bad idea?
그게 나쁜 생각이라고 하는 거지?

Are you trying to say that~? …라고 말하려는 거야?
Example Are you trying to say that this book is wrong?
이 책은 안좋다고 말하려는 거야?

내가 말하는 내용을 다시 한번 분명히 말할 때

16 오해 내 말이 그거야

That's my point 내 말이 그거야

That's not the point 핵심은 그게 아니라고

What I'm trying to say 주어+동사 내가 말하고자 하는 건…
Example What I'm trying to say is we're short-handed
내 말은 일손이 부족하다는 거야

What I'd like to say is that 주어+동사 내가 말하고 싶은 건…
Example What I'd like to say is that you're not qualified for this job
내가 말하고 싶은 건 당신은 이 일에 자격이 안 된다는 겁니다

What I'm saying is 주어+동사 내가 말하는 건…
Example What I'm saying is we have to work overtime this week
내 말은 이번 주 야근해야 된다는 거야

What I said was 주어+동사 내가 말한 건…
Example What I said was we have to work overtime this week
내 말은 이번 주 야근해야 된다는 거야

I mean,~ 내 말은…

Example I mean, I don't like to be with you 내 말은, 너하고 함께 하고 싶지 않아

I'm just saying (that) 주어+동사 내 말은 단지 …라는 거야

Example I'm just saying that we should get together more often

그냥 우리가 자주 만나야 된다는 거야

상대방에게 숨기지 말고 솔직히 말하자고 할 때

17 오해 솔직히 말해

Be honest 솔직히 털어놔

You have to be honest with me 너 나한테 솔직히 말해

I'll be honest with you 네게 솔직히 털어놓을게

Level with me 솔직히 말해봐

I'll level with you 솔직히 말할게

Tell me the truth 사실대로 말해

You've got to come clean with me! 나한테 실토해!

Give it to me straight 솔직히 말해봐

Don't beat around the bush 말 돌리지 마, 핵심을 말해

Let's cut to the chase 단도직입적으로 물어볼게

상대방의 말이 놀랍거나 혹은 못 믿겠을 때

18 확인 정말야?

Are you serious? 정말이야?, 농담 아냐?

Are you for real? 정말이야?

Are you sure (about that)? 정말이야?

Is that true[right]? 정말이야?

Is that so? 확실해?, 정말 그럴까?

You mean it? 정말야?

Do you mean that? 정말야?

You're kidding! 농담하지마!, 장난하는 거지!

Are you kidding? 농담하는 거야?, 무슨 소리야?

No kidding! 설마!, 너 농담하냐!, 진심이야!

You're not kidding 정말 그렇네

Is this some kind of joke? 장난하는 거지?

You must be joking 농담하는 거지

Did I hear you right? 정말이니?, 내가 제대로 들은 거야?

Get out of here! 농담하지 마!

Really? 정말?

Oh yeah? 어, 그래?

You bet! 정말!

19 확인 진심이야

I mean it 진심이야

I mean business 진심이야

I don't mean maybe! 장난아냐!

I'm not kidding 정말이야, 장난아냐

I kid you not 장난삼아 하는 말 아냐

I'm telling the truth 진짜야

I'm not lying 정말이라니까

I am (dead) serious (정말) 진심이야

I'll bet 틀림없어, 정말이야, 확실해, 그러겠지

보충설명 기본적으로 I'll bet은 상대방의 말에 수긍하는 표현이지만 "그러겠지," "어련하시겠어"라는 빈정대는 뜻으로도 쓰인다.

I bet (you) 맹세해

I'll bet you 내 너한테 맹세하마

I'd bet my life on it 그건 내가 맹세해

I'll say 정말이야

You can bet on it 그럼, 물론이지

You can bet 주어+동사 …인 게 틀림없어

Example You can bet she wants to go 걔가 가고 싶어하는 게 틀림없어

Believe me 정말이야

Believe you me 정말 진심이야

How true 정말 그렇다니까

---

20 확인 날 믿어줘

Take my word for it 진짜야, 믿어줘

You have my word 내 약속이지

I give you my word 약속할게

Mark my words! 내 말 잘 들어!

(You can) Trust me 믿어봐

You'd better believe it 맞아, 정말야

I promise (you)! 정말이야

보충설명 I promise와 I promise you는 같은 의미이지만 I promise you의 의미가 다소 강함.

Promise? 약속하는 거지?

I swear 맹세해

I swear to God[you] 하나님께[네게] 맹세코

I swear I told you all about it 맹세코 다 얘기한 거라니까

Believe what I say 내 말 믿어줘

You can take it from me 그 점은 내 말을 믿어도 돼

Have faith in me 날 믿어줘

It may sound strange, but it's true
이상하게 들리겠지만 진짜야

---

21 확인 어째서?

How come? 어째서?, 왜?

How come 주어+동사? 왜 …하는 거야?

Example How come you're late? 어쩌다 이렇게 늦은 거야?

What makes you think so?
왜 그렇게 생각하니?, 꼭 그런건 아니잖아?

What makes you so mad? 뭐 때문에 그렇게 화난거야?

How did it happen? 이게 어떻게 된 거야?

What brings you here? 무슨 일로 왔어?

What for? 왜요?, 뭣 때문에?

For what? 왜?, 뭣 때문에?

What're you doing this for? 왜 그러는 거야?

보충설명 What ~ for? 어째서…?, 무엇 때문에…?

Why do you think that? 왜 그렇게 생각하는 거야?

Why do you say that? 왜 그렇게 말하는 거야?

Why did you do that? 왜 그랬어?

Why would you say that? 왜 그런 말을 하는 거야?

What's the reason? 이유가 뭔대?

Tell me why 이유를 말해봐

I was just wondering 그냥 물어봤어

◆ **Can you say this word for me?** 이 단어 어떻게 말해요?

◆ **I'm not sure how to say this word** 이 단어 어떻게 말하는 지 모르겠어요

◆ **How do you pronounce this word?** 이 단어 어떻게 발음해요?

◆ **What's the pronunciation of this word?** 이 단어 발음이 어떻게 돼요?

◆ **Please spell that word for me** 이 단어 철자 좀 말해줘요

◆ **What does 'tofu' mean?** 'tofu'가 무슨 의미예요?

◆ **Can I say it like this?** 이거 이렇게 말해도 되나요?

◆ **I wonder if this is the correct expression** 이게 올바른 표현인 지 모르겠어요

◆ **I wrote "to say the lease of." Is this correct?**
"to say the least of"라고 썼는데 맞나요?

◆ **Is it okay to say "As I said before~"?** "As I said before"라고 말해도 되나요?

◆ **Can I use this expression in a situation like this?**
이런 상황에서 이 표현을 써도 돼요?

◆ **Would it be rude to say "Never mind" to the teacher?**
선생님께 "Never mind"라고 해도 무례가 아닌가요?

A: Leave a message that Mr. Horowitz called.
호로비츠가 전화했다고 전해줘요.

B: OK. Please spell your name for me.
예, 성함 철자 좀 알려주세요.

A: Is it okay to say "I wish you good luck"?
I wish you good luck 이라고 말해도 돼요?

B: No, that sounds odd. Just say "good luck."
아니, 좀 이상해. 그냥 good luck이라고 해.

Chapter **07** 생각 | 의견

01 생각 내 생각엔 말야

The way I see it 내가 보기엔

As far as I can see 내가 보기엔

As I see it 내가 보기로는
Example As I see it, we need to save more money
내가 보기로는 좀 더 저축해야 돼

The way I look at it is~ 내가 보기엔 …이야
Example The way I look at it is that we have to wait until he's back
걔가 돌아올 때까지 기다려야 할 것 같아

The thing is (that) 주어+동사 중요한 건 …라는 거야
Example The thing is I need to find a date
중요한 건 데이트 상대를 찾아야 된다는 거야

The point is that 주어+동사 요점은 …라는 것이야
Example The point is that we are bankrupt 요점은 우리가 파산했다는 겁니다

My opinion in a nutshell is that 주어+동사 내 의견은 한마디로 …이야
Example My opinion in a nutshell is that he will win the race
내 의견은 한마디로 경주에서 걔가 이길거라는 거야

I (will) tell you what I think 내 생각을 말하면 이래

This is what we'll do 우리 이렇게 하자

Here's my plan 내 생각은 이래

Here's my idea 내 생각 들어봐

Here's the deal 이렇게 하자, 이런 거야

Here's the thing 내 말인 즉은, 그게 말야, 문제가 되는 건

If you ask me 내 생각은, 내 생각을 말한다면

02 생각 …인 것 같아

I think~ …것 같아
Example I think it would be better if you went to bed
잠자러 가는 게 좋을 것 같은데

I guess~ …인 것 같아

Example I guess he got the contract

내 생각에는 걔가 계약을 따낸 것 같아

It seems (like) that~ …인 것 같은데

Example It seems like that I have lost my wallet

지갑을 잃어버린 듯해요

I feel like 주어+동사 …할 것 같아

Example I feel like my head is going to explode!

머리가 폭발할 것 같아!

It looks like[as if]~ …처럼 보여

Example It looks like you don't like your meal at all

밥이 네 입맛에 전혀 맞지 않나 보구나

It sounds like~ …한 것 같아

Example It sounds like you need a new mouse

새 마우스가 필요할 것 같은데

I'm afraid I don't know what to say 뭐라고 해야 할지 모르겠어

I doubt that they'll know what to do 걔들이 뭘 해야 하는 지 모를걸

I doubt~ 과연 …일까 의심스러워

Example I doubt you'll be able to get soccer tickets

네가 표를 못 구할 것 같아

I suspect~ 아무래도 …인 것 같아

Example I suspect that my son has been smoking

웬지 우리 아들이 담배피우는 것 같아

I have a feeling ~ …인 것 같아

Example I have a feeling that they are not going to show up

걔들이 안 올 것 같아

I have a hunch that~ …라는 느낌이 들어

Example I have a hunch that he's lying

걔가 거짓말하는 것 같아

I bet 주어+동사 난 틀림없이 …라고 생각해

Example I bet you will find a new boyfriend soon

곧 틀림없이 새로운 남친을 만나게 될거야

Let's just say 주어+동사 …라고 생각해

Example Fine, then let's just say she's not my type

좋아, 그럼 걘 내 타입이 아닌 것 같아

03 생각 네 생각은 어때?

How[What] about you? 네 생각은 어때?

How about it? 그거 어때?

What do you think? 네 생각은 어때?, 무슨 말이야? 그걸 말이라고 해?

What do you think of[about] that? 넌 그걸 어떻게 생각해?

What do you think~? 어떻게 …를 생각해?
> Example What do you think will happen? 어떻게 될 것 같아?

What is your opinion? 네 의견은 어때?

What is your feeling about this? 여기에 대해 네 생각은 어때?

What do you think is the best? 뭐가 최선인 것 같아?

Which is better, A or B? A와 B중에서 어떤 게 좋아?
> Example Which is better, getting married or being single?
> 결혼과 싱글 중 어떤 게 좋아?

Is it "yes" or "no"? 그렇다는 거야 안 그렇다는 거야?

Yes or no? 찬성야 반대야?

Does it work for you? 네 생각은 어때?, 너도 좋아?

Do you like it? 좋았어?

Did you have fun? 재밌었어?

Don't you think so? 그렇게 생각되지 않아?

Like this? 이렇게 하면 돼?

04 생각 어땠어?

How was it? 어땠어?

How did you like it? 어땠어?

How'd it go? 어떻게 됐어?, 어땠어?

How did it go at the doctor's? 병원에 간 일은 어땠어?

How would you like + 명사~? …는 어때요?, 어떻게 (준비) 해드릴까요?

How would you like 다음에 'to+동사' 가 오면 권유의 문장으로 「…하는 게 어때?」라는 의
미이다.

Example How do you like this suit? 이 옷 어때?

How would you like it if 주어+동사~? …한다면 어떻겠어?
Example How would you like it if we switched offices?
사무실을 바꾸면 어떻겠어?

What do you say? 어때?

What do you say to + 명사[동사~ing]? …하는 게 어때?
Example What do you say to going for a drink tonight?
오늘 밤 한잔 하러 가는 거 어때요?

What do you say (that) 주어+동사? …어때요?
Example What do you say that we eat some lunch? 점심 좀 먹는 게 어때?

What would you say? 어떻게 할 거야?, 넌 뭐라고 할래?

What would you say if 주어+동사~? …한다면 어떨까?
Example What would you say if I wanted to stay home?
내가 집에 더 있는 건 어떨까?

내가 좋아한다고 말할 때

05 기호 그거 좋은데

I like that 그거 좋은데, 맘에 들어

would를 삽입해서 I'd like that하면 "그러면 좋겠다,"
"그렇게 한다면 난 좋다"라는 표현으로 상대방의 제안이나
권유에 찬성을 뜻하는 표현이 된다.

I love it! 정말 좋다, 내 맘에 꼭들에!

I like A better than B 난 B보다 A가 좋아

I began to like Bulgogi 불고기를 좋아하게 됐어

I've started to like Pasta 파스타를 좋아하기 시작했어
Example I like tea better than coffee 차보다는 커피가 좋아

I prefer A to B 난 B보다 A가 좋아
Example I think I prefer Suwon to other cities in Korea
한국에서 수원이 타도시보다 더 좋아

I'm fond of reading novels 소설 읽는 걸 좋아해

I want + 명사 ···를 원해, 필요해

Example I want a straight answer 분명한 답을 듣고 싶어

I want to + 동사 ···하기를 원해, ···해야 해

Example I want to get her number 전화번호를 알아내고 싶은 걸

I'd like + 명사 ···를 원해

Example I'd like a round-trip ticket to New York
뉴욕행 왕복항공권을 주세요

I'd like to + 동사 ···했으면 해

Example I'd like to go out for lunch on Friday
금요일에 같이 점심 먹으러 갔으면 하는데

I'd love to + 동사 ···하고 싶어

Example I'd love to go, but I've got too much work to do
가고 싶지만, 할일이 많아

I'd love it if~ ···하면 좋을텐데

Example I'd love it if you would do it 네가 그걸 한다면 좋지

I need + 명사 ···가 필요해

Example I need the money 돈이 필요해

I need to + 동사 ···해야 해

Example I need to take the rest of the day off 오늘은 그만 쉬어야겠어요

I feel like ~ing ···가 하고 싶어

Example I feel like having a nice cold beer right now
지금 시원한 맥주가 당기는데

I can't wait (to+동사) 지금 당장이라고 하고 싶어

Example I can't wait to see the results of the test
시험 성적을 알고 싶어 죽겠어

I'm willing to + 동사 기꺼이 ···하고 싶어

Example I'm willing to pay as much as 2,000 dollars for it
2천달러 정도 낼 의향이 있어

I'm looking forward to doing it 무척 기다려져

You up for it? 하고 싶어?

I'm just not up for it tonight 오늘 밤에는 생각없어

I'm eager to + 동사 ···를 무지 하고 싶어

Example I'm eager to start my vacation
어서 휴가를 갔으면 해

I'm dying to + 동사 ···하고 싶어 죽겠어

Example I'm dying to meet her 걔를 만나고 싶어 죽겠어

I'm itching to + 동사 몹시 ···하고 싶어

Example I'm itching to go travelling again

　　　　　다시 여행 가고 싶어서 견딜 수가 없어

Hopefully! 바라건대!, 그랬음 좋겠다!

Good enough! 딱 좋아!

I'm a real fan of~ 난 ···를 정말 좋아해

Example Well, I'm a real fan of Manchester United

　　　　　음, 난 맨유가 정말 좋아

내가 싫어한다고 말하기

06 기호 싫어

I don't like it 싫어해

I hate it 싫어해

I'm not into it 그런 건 안해요

I don't want to get involved 끼어들고 싶지 않아

I'm not going to be part of it 난 끼고 싶지 않아

That's not for me 내 것이 아닌데, 그런 건 나한테는 안 어울려

I don't care for it 난 싫어

That's not my cup of tea 내 취향이 아냐

That's not my thing 난 그런 건 질색이야

The last thing I want to do is 주어+동사 가장 하고 싶지 않은 건 ···이다

Example The last thing I want to do is lay anyone off

　　　　　누굴 해고한다는 게 가장 싫은 일야

07 기호 …면 좋겠어

I hope 주어+동사~ …면 좋겠어

Example I hope you like it 네 맘에 들었으면 좋겠어

I hope to + 동사 …하기를 바래

보충설명 I wish to 또한 「…하기를 바란다」이지만 I hope to에 비해 다분히 공식적인 경우에 쓰인다.

Example I hope to enroll in a course this summer

올 여름에 한 과목 등록하고 싶어

I hope so 그랬으면 좋겠어

I hope not 그러지 말았으면 좋겠다, 아니라면 좋을텐데

It would be nice if 주어+동사 …한다면 좋을 텐데

Example It would be nice if we could take a vacation

우리가 휴가를 얻는다면 좋을 텐데

It'll be good[nice; wonderful] to + 동사 …하면 멋질 거야

Example It'll be good to see my family again

가족을 다시 보는 건 멋질거야

I'd rather A than B A하느니 차라리 B할 거야

Example I'd rather play computer games than study

공부를 하느니 컴퓨터게임을 할거야

If only I could~ …할 수 있다면 좋을 텐데

Example If only I could remember her name

그 여자 이름을 기억하면 좋겠는데

I wish 주어+동사 …였으면 좋겠어

Example I wish I had a little time for fun 놀 시간이 좀 있으면 좋겠어

Example I wish you would get out of my face! 네가 꺼져줬으면 좋겠어!

If I + 과거, I would + 동사 …이면 …할 텐데

Example If I had his phone number, I would call him

걔 전화번호를 알면 전화할텐데

If I had + pp, I would[could; might] have + pp …였다면 …했을 텐데

Example If I had never met my wife, this would never have happened

와이프를 만나지 않았더라면 이런 일이 생기지 않았을텐데

08 관심 그건 내게 중요한 문제야

It matters to me
그건 내게 중요한 문제야

It doesn't matter to me
난 아무래도 상관없어요

It doesn't matter 상관없어

I'm (not) interested in~
…에 관심이 있(없)어

Example I'm interested in the new yoga class 새로 생긴 요가교실에 관심이 있어

I'm involved in~ …을 하고 있어
Example I really don't want to get involved in it
정말이지 거기 끼고 싶지 않아

I'm into~ 난 …에 관심이 많아
Example Thanks! I'm really into health food now
고마워! 요즘 건강식에 관심많아

Something appeals to me …가 끌리다
Example I know, but nothing appeals to me today
그래, 하지만 오늘은 딱 끌리는 게 없어

I don't care (about it) (상대방의 부탁, 제안에 대해 승낙하며) 상관없어

I don't care if[what; how much]~ 난 (뭐라도, 얼마나 ~해도) 상관없어
Example I don't care what they say 걔들이 뭐래든 상관없어

I couldn't care less 알게 뭐람

It makes no difference to me 상관없어

It doesn't make any difference 상관없어

It's not going to make any difference 전혀 상관없어

It's gonna make a difference 차이가 있을 거야

What's the difference? 그게 무슨 상관이야?

What difference does it make? 그게 무슨 차이야?

It doesn't mean anything to me 난 상관없어

It's not my concern[business] 난 관심없어

It's not my problem 나하고 상관없어

I have nothing to do with this 난 아무 관련이 없어

It doesn't have anything to do with me 난 모르는 일이야

Who cares? 누가 신경이나 쓴대?

So what? 그래서 뭐가 어쨌다고?

So shoot me 그래서 어쨌다는 거야

Whatever! 뭐든지 간에!

The hell with that 알게 뭐람! 맘대로 해

To hell with tradition 전통따위 알게 뭐람

I don't give a shit[damn, fuck] 난 알 바 아냐

Chapter **08** 동의 | 반대

01 긍정 그런 것 같아

I'm afraid so (안타깝게도) 그런 것 같아

I guess so 아마 그럴 걸

I think so 그래요

I believe so 그럴 거라 생각해

I suppose (so) 그럴 걸

It might be true 사실일 수도 있어

It could be 그럴 수도 있어

It's possible 그럴 수 있어

Sort[Kind] of 어느 정도는, 다소

Yes and no 글쎄 어떨지

Maybe yes, maybe no 어느 쪽이라고 말해야 할지

02 긍정 물론이지

Absolutely! 물론이지!

보충설명 반대로 Absolutely not!하면 「물론 아니지」란 의미가 되며 비슷한 표현으로는 Certainly!(확실해) – Certainly not!(정말 아냐) 그리고 Definitely!(틀림없어)– Definitely not!(절대 아냐)이 있다.

Of course 물론이지, 확실해

Sure 물론, 당연하지

Sure thing 물론이지, 그럼

It sure is 그렇고 말고, 맞고 말고

That's for sure 확실하지, 물론이지

(It's) For sure 물론이야

No doubt 분명해

There is no doubt about it! 틀림없어!

You bet 확실해, 물론이지

03 긍정 알았어

All right 알았어

All right, already! 좋아 알았다구!, 이제 그만해라!

All right then 좋아 그럼

All right, I get it 좋아 알겠어

All right, I see 좋아 알았어

Okay 좋아

> 보충설명 Okay나 All right은 상대방의 말에 동의하는 표현이며, That's okay나 That's all right은 역시 상대방의 말에 동의하는 표현으로도 쓰이지만 상대방의 사과에 괜찮다는 「용서의 표현」으로도 쓰인다. 이때는 No problem과 의미가 유사하다.

Okey-dokey [Okie-dokie] 좋아, 됐어

That's great 아주 좋아, 잘 됐어

That's nice 좋아, 잘했어

That's cool 좋아

That's terrific[wonderful] 끝내주네[훌륭해]

That's really something 거 굉장하네

I'd like that 그러면 좋겠다, 그렇게 한다면 난 좋다

That would be great[perfect] 그럼 좋겠어

(That) Sounds good (to me) 좋은데

Sounds great 아주 좋아

Sounds like a plan 좋은 생각이야

Sounds like fun 재밌을 것 같은데

Sounds interesting 재미있겠는데

Sounds like a good idea 좋은 생각 같은데

04 동의 맞아, 그래

That's right 맞아, 그래

You're right 네 말이 맞아

You're exactly right 정말 맞아

I think you're right (about that) (그 점에 있어서) 네가 옳은 것 같아

You're right on the money 네 말이 맞아

That's a good point 좋은 지적이야, 맞는 말이야

You have a point there 네 말이 맞아

You've got a point 맞는 말이다

You got that right 네 말이 맞아

That's correct 맞아

You're correct 네가 맞아

That's it 바로 그거야, 그게 다야, 그만두자

That's it? 이걸로 끝이야?

Tell me about it! 그 얘기 좀 해봐!, 그게 맞아!, 그렇고 말고!

You're telling me! 누가 아니래!, 정말 그래!, 나도 알아!

Big time 그렇고 말고, 많이

In a word, yes 한마디로 말해서 그래

In a sense he's right 어떤 의미에서 걔 말이 맞아

상대방의 말에 동의하기

05 동의 네말에 동의해

I agree 그래

I agree with you 100% 전적으로 동감이야

I couldn't agree with you more 정말 네 말이 맞아

I can't argue with that 두말하면 잔소리지, 물론이지

I can't disagree with you 네 말이 맞아

You can say that again 그렇고 말고, 당근이지

You could[might] say that 두말하면 잔소리지

You said it 네 말이 맞아

Well said 그 말 한번 잘했어, 맞는 말이야

I'm with you 동감이야, 알았어

I'm with you there 나도 그 말에 공감해

I feel the same way 나도 그렇게 생각해

I'm like you 나도 너랑 같은 생각이야

We're on the same page 우린 같은 생각이야

I'm on your side 난 네 편이야

Same here 나도 그래

So am I 나도 그래

So do I 나도 그래

Go ahead 그렇게 해

Yes, please do 어, 그렇게 해

상대방의 말에 나도 그렇다라고 찬성하기

06 찬성 난 찬성이야

I'm for it 난 찬성이야

I'm for giving him another chance 걔에게 기회를 한 번 더 주는데 찬성야

I'm for the basic idea 기본적인 생각은 찬성야

I'm in favor of it 찬성이야

Let's do it 자 하자, 그러자

That's more like it 그게 더 낫겠어

I don't see why not 그래

I'll drink to that! 옳소, 찬성이오!

Why not? 왜 안해?, 왜 안되는 거야?, 그러지 뭐

A deal's a deal 약속한 거야

(It's a) Deal! 그러기로 한 거야!, 내 약속하지!

(It's a) Done deal 그러기로 한 거야

It's settled! 그렇게 하자!

I'm standing behind you 내가 뒤에 있잖아

I'll stand by you 네 옆에 있어줄게

07 찬성 괜찮아

That's all right 괜찮아, 됐어

보충설명 고맙다는 혹은 미안하다는 말에 대한 답변으로 자주 쓰이는 표현

I'm all right with that 난 괜찮아

They seem all right with it 걔네들 괜찮은 거 같아

That's fine (with me) (난) 괜찮아

That will be fine 괜찮아질 거야

That's okay (with me) 괜찮아, 난 상관없어

Are you all right? 괜찮아?

보충설명 All right?은 「알겠니?」라고 상대방에게 물어보는 말.

Are you okay? 괜찮아?

Is it all right? 괜찮겠어? 괜찮아?

I'm cool with[about] that 난 괜찮아, 상관없어

Are you cool with this? 이거 괜찮아?

I can live with that 괜찮아, 참을 만해

보충설명 I'm cool with that과 같은 맥락의 표현으로 의미는 It's okay with me 혹은 I will agree with that이다.

It works for me 난 괜찮아, 찬성이야

I have no problem with that 난 괜찮아요

It suits me (fine) 난 좋아, 내 생각엔 괜찮은 것 같아

I'm easy (to please) 네 결정에 따를게, 난 어느 쪽도 상관없어

I'm happy either way 난 아무거나 좋아

Either will do 아무거나 괜찮아

08 찬성 그럼요

Be my guest 그럼요

Whatever you ask 뭐든 말만 해

Whatever you say 말만해, 전적으로 동감이야

Whatever you want to do 네가 하고 싶은 거 뭐든 좋아

Whatever it takes 무슨 수를 써서라도

Whatever turns you on 뭐든 좋을 대로

I am all yours 얼마든지, 뭐든지 다

Suit yourself 마음대로 해

You name it 말만 해

You are on 그래 좋았어

보충설명 특히 내기를 받아들일 경우에 쓰는 표현.

So be it (그렇게 결정됐다면) 그렇게 해

Anything you say 말만 하셔

Anytime 언제든지

생각 좀 해본다고 하면서 시간을 벌기

09 부정 생각 좀 해보고

I'll think about it 그거에 대해 생각해볼게

I'll think it over 검토해볼게

Let me think about it 생각 좀 해볼게

Let me have time to think it over
생각할 시간 좀 줘

We're having second thoughts about it 다시 생각해봐야겠어

Let me sleep on it 곰곰이 생각해봐야겠어

I'll see what I can do 내가 어떻게 할 수 있는지 좀 보고

I never looked at it that way before 전에 그렇게 생각해 본 적이 없는데

상대방의 말에 가볍게 부정하기

10 부정 그런 것 같지 않은데

I don't think so 그런 것 같지 않은데

I don't believe so 그런 것 같지 않은데

I guess not 아닌 것 같아

I suppose not 아닐 걸

I expect not 아닌 것 같아

I'm afraid not 아닌 것 같아

I'm afraid (that) 주어+동사 …가 아닌 것 같아
Example I'm afraid it's too late for that now
지금 그거 내세우기에는 너무 늦었다고 봐

I don't see that 난 그렇게 생각 안하는데, 그런 것 같지 않아

I don't see it (that way) 난 그렇게 생각하지 않아

I don't see that happening 그렇게는 안될 걸

That can't happen 말도 안돼, 그렇지 않아

I can't say 주어+동사 …라곤 말 못하지
Example I can't say he is innocent 걔가 무죄라고는 말 못하지

It's not what you think 그건 네 생각과 달라, 속단하지 마라

That's what you think 그건 네 생각이고

This is a totally different situation 전혀 다른 상황야

That's another[a different] story
그건 또 다른 얘기야, 그건 또 별개의 문제야

I have a different opinion 내 생각은 달라

Speak for yourself 그건 그쪽 얘기죠, 당신이나 그렇지

Not me 난 아냐

I wouldn't do that 나라면 그렇게 안하겠어

I didn't do it 내가 안 했어

I didn't cause this 내가 이런 건 아냐

Me neither 나도 안그래

Neither did I 나도 안그랬어

Neither do I 나도 안그래

Neither am I 나도 안그래

Neither will I 나도 안 그럴 거야

Neither can I 나도 못해

11 거절/반대 그러고 싶지만 안되겠어

I wish I could, but I can't 그러고 싶지만 안되겠어

I'd like[love] to, but~ 그러고 싶지만…
Example I'd like to, but I'm on call today 그러고 싶은데, 난 오늘 대기해야 돼

I'd have to say no 안되겠는데

I don't feel like it 사양할래, 그러고 싶지 않아

I'm sorry, but~ 미안하지만…
Example I'm sorry, but I don't have any money with me right now
미안하지만 지금 수중에 돈이 하나도 없어

No, thank you 고맙지만 사양하겠어요

No, thanks 고맙지만 됐어요

Nothing for me, thanks 고맙지만 난 됐어요

I'd rather not 그러고 싶지 않아

I'd rather you didn't 안그랬으면 좋겠는데

Not right now, thanks 지금은 됐어요

Not now 지금은 아냐

Not here 여기서는 말고

Not always 항상 그런 건 아니야

Not exactly 꼭 그런 건 아니야

Not really 실제로는 아니야

Not yet 아직은 아냐

Not anymore 이젠 됐어, 지금은 아니야

I don't think it was very good 안 좋았다고 생각해

That (all) depends 상황에 따라 다르지, 경우에 따라 달라

12 거절/반대 네가 틀렸다고 생각해

I think you're wrong 네가 틀렸다고 생각해

You're dead wrong 넌 완전히 틀렸어

You got the wrong idea 틀린 생각이야

You're on the wrong track 네가 잘못 생각했어

You're way off the mark 네가 아주 어긋났어

That's not right 그렇지 않아

It doesn't work 제대로 안돼, 그렇게는 안돼

It doesn't work that way 그렇게는 안 통해

It won't work 효과가 없을거야

That's not true 그렇지 않아, 사실이 아니야

I won't 싫어, 그렇게 안할래

Let's not 그렇게 하지 말자

It's not a good idea 별로 좋은 생각이 아니야

I can't do anything about it 어쩔 수가 없어

I can't make that happen 그렇게는 안되지

I don't buy it 못 믿어

We aren't buying your story 네 얘기 믿을 수 없어

I can't accept that 인정 못해

That's not how it works 그렇게는 안돼

That's not how we do things here 여기선 그렇게 하는 게 아냐

I don't[can't] agree with that[you] 그거에[네게] 동의할 수 없어

┌─────────────────────────────────────┐
│ 상대방의 부탁, 제안 등에 강하게 거절하기 │
└─────────────────────────────────────┘

13 거절/반대 절대 안돼!

No way! 절대 안돼!, 말도 안돼!

Not on your life! 결사반대야, 절대 안돼!

No, no, a thousand times no! 무슨 일이 있어도 안돼, 절대로 싫어

Not by a long shot 어떠한 일이 있어도 아냐, 어림도 없지

Not a thing 전혀

No, not a bit 아니, 조금도 안돼

Not that way! 그런식으론 안돼!

Not a chance! 안돼!

(There is) No chance! 안돼!

I said no 안 된다고 했잖아, 아니라고 했잖아

I'm dead set against it 난 결사 반대야

It's out of the question 그건 불가능해, 절대 안돼

No means no 아니라면 아닌 거지

Over my dead body 내 눈에 흙이 들어가기 전엔 안돼

That's impossible 그건 불가능해

It's never going to happen 그건 절대 안돼

보충설명 happen 대신에 work를 써도 된다.

It's not even a possibility 절대 그런 일 없을거야

상대방의 말에 나도 알고 있다고 말하기

14 알아 알겠어

I know (that) 알아, 알고 있어

보충설명 I know는 이미 알고 있다(I had that information already)라는 의미이고 I see는 상대방이
뭔가 설명하거나 보여주고나서 이해했다(I understand)라는 의미로 쓰인다.

I know what I'm saying 나도 알고 하는 말이야, 내가 알아서 얘기한다구

I know what I'm talking about 나도 다 알고 하는 얘기야

I know what I'm doing 나도 아니까 걱정하지만, 내가 다 알아서 해

Do you know what you're doing? 잘 알겠지?, 어떻게 하는지 알지?

I've been there 무슨 말인지 충분히 알겠어, 정말 그 심정 이해해, 가본 적 있어

We have all been there 우리도 다 그런 적 있잖아

Been there done that (전에도 해본 것이어서) 뻔할 뻔자지

I can see it in your eyes 네 눈에 그렇게 쓰여 있어

It's written all over your face 네 얼굴에 다 쓰여있어

아무도 모른다고 강하게 반어적으로 말해보기

15 몰라 누가 알겠어

Who knows? 누가 알겠어?

Who knows what[where] ~? 무엇이[어디서] …한지 누가 알아?

Example Who knows what could happen? 무슨 일이 일어날 지 어떻게 알아?

Who can tell? 누가 알겠어?

Nobody knows 아무도 몰라

God (only) knows! 누구도 알 수 없지!

Heaven[Lord; Christ] knows! 아무도 몰라!

That's anybody's guess 아무도 몰라

There's no way to tell 알 길이 없어

상대방의 물음에 잘 모르겠다고 말하기

16 몰라 잘 모르겠어

I have no idea 몰라

I have no idea what you just said 네가 무슨 말 하는지 전혀 모르겠어

I didn't know that 모르고 있었지 뭐야

I don't know about that 글쎄

I don't know for sure 확실히 모르겠는데

I don't know for certain 확실히 몰라

I'm not sure 잘 모르겠어

I'm not sure about that 그건 잘 모르겠는데

I'm not sure 주어+동사 …를 잘 모르겠어

Example I'm not sure I agree with you 네 말이 맞는지 모르겠어

I can't say (for sure) 잘 몰라, 확실히는 몰라

You got me 난 모르겠는데, 내가 졌어

You got me there 모르겠어, 네 말이 맞아

Beats me 잘 모르겠는데, 내가 어떻게 알아

Search me 난 몰라

Not that I know of 내가 알기로는 그렇지 않아

Not likely 그럴 것 같지 않은데

Don't ask me 나한테 묻지마

Your guess is as good as mine 모르긴 나도 매한가지야

I don't understand (it) 왜 그런지 모르겠어, 알 수가 없네

I don't see why 이유를 몰라

17 몰라 내가 어떻게 알아?

How should I know? 내가 어떻게 알아?

How can I tell? 내가 어떻게 알아?

What can I do? 내가 (달리) 어쩌겠어?

What more[else] can I do? 달리 방도가 있어?

What can I tell you? 뭐라고 얘기하면 되지?, 어쩌라구?

What can I say? 난 할 말이 없네, 나더러 어쩌라는 거야?, 뭐랄까?

What do you want me to say? 무슨 말을 하라는 거야? 나보고 어쩌라고?

(I) Can't help it 나도 어쩔 수 없어

It can't[couldn't] be helped 어쩔 수 없[었]어

I'm sorry, but I couldn't help it 미안하지만 어쩔 수가 없었어

You tell me 그거야 네가 알지

I wouldn't know 내가 알 도리가 없지, 그걸 내가 어떻게 알아

I have no other choice but to do so
그렇게 하는 거 외에는 달리 방법이 없어

I had no choice (in that matter) 그 문제에서 달리 방법이 없어

It was my only choice 나의 유일한 선택이었어

I don't have any idea 모르겠어

I do not have the slightest idea 나야 전혀 모르지

I don't have a clue 전혀 모르겠어

There was nothing else I could've done 달리 방법이 없어

Talking about Me & You

03

나와 너를 말하기

01 Talking about Me 대부분 지현이라고 불러

반가워. 민지현이라고 해. 대부분 지현이라고 부르지
Hi. I'm Ji-hyun Min. Most people just call me Ji-hyun

내 이름은 이민수이야. '이' 는 성이고 '민수' 는 이름이지
My name is Lee Min-soo. Lee is my family name, and Min-soo is my first name
- My family name, 'Gil,' is pretty rare in Korea
  성이 '길' 인데 한국에선 드문 성이야

이달 21일이 내 24번째 생일야
The 21st of this month is my twenty-fourth birthday
- I was born in Seoul in 1974 1974년 서울에서 태어났어
- I was born on August 10, 1983 1983년 8월 10일에 태어났어

다음 주 월요일이면 나 30살 돼
I'm going to be thirty next Monday
- I turned thirty-one last month 지난 달에 31살이 되었어

난 캐나다에서 왔는데 토론토에서 나고 자랐지
I'm from Canada, born and raised in Toronto.

난 식구들하고 옥수동에 살아. 그 동네에 관해서 들어봤을 거야, 그렇지?
I live with my family in Ok-su Dong. You've probably heard about that area, right?

난 고려대학교 근처의 종암동에 살아. 그 동네 알아?
I'm living over in Jong-am Dong, near Korea University. Do you know that neighborhood?

23살 때 고향을 떠나왔어
I left my hometown when I was twenty-three
- It's located about 30 kilometers from Daegu 대구에서 한 30킬로 미터 지점에 있어

자전거타고 역에 가
I go to the station by bike
- I ride my bike to the station 자전거타고 역까지 가
- My house is about 300 meters from the station 집은 역에서 300미터 떨어진 곳에 있어

아파트 건물 2층에 살아
I live on the second floor of an apartment building
- I live in an apartment 아파트에서 살아
- My house has five rooms 집에는 방이 5개야

월세로 50만원을 내고 있어
I pay 500,000 won a month for rent
- I'm going to rent a larger room 더 큰 방을 얻을려고 해
- How much is your rent? 월세가 얼마야?

거기서 5년 째 살고 있어
I have lived there for five years

02 Talking about Me 서른 살에 결혼했어

서른 살에 결혼했어
I got married at the age of thirty

- I got married when I was thirty-one 서른 한 살에 결혼했어
- We have been married for 10 years 우린 10년 전에 결혼했어
- I'm married 유부남(녀)야

오는 12월에 결혼할거야
I'm getting married next December
- I got to know my wife through one of my friends 아내 친구 통해서 알게 됐어

결혼기념일은 6월 15일이야
Our wedding anniversary is June 15th

- We went to Cheju Island for our honeymoon   제주도로 신혼여행갔었어
- We're going to have a baby in July   출산예정은 7월야

2년 전에 이혼했고 지금은 혼자야
I got divorced two years ago, so I'm single now
- That was my first, and her second marriage   난 초혼이고 아내는 재혼이었어

식구는 3명야
There are three in my family
- We are a family of five   식구가 다섯이야

애가 둘이야
I have two children
- I have a son and two daughters   아들 하나고 딸이 둘야
- I have a son in middle school   중학교 다니는 아들 하나야
- I don't have any children   애가 없어
- My son is a high school student   아들은 고등학생야

남자형제가 셋 있고, 누이가 둘 이야
I have three brothers and two sisters
- I have two brothers   형이 둘이야
- I'm an only child   외아들(외동녀)야
- I have no brothers or sisters   형제가 없어

난 5형제 중 둘째야
I'm the second of five brothers and sisters
- I'm the oldest   장남(녀)야
- I'm the youngest of three sisters   3자매 중에서 막내야

아들이 공부를 안할려고 해서 걱정야
I'm worried about my son because he doesn't like to study
- He doesn't like to study   공부하는 걸 싫어해
- My son won't listen to us at all   아들놈이 우리말을 전혀 듣지 않으려고 해

부모님은 다 건강하셔
My parents are in good health
- My father retired last year   아버지는 작년에 퇴직하셨어
- My parents live on their pensions   부모님은 연금으로 사셔

우린 맞벌이 부부예요
We're a working couple

· My wife is a housewife 와이프는 전업주부야

애완동물을 안 키워
I don't have any pets

· I have a dog 강아지를 키워
· It's a female named Mimi 숫놈이고 이름은 미미야

03 Talking about Me 내 혈액형은 B형야

내 혈액형은 B형이야
I have type B blood

키는 175센티야
I'm 175 centimeters tall

· I'm about 5 feet 5 inches tall 키는 한 5피트 5인치야
· I weigh 74 kilograms now 지금 74킬로 나가
· I'd like to gain some weight 살이 쪘으면 해

노안이 돼서 조그만 글자를 읽기가 힘들어
My eyes are getting weak, so it's hard to for me to read small letters

· I'm afraid I'm becoming forgetful 점점 깜박하는 게 걱정돼
· I'm losing my hair these days 요즘 머리가 빠져

푸시업을 30개 할 수 있어
I can do 30 push-ups

· I can run 100 meters in 14 seconds 100 미터를 14초에 뛸 수 있어
· I walk up and down the stairs instead of taking elevators
  엘리베이터 대신 계단으로 오르내리고 있어

요즘 충분한 운동을 못하고 있어
I haven't been getting enough exercise recently

건강을 유지하기 위해 일찍 일어나고 있어
I get up early to keep me in good health

· Getting up early is the secret of my good health 일찍 일어나는게 내 건강비결야

나의 성격 그리고 신조 등을 말할 때

04 Talking about Me 난 사교적이야

난 사교적이야
I'm sociable

· I'm optimistic 난 낙천적이야
· I'm pessimistic 난 부정적이야

내 강점중의 하나는 신중하다는 거야
One of my strong points is that I'm cautious

· I really like jokes very much 정말 조크를 아주 좋아해

난 너무 수동적이야
I'm too passive

· Being passive is one of my weak point
  수동적인 게 내 약점중 하나야
· I've become quite conservative lately
  최근 내가 아주 보수적으로 되었어

난 쉽게 화를 내는 경향이 있어
I'm afraid I tend to lose my temper easily

내가 좋아하는 속담으로는 "현재를 즐겨라!"야
My favorite saying is "Seize the day!"

"불굴의 의지로 끝까지 최선을 다하자"라는 슬로건으로 좋아해
I like the slogan, "Just do it."

· "Get real" is my motto "현실을 직시하라"가 내 모토야
· It's important to be punctual 시간을 지키는 게 중요해

05 Talking about Me 1992년에 대학 졸업했어

1992년에 대학교를 졸업했어
I graduated from college in 1992

. . . .

1998년에 고려대학교에 진학했어
I started Korea University in 1998

· I'm a Yonsei graduate 연세대학교 졸업했어

. . . .

경영학을 전공했어
I majored in business administration

· My major was English literature 내 전공은 영문학이야
· My graduation thesis was about "the Big Bang" 졸업논문은 "빅뱅"이야
· I'm majoring in economics 경제학을 전공하고 있어

. . . .

난 조선대학교에 다니고 3학년이야
I'm a third-year student at Chosun University

. . . .

서울대학교에서 법학을 공부하고 있어
I'm studying law at Seoul National University

. . . .

언젠가 형사 사건 전문 변호사가 되고 싶어
I hope to be a criminal defense lawyer someday

. . . .

난 서강대학교에서 생물학을 공부하고 있는데, 환경과학에 굉장히 흥미가 있어
I'm studying biology at Sogang University. I'm really interested in environmental science

. . . .

매주 월요일과 수요일에 영어회화 수업을 듣고 있는데, 강사가 굉장히 잘 가르쳐서 학생들을 항상 웃게 만들지
I'm taking an English conversation class on Mondays and Wednesdays. My teacher is really great and always makes us laugh

약사증을 따고 싶어
I want to get a pharmacist's license
· I want to qualify as a lawyer 변호사 자격을 따고 싶어

금년도에 졸업하기를 바래
I'm hoping to graduate this year

공부를 해서 석사학위를 받으려고 해
I'm planning to study for a master's degree

졸업해서 직장 구하기를 바라고 있어
I'm looking forward to graduating and getting a job

이번주 우리 대학은 중간고사 기간야
Our university is having mid-term exams this week

고려대학교는 법대쪽이 유명해
Korea University is well known for its law program

전공을 바꿔서 다른 흥미로운 전공을 택했으면 해
I wish I could change my major to a more interesting subject

나의 직장 및 내가 하는 일에 대해 말할 때

06 **Talking about Me** 사무직일 해요

사무직일 해
I'm an office worker
· I'm a cashier 출납하는 일 해
· I'm secretary to the president 사장비서야

파트타임으로 일 해
I'm a part-timer
· I'm a freelance writer 프리랜서 작가야
· I work freelance as a designer 프리랜서로 디자이너일을 해

공무원이야
I'm a government employee

- I work for a trading company 무역회사다녀
- The company I work for is a travel agency 내가 다니는 회사는 여행사야

내 직책은 영업차장야
My title is assistant sales manager

우린 여성화장품을 수입해서 판매해
We import and sell cosmetics for women

- We make computer parts 컴퓨터 부품을 제조해

우리 사무실은 중앙빌딩 3층에 있어
Our office is on the third floor of the Jungang Building

- Do you see the Lotteria? Our office is behind it 롯데리아 보여? 사무실은 그 뒤에 있어
- Our office is in a white five-story building 우리 사무실은 하얀 5층 건물에 있어
- There're parking space next to our office building 회사건물 옆에 주차장이 있어

사무실가는 데 한 50분 걸려
It takes about 50 minutes to get to the office

- I drive to work 차로 출근해

사당역에서 2호선으로 갈아타
I change to the green line at Sadang Station

- Every commuter train is overcrowded during rush hour 러시아워에 모든 전철은 다 만원야
- I usually enjoy reading books on the train 전철에서 보통 책을 읽어
- I always have to stand on the train 난 항상 전철에서 서 있어
- A monthly commuter pass costs me 10,000won 전철 월정액권은 만원야

수입회사를 운영해
I have my own importing company

- I'm self-employed 사업해
- I have about 20 people working for me 종업원이 한 20여 명야
- I run a boutique 미용실을 하고 있어

지금 실직상태야
I'm out of work now
- I don't have a job now 현재 직업이 없어
- I'm not working right now 현재 놀고 있어

전직하고 있는 중야
I'm changing jobs
- I'm job hunting now 현재 직장을 알아보고 있어
- I'm retiring next year 내년에 퇴직해

여기 내 명함야
Let me give you my card

07 **Talking about Me** 근무시간은 5~7시까지야

근무시간은 5시부터 7시까지야
Our working hours are from five to seven

주 5일제 근무하고 있어
We're on a five-day week
- Our company is on five-day week 우리 회사는 주 5일 근무야

토요일마다 쉬어.
We're off on Saturdays.
- We're off on every other Saturday 격주 토요일은 쉬어

거의 매일 야근야
I work overtime almost every day

휴일에도 난 고객들과 골프를 쳐야 돼
Even on holidays, I sometimes go play golf with clients

일년에 수차례 해외출장을 가
I go abroad on business several times a year

이번 달에 일정이 아주 바빠
I have a heavy schedule this month
- We're busy as bees during the fiscal term 결산기간동안엔 엄청 바빠

급여로 세금떼고 월 3백만원 정도 받아
I'm paid about 3,000,000won a month, after taxes
- My work is paid by the hour 시급으로 일해
- I'm paid on an hourly basis 시급으로 돈을 받아
- I get 3,000 won an hour 시급 3천원받아

능력급으로 받고 있어
We're paid according to ability

7월과 12월에 보너스를 받아
We receive a bonus in July and December

보통 패스트푸드 식당에서 점심을 먹어
I usually have lunch at a fastfood restaurant
- I like to have noodles for lunch 점심으로 국수먹는 걸 좋아해
- I bring my own lunch every day 매일 점심을 가져와

우린 12시부터 1시까지 점심식사 시간야
We have an hour's lunch break, from twelve to one

퇴근 후 종종 동료들과 술한잔 하러 가
I often go for a drink with my co-workers after work

08 Talking about Me 여행하는 걸 좋아해

여행을 무척 좋아해
I like traveling very much
- Traveling is one of my favorite hobbies 여행은 내가 가장 좋아하는 취미생활야

뉴욕에 한번 간 적 있어
I've been to New York once
- I took a trip to Canada in 1999 1999년에 캐나다에 여행갔었어
- Chicago is a really nice place to visit 시카고는 정말 가보기 좋은 곳이야
- I've never been abroad 해외에 나가 본 적이 없어

한달에 다섯번 요리강의를 들어
I go to cooking class five times a month
- I enjoy baking cakes during my holidays 휴일마다 케익 굽는 걸 좋아해

일년에 4권 이상의 책을 읽어
I read more than 4 books a year
- I usually read a book each month, depending on how busy I am
  얼마나 바쁘냐에 따라 다르지만, 나는 대체로 매달 한 권 정도의 책을 읽어

위성 TV 그리고 케이블 TV 보는 걸 좋아해
I enjoy satellite TV and cable TV, too
- I like watching good movies on TV TV에서 좋은 영화 보는 걸 좋아해

음악을 무척 좋아해
I'm a fan of music

한달에 4, 5섯 번은 영화관에 가
I go to the movies four or five times a month

- My favorite actress is Angelina Jolie 내가 제일 좋아하는 여배우는 안젤리나 졸리야
- I was deeply moved by "Alexander" 알렉산더 를 보고 감동받았어

기타를 쳐
I play the guitar
- I can play the clarinet a little 클라리넷을 조금 불 수 있어

가끔 락 콘서트를 보러 가
I sometimes go to rock concerts
- Queen's "We Are the Champion" is a song I enjoy singing
  퀸의 챔피언은 내가 즐겨 부르는 노래야

· I'm not good at singing   노래를 잘 못 불러

쉬는 날에는 박물관에 가는 걸 좋아해
I like to go to museums on my days off

그림을 그리진 않지만 그림감상을 무척 좋아해
I don't draw pictures, but I like to look at artwork very much

고전음악 감상을 좋아해
I like listening to classical music
· I often buy folk music CDs these days   요즘 종종 포크음악시디를 사
· I listen to CDs whenever I have free time   시간날 때마다 CD를 들어

나의 운동생활에 대해 말할 때

09 Talking about Me 난 야구를 좋아해

난 야구를 좋아해
My favorite sport is baseball

축구를 무척 좋아해
I'm a huge soccer fan
· I support FC Seoul   FC 서울을 응원해

실외운동보다는 실내운동을 좋아해
I prefer indoor sports to outdoor sports

스포츠를 보는 것도 좋아하고 하는 것도 좋아해
I like both watching and playing sports

TV로 K-1 경기 보는 걸 좋아해
I like to watch K-1 on TV

건강을 위해 매일 조깅해
I jog every day for my health
· I started jogging   조깅을 시작했어
· I jog every morning   매일 아침 조깅해

일주일에 두 번 헬스클럽에 가
I go to the sports[fitness] club twice a week

다음 달에 에어로빅을 시작할거야
I'm going to start doing aerobics next month
- I belong to a tennis club 테니스 클럽에 들었어

퇴근 후에 보통 운동을 해
I usually work out after work
- I usually go to the gym after work 보통 퇴근 후에 체육관에 가

골프를 친 지가 1년 밖에 안됐어
It's only been a year since I started playing golf
- My golf handicap is 20 핸디캡이 20야
- My score was 3-under-par 69 3언더파로 69타야
- I took up golf two months ago 골프를 두달 전에 시작했어

골프를 잘 쳐
I'm good at playing golf
- I finished the round at 2 under par 2언더파로 라운드를 마쳤어
- I'm into golf 골프를 쳐

매 겨울마다 스키를 타
I enjoy skiing every winter
- I can't wait to go skiing 스키타고 싶어 죽겠어

수영강습을 들어
I'm taking swimming lessons
- I'd like to go rafting 래프팅하는 걸 좋아해

요즘 충분한 운동을 못하고 있어
I haven't been getting enough exercise lately
- You need exercise 넌 운동 좀 해야 돼

10 Talking about Korea 음력 새해를 설날이라고 해

한국에서는 음력 새해를 「설날」이라고 하죠
In Korean, the word for the Lunar New Year is Sul-nal

한국에는 새해가 두번 있어요. 하나는 양력 1월 1일, 또 하나는 음력 1월 1일입니다
There are two New Year's days in Korea. One is January 1st on the solar calendar, and the other is on the lunar calendar

「설날」은 한국에서 가장 큰 전통 명절입니다
Of the many traditional holidays in Korea, Sul-nal is one of the biggest

설날에 한국 사람들은 고향집을 찾아가기 때문에 전국의 교통이 상당히 혼잡합니다
Koreans travel home during Sul-nal, which causes heavy traffic throughout Korea

설날에는 집안 어른들이 자녀나 손주들에게 새해를 기념하는 특별한 절을 받는데, 이를 「세배」라고 해요
On Sul-nal, parents and grandparents expect their offspring to perform a special New Year's bow, called sae-bae in Korean

한국 사람들은 설날에 쫀득쫀득한 쌀떡으로 만든 「떡국」을 먹습니다
On New Year's day, Koreans eat tok-guk, a soup made with slices of rice paste

설날에는 장남의 집에 온 가족이 모입니다
The eldest son hosts a party on New Year's

한복은 예를 들어 설날이나 추석 같은 명절과 전통의식용으로 입어
The hanbok is worn for traditional ceremonies and festivals, like Sulnal or Chusok, for example

11 | Talking about Korea 미래를 보려고 점을 봐

새해가 시작되면 점을 보는 한국 사람들이 많습니다
At the start of the year, many Koreans visit a fortune-teller

한국에서는 자신들의 미래를 알아보려고 점장이에게 찾아가는 사람들이 많아
A lot of people in Korea visit fortunetellers to have their future predicted

한국 사람들은 옛부터 중대사를 앞두고 점을 봤습니다
Koreans have traditionally sought divination before important events

무료로, 혹은 요금을 받고 운세를 알려주는 인터넷 사이트도 많아졌습니다
It has become common for Internet sites to offer both predictions for a free and predictions which are free of charge to Internet users

점술을 연구하는 사람들을 고용하여 손님들의 점을 봐주는 사주까페도 많아요
There are a lot of coffee shops specializing in telling fortune. They hire students who are studying fortune telling for customers to consult

한국사람들 사이에는 시험과 관련해서 미신이 많아요
Koreans have a lot of superstitions associated with the exams

시험이 다가오면, 수험생들은 보통, 행운을 기원하는 여러 종류의 선물을 받지요
As an examination draws near, students who are preparing for it are usually given presents for good luck

한국말로 찐득찐득하게 「붙는다」는 말과 시험에 「붙는다」는 말이 똑같이 「붙다」거든요.
그래서 찐득찐득한 엿을 선물하는 거랍니다. 엿은 한국 고유의 사탕이에요
The word for both "stick" and "pass" in Korean is but-da,

which is why sticky Yot candy is given. Yot is a traditional Korean taffy

12 Talking about Korea 서울교통은 너무 막혀

서울의 교통상황이 이렇게 나쁜 줄 미처 몰랐어요
I had no idea that traffic was this bad in Seoul

차들이 몰리는 출퇴근 시간은 교통정체 때문에 정말 골칫거리야
Rush hour is a real headache with these traffic jams

고급차를 선호하는 사람들이 많아서 고급차들이 불티나게 팔립니다
Many people prefer luxurious cars, and they are selling like hot cakes

한국의 교통사고 사망률은 다른 나라들과 비교해서 아주 높은 편입니다
The death rate from traffic accidents in Korea is very high compared to other nations

주차공간이 부족해서, 주차하는 게 마치 전쟁을 치르는 것 같아요
Parking is a nightmare, as there are not enough spaces for cars

도로에서 다른 차에 길을 내주게 되면 손해본다고 생각하는 운전자들이 많아요
Many drivers feel like they are being victimized when they give other drivers a break

이 푸른색 차선은 정해진 시간동안에는 버스만이 이용할 수 있습니다
Blue lanes are for buses only during specific hours
· Only buses are permitted to use the blue lanes during specific hours.
일정시간동안 버스만이 푸른색 차선을 통행할 수 있어

목적지까지 더 편하고 느긋하게 갈 수 있기 때문에 저는 자주 지하철을 탑니다
I often take the subway because I find that I arrive at my destination feeling more relaxed

휴가에 대하여 말할 때

13 Talking about Korea 대부분 7, 8월에 휴가 가

6월과 7월에 적어도 연 강수량의 반이 내려요
We get at least half of our annual rainfall in June and July
- More than half of our rainfall comes in June and July
  강수량의 반이상이 6,7월에 내려요
- We receive more than fifty percent of the year's rainfall in June and July
  연강수량의 50%이상이 6월과 7월에 내려요

8월은 여름 중에서도 날씨가 가장 좋은 달이죠
August is the nicest of the summer months
- Of all the summer months, August is the nicest   여름중에서 8월이 가장 좋아요

대부분 7월에서 8월 사이에 휴가를 갖지요
Most Koreans take their vacations between the months of July and August

한국사람들은 여름에 보통 일주일 정도 휴가를 갖습니다
Koreans usually have around a week off in the summer

보통 가족이나 친구들과 함께 휴가를 보내요
Koreans usually spend their vacations with family and friends

여름휴가 때는 휴가여행을 계획하는 사람들이 아주 많은데, 해외로 나가려고 하는 사람들이 점점 많아지고 있습니다

A large number of people plan getaway trips for their summer holidays, and more and more Koreans want to use this time to go abroad

꽉 막힌 도로와 혼잡한 휴양지를 피하려고 성수기 전후로 휴가를 계획하는 사람들도 있습니다
In order to avoid sitting in traffic and experiencing crowded resorts, some people plan their vacations after the peak season

결혼문화를 말할 때

14 Talking about Korea 여자들이 결혼을 늦게 해

한국의 젊은 세대들, 특히 여자들은 부모세대들보다 결혼하는 시기가 더 늦습니다
A lot of the younger generation in Korea, especially women, are waiting longer than their parents to get married

과거에는 여자들이 서른 살이 넘으면 결혼하기에는 늦은 나이라고 여겼지만, 요즘에는 서른 살이 되야 비로소 결혼하는 여자들이 많습니다
It used to be that a woman over thirty was considered too old to marry. But these days, many women don't marry until they're thirty years old

백년가약을 맺기 전에 동거를 해봐야 한다고 생각하는 젊은이들도 꽤 있어.
There are a lot of young people that think couples should definitely live together before they tie the knot
· Our parents just can't get why our generation thinks unmarried couples should live together 부모님 세대는 왜 우리 세대가 동거를 해야하는지 이해 못해서

혼전동거는 연인들이 서로 잘 맞는지 알 수 있는 좋은 방법인 것 같아
I think living together before marriage is a great way for couples to know for sure if they are compatible

난 종교적인 이유로, 결혼 전에 동거하는 건 정말 옳지 않다고 생각해
I really think it is wrong to live together before marriage because of my religious beliefs

동거하는 게 옳지 않은 일이라고는 생각하지 않지만, 나의 경우라면, 그렇게 안할거야
I don't think it's wrong to live together, but personally, I wouldn't do it

과거와는 달리 직업을 갖고 있는 한국 여성들이 많으며, 이들은 결혼을 미루는 경향이 있습니다
Many Korean women have a job, unlike in the past, and they tend to put marriage on a back burner

결혼을 한다해도, 일하는 여자들은 아이 갖는 일을 미루려는 경향이 있습니다
Once they're married, working women tend to put off starting a family

또한 젊은이들 중에는 아예 결혼은 반드시 해야 하는 것은 아니라고 생각하는 이도 많죠
Many young Koreans think marriage isn't necessary in the first place

심지어는 결혼을 완전히 포기하고 독신 생활을 즐기기로 결심한 여자들도 있습니다
Some Korean women have even decided not to get married at all, and to simply enjoy being single for life

한국의 이혼율이 최근 상승하고 있습니다
Korea's divorce rate has grown in recent years

통계에 의하면 이혼의 가장 큰 이유는 배우자의 부정(不貞)이었다고 합니다
According to the statistics, the number one reason for divorce was unfaithfulness

요즘에는 아내측의 부정이 이혼 사유로 꼽히고 있는데, 반면 과거에는 남편측에서 대부분 부정을 저질렀죠
Nowadays, adultery on the part of wives has become a major reason for divorce, while in the past, it was done by husbands

심지어는 사오십년 동안 결혼 생활을 해온 나이든 부부들도 이혼을 하고 있습니다
Even older couples are divorcing after 40 or 50 years of marriage

15 Talking about Korea 미국의 추수감사절과 비슷해

추석은 음력 8월 15일인데, 일년 중 가장 풍요로운 때야
Chu-sok is celebrated on August 15th of the lunar calendar, around the time of the year's harvest

미국의 추수감사절과 흡사해요
Chu-sok is somewhat similar to the American Thanksgiving

다른 점 중의 하나는 조상에게 경의를 표한다는 점인데 이걸 「차례」라고 하지요
Chusok and Thanksgiving are a little different because during Chusok, we honor our ancestors

추석은 가족과 친구들을 만나러가는 시기로, 이 때의 교통상황은 정말 악몽같죠
Chu-sok is a time to visit families and friends. Traffic at this time of year is an absolute nightmare

서울에 사는 사람들은 대개 서울을 떠나 부모를 찾아뵙지만 요즘엔 아들딸을 보러 서울로 올라오는 부모들도 많습니다
Usually people in Seoul go to visit their parents, but many parents now make a trip to Seoul to see their sons or daughters

추석에는 조상의 묘소에 가 차례를 드리고 묘지를 보살피죠. 이것을 「성묘」라 해요
On Chu-sok, people visit their ancestors' graves to attend a worship service and to care for the grave. This is called Sung-myo

추석에 한국 사람들은 「송편」을 먹는데, 「송편」은 솔잎 위에 얹어서 찐 쌀떡입니다
On Chu-sok, Koreans eat Song-pyun, a cake made of rice and cooked on top of pine needles

16 Talking about Korea 건강에 관심이 많아

최근에 한국 사람들은 자신의 몸매와 건강에 관심을 아주 많이 갖게 되었어요
It has become really popular lately for Koreans to pay a lot of attention to their bodies and their health

요즘 한국에서는 남자든 여자든 건강미가 풍기는 몸매를 원해요
What both men and women want is a healthy, good looking body

다이어트를 하는 여자들이 많은데, 다른 계절에 비해 노출이 심해지는 여름에 특히 많아요
A lot of women go on diets, especially in the summer, when their bodies are more exposed than in other seasons

빨리 날씬해지려고 지방흡입 수술을 받는 사람들도 있어요
Some people have liposuction, in order to become slender quickly

한국 사람들 중에는 담배를 피우는 사람들이 많습니다. 성인 남성 중에는 담배를 피우는 사람이 절반을 넘고, 여성과 청소년 흡연자의 숫자도 점점 늘고 있어요
Many people smoke in Korea. Over half of male adults smoke, and the number of female and teenage smokers is increasing

보약은 일종의 전통적인 한국 강장제(强壯劑)라고 할 수 있지요
Boyak is a kind of traditional Korean medicine for improving health

인삼이 노화를 방지하고 질병치료와 면역체계에 도움이 돼요
Ginseng is said to slow aging, cure illnesses and boost immune systems

17 Talking about Korea 인터넷이 너무 편리해

대금을 지불하거나 편지를 쓰고 정보를 찾아내는 것이라면 인터넷이 정말 너무 편리해요
The Internet is so convenient when it comes to paying bills, writing letters, and finding information

좋아하는 사이트에 가서 농담거리와 음악, 게임 같은 재밌는 것들을 다운받아요
I go to my favorite sites and download lots of neat things, like jokes, music, and games

내 컴퓨터는 더 이상 문서 작성용만으로 쓰는 것이 아니라 이제는 오락센터예요
My computer is no longer just used for word processing. It is also an entertainment center

인터넷을 많이 사용하면서 생기는 문제들 중의 하나는 가끔씩 시간을 잊어버린다는 건데, 시간이 얼마나 지났는지도 모르고 접속한 채 시간을 보내죠
One of the problems with using the Internet so much is that I often lose track of time and I spend hours on-line without noticing how much time has passed

인터넷에는 포르노 사이트, 도박 사이트, 자살 사이트 등, 문제있는 사이트들이 굉장히 많아요
There are many controversial sites on the Net, such as porn sites, gambling sites, suicide sites, etc.

이런 유해한 사이트들은 심지어 아이들도 아주 쉽게 접속할 수 있는데, 특히 스팸메일이나 블로그를 통해 쉽게 접할 수 있어요
It's easy for young children to access these sites, usually through spam emails or blogs

한국인들은 인터넷을 잘 활용하고 있다고 스스로 자랑스럽게 생각하고 있어요
We are proud of ourselves as Koreans for using the Net well

18 Talking about Korea 핸드폰이 잘 보급되어 있어

한국의 핸드폰 산업은 고도로 발달했어요
The cellphone industry in Korea has reached a high level of sophistication

한국은 핸드폰이 다른 어느 나라보다도 더 많이 보편화되어 있습니다. 한국 사람들 대부분이 핸드폰을 갖고 있지요
Cellphones are more popular in Korea than any other country. Most Koreans own a cellphone

핸드폰이 통화기능 뿐만 아니라, 여러가지 다른 일도 하는데 사용돼요
Cellphones are used for making phone calls and many other tasks

핸드폰으로 문자 메시지를 주고받는 것은 보편화되어 있어요
It's popular for people to exchange text messages with their cellphones

인터넷 기능을 갖춘 핸드폰으로는 인터넷 검색도 할 수 있고, 게임을 즐길 수도 있으며 심지어 인터넷 채팅방에 접속하는 것도 가능해요
Cellphones with an Internet option allow us to surf the Net, play games, and even enter chat rooms

핸드폰은 성능이 향상되어 은행업무를 볼 수 있는 기능도 추가되었어요
Cellphones have been upgraded to include the option of banking

핸드폰을 무절제하게 사용하여 어마어마한 액수의 고지서를 받아들게 되는 사람들도 있습니다. 특히 미성년자들 중에 많죠
Some people - especially minors - use cell phones recklessly, and end up with high bills

19 Talking about Korea 인사동은 전통의 거리

인사동은 한국 문화의 거리로 한국의 전통 골동품을 살 수 있는 곳이예요
Insa-dong is a street where visitors can see Korean culture and buy traditional Korean antiques

---

만약 고국에 있는 가족이나 친구에게 줄 특별한 선물을 찾고 있다면 이곳이 가장 적당한 장소일 거예요
If you are looking for a special gift for someone back home, Insa-dong would be the best place to get it

---

판문점은 서울에서 자동차로 한 시간 반 거린데, 군사분계선에 걸쳐 있어요. 판문점을 방문하는 사람은 왜 이곳이 평화를 유지해야 하는 것이 얼마나 중요한 지를 실감하게 될 거예요
Panmunjom is about an hour and a half outside of Seoul by car, straddling the Military Demarcation Line. Visitors can see why it is important that the area should remain peaceful

---

제주도는 우리나라에서 가장 큰 섬으로 여자, 돌, 바람이 많아 「삼다도」로 알려져 있어요.
Cheju Island is the largest of Korea's islands, and it is known as the island of three "many's": many women, many rocks, and much wind.

이건 돌하르방[石祖]이예요. 이 지역의 구멍이 숭숭 뚫려 있는 화산암을 크고 작은 형태로 조각한 것이죠
The dolharubang(stone grandfather) is sculptured in large and small sizes from the porous lava stone of the area

---

민속촌은 수세기 전 생활양식을 재현해 놓은 한국의 민속 마을이예요
Minsokch'on is a Korean folk village that recreates the lifestyles of several centuries ago

---

민속촌에는 공예품 제작을 통해 전통문화를 보존하고 있는 장인(匠人)들이 있어요

In the Minsokch'on, there are artisans and craftsmen who preserve the traditional culture through their artwork

남대문 시장은 값싼 물건들과 사람들로 가득한 상가들이 아주 많이 있어요
The Namdaemun Market has tons of stores. There are great bargains and lots of people there

동대문 시장은 요즘에 남대문 시장보다 더 인기가 많아지고 있는 또 다른 시장이죠
The Tongdaemun Market is another market that's becoming more popular than the Namdaemun Market these days.

우리나라 동해안에 설악산이라는 곳이 있어요
There is a mountain on the east coast of Korea called Mt. Sorak

설악산은 높이 솟은 화강암 봉우리들과 수풀이 우거진 푸른 계곡들, 울창한 숲과 폭포, 개울이 있는 멋진 곳이지요
Mt. Sorak is a lovely area, with granite peaks, lush green valleys, dense forests, waterfalls and streams

사물은 네 개의 전통적인 타악기인 꽹과리와 징, 장구와 북을 가리켜요
Samul refers to 4 traditional percussion instruments: the small and large gong, the hourglass drum, and the barrel drum

사물놀이는 농악과 무속 음악의 민속 가락에 뿌리를 두고 있어요
Samul-nori has its roots in both the folk rhythms of farmers' music and Shamanistic music

탈을 쓰고 하는 무용극인데, 거드름을 피우는 양반들과 승려들을 비웃는 사회 풍자극이예요
A talchum is a mask dance-drama which began as a social satire that made fun of snobby aristocrats and monks

씨름은 전에는 명절때마다 경기를 열면서 인기가 많았어. 하지만 지금은 인기를 많이 잃었지
Ssireum used to be more popular. This sport was used to open games on festival days. But it has lost a lot of popularity

20 Talking about Korea 한국음식 먹어봤어요?

지금까지 한국식당에서 식사할 기회가 많았나요?

Have you had much of a chance to eat out at Korean restaurants?

· Have you had an opportunity to eat at a Korean restaurant?

한국식당에서 식사해보신 적 있어요?

김치는 한국 전통음식인데, 대개 반찬으로 내놔요. 김치는 소금물에 절인 채소같은 건데, 배추와 무, 파와 마늘을 한데 버무린 거구요

Kimchi is a traditional Korean food. We usually serve it as a side dish. It is made from a variety of pickled vegetables; cabbages, turnips, green onions and garlic, all mixed together

불고기는 여러시간 동안 양념에 재워 두기 때문에 고기가 굉장히 연해. 마늘과 간장, 설탕, 참기름, 후춧가루와 양파, 생강, 술로 만든 양념예요

Bulgogi is incredibly tender because it has been marinating in a sauce for hours. The marinade is made from garlic, soy sauce, sugar, sesame seed oil, black pepper, onions, ginger and wine

떡은 일종의 쌀로 만든 케이크로 보통 설날이나 추석, 결혼식날 같은 특별한 경우에 먹어요

T'tok is a kind of rice cake, and Koreans generally eat t'tok on special occasions, such as New Year's Day, the Harvest Moon Festival, and on wedding days

비빔밥은 한국에서 대중적인 음식으로 여러 야채들과 밥 그리고 매운 고추장을 비벼서 만들어요

Bibimbop is a popular Korean dish that is made from a mix of vegetables, rice, and spicy pepper sauce

설렁탕은 조선시대부터 유래한 음식으로 주 성분은 소의 내장, 그리고 소의 뼈 등이예요

Sulrungtang is a dish that originated in the Chosun period

and its ingredients consist of tripe, and certain beef bones

김치찌게는 우리나라에서 유명한 찌게로 김치와 여러 야채들 그리고 밥반찬들을 섞어서
만들어요
Kimchi chigae is a well known stew that blends kimchi,
certain vegetables and a side dish of rice

삼겹살은 고기이고 사람들이 바로 앞에서 그릴로 구워서 상추에 싸서 먹는 음식이예요
Samguypsal is composed of meat that is cooked on a grill in
front of diners before being wrapped in lettuce and consumed

김밥은 단순하고 원형모양의 음식으로 밖은 김이 싸고 있고 안쪽에는 밥 그리고 가운데
에는 야채, 계란, 그리고 고기나 생선을 넣어 만들어요
Kimbop is a simple, round shaped snack that consists of an
outer layer of seaweed, an inner layer of rice, and a center of
various ingredients including vegetables, eggs, and possibly
meat or fish

라면은 요리하기 쉬운 음식으로 세계적으로 알려졌으며 독특하고 매운 한국적인 맛으로
도 먹을 수 있어요
Ramyen noodles are known worldwide for being easy to
prepare, and are available here with a distinctive, spicy
Korean flavor

자장면은 중국에서 유래된 국수요리로 한국에선 특히 점심식사때 많이들 먹어요
Jajangmyun is a noodle dish which originated in China and
which is very popular in Korea, especially when eaten during
lunch

21 **Talking about You** 너 참 인상이 좋아

너 인상이 참 좋다
You're fairly good-looking
· He looks like Ashton Kutcher 걔는 애쉬튼 커처처럼 생겼어

넌 나보다 어려보여
You look younger than me
· He looks old for his age 걔는 나이에 비해 늙어보여
· He looks older than he is 걔는 실제보다 나이가 들어보여
· You look young for your age 너는 나이에 비해 어려보여

걔는 취향이 고상해
He has a taste for luxury
· She's a smart dresser 걔는 옷을 아주 잘 입어

걔는 좀 섹시해
He's sort of sexy
· He's very popular with the girls 걔는 여자들한테 인기가 좋아
· She's wearing a lot of makeup 걔는 화장을 떡칠해

너 배 나왔어
You have a pot belly
· He's bald 걔는 대머리야

걔는 매우 날카로워
She's very sharp
· He's a wise guy 걔는 현명한 친구야
· He's wise for his age 걔는 나이에 비해 현명해

걔는 진짜 완벽주의야
He's a perfectionist
· He has good judgement 걔는 분별력이 좋아

너는 아주 대담해
You have a lot of nerve

- He's got a lot of nerve 걔는 아주 대담해
- You're very brave 넌 매우 용감해
- You're bold 너는 대담해

쟤는 정말 말을 잘해
She's a smooth talker

- He's flexible in his thinking 걔는 생각이 유연해

걔는 어울리기 쉬운 친구야
He's easy to get along with

- He's very friendly 걔는 매우 우호적이야
- She's a good mixer 걔는 매우 잘 어울려

성격이 좋은 사람야
He's an easy-going person

- He knows a lot of people 걔는 사람들을 많이 알아
- He's the outgoing type 걔는 외향적이야

걔는 마음이 따뜻한 친구야
He's a warm-hearted guy

- You're so generous 너는 정말 맘씨 좋아
- She's always willing to help out 걔는 항상 도와줄려고 해
- He just can't turn down a request 걔는 단지 거절을 못하는 거야

걔는 정말 수완가야
He's a real go-getter

걔는 약속을 일단하면 절대로 말을 바꾸지 않아
Once he makes a promise, he never goes back on his word

- He's not the type to break his word
  약속을 깨는 타입을 아니야

걔는 매너가 좀 거칠지만 실은 괜찮은 녀석이야
He has a rough manner, but deep down, he's a nice guy

- He is good humored 걔는 유머감각이 좋아
- He's very modest man 걔는 점잖은 사람야

22 **Talking about You** 걔는 내성적이야

걔는 매우 내성적이야
He's so reserved
- He's shy 걔는 수줍어 해
- You're too timid 너는 너무 소극적이야

걔는 쉽게 화를 내
He gets angry easily
- He loses his temper quickly 걔는 쉽사리 성질을 부려
- He has a bad temper 성질이 못됐어
- He has a short temper 성질이 안좋아

걔는 매우 민감해
She's so sensitive
- She shows her feelings easily 걔는 쉽게 자기 감정을 노출해

걔한텐 뭔가 이상한 게 있어
There's something strange about her
- She's not herself today 걔는 오늘 제정신이 아니야
- She's not acting like herself 걔는 자기 답지 않게 행동을 하고 있어
- He's weird 걔는 이상해

걔는 냉소적이야
He's sarcastic
- He's very outspoken 걔는 말을 거침없이 해
- He's talkative 걔는 수다장이야

걔는 종종 말도 안되는 이야기를 해
He often says absurd things
- He often says ridiculous things 걔는 종종 우스운 이야기를 해
- He lacks common sense 걔는 상식이 부족해

걔는 책임감이 없어
He has no sense of responsibility

개는 자기가 모두 다 아는 것처럼 행동해
He acts like he knows it all
- He's acting like a hot shot 개는 자기가 대단한 사람인양 행동해
- He's acting big 개는 거물처럼 행동해

개는 거래하기 힘든 사람야
He's hard to deal with
- He's a difficult man to deal with 개는 거래하기 어려운 사람야

그 사람은 자신이 틀렸다는 걸 절대로 인정 안 해
He never admits he is wrong
- That man never admits defeat 저 남자는 패배를 절대로 인정하지 않아
- He can't handle defeat 개는 패배했을 때 어떻게 할 줄 몰라

개는 이기적이야
He's selfish
- He's self-centered 개는 자기 중심적이야
- He only cares about himself 개는 오직 자기만 생각해
- He's stingy 개는 인색해

개는 항상 양다리를 걸쳐
He always sits on the fence
- He's very vague 개는 분명하지가 않아

개는 매우 공격적이야
He's very offensive

너는 정말 문제다
You're really causing a problem
- He's a brown noser 개는 아첨꾼이야

다른 사람의 능력을 말할 때

23   **Talking about You** 걘 실망시키지 않을거야

개는 널 절대로 실망시키지 않을 거야
He'll never let you down

- He gets things done efficiently 개는 효율적으로 일을 처리해
- He's efficient 개는 실력있어
- He handles things quickly 개는 일을 빨리 처리해

개는 센스가 빨라
He has a quick mind
- He catches on quickly 개는 빨리 알아들어

개는 사무실의 자랑거리야
He's the pride of our office
- He's a real asset 개는 정말 인재야

그들은 개를 아주 높게 평가해
They have a high opinion of her
- The boss has high expectations of him 사장은 개한테 많은 기대를 하고 있어

개는 일을 무리없이 잘 처리해
He's a smooth operator
- He's a fast worker 개는 일을 빨리해

개는 일을 잘 해
He's good at his job
- She really knows her job 개는 일을 잘 해

개의 생각은 매우 독창적이야
His ideas are unique

개는 정말 일벌레야
He's a real workaholic

개는 정말 무용지물야
He's good for nothing
- He isn't good for anything 개는 할 수 있는 게 아무 것도 없어
- He's a nobody 개는 별 볼일 없는 친구야

개는 사람 다룰 줄 몰라
He just doesn't know how to handle people

개는 일처리 능력이 없어
He's not capable of doing the work

개는 똑똑하지가 않아
He isn't so smart

- He has poor judgement 개는 분별력이 없어
- He's simpleminded 개는 단순해
- His best days are behind him 그 사람 좋은 시절은 다 갔어

개는 한물간 사람야
He's a has-been

- He's history 개 한물 갔어
- He's a goner 그 사람 한물 간 사람이야

너는 한심한 놈이야
You're (such) a loser

- He's a loser 개 골통야
- You are not so great 그렇게 잘난 것도 없으면서

Supplements

Let's Speak Now!

지금까지 학습한 표현들을 이용해
실제 대화해 보는 시간

Easy Talk 이제 이 정도는 말할 수 있어야 `Level 1`
Real Talk 이 정도까지 말할 수 있으면 So Good `Level 2`
Magic Talk 혹 이정도까지 가능하면 당신은 이미 네이티브 `Level 3`

Easy Talk

01

A : How come you're late?

B : I got caught in traffic.

A : Next time you should leave earlier.

> **우리말** A: 어쩌다 이렇게 늦은 거야?
>
> B: 차가 밀려서.
>
> A: 다음 번엔 좀더 일찍 출발하도록 해.

02

A : Do you want to come with us for drinks?

B : Why not?

A : I'll come by your office when I'm through.

> **우리말** A: 우리랑 같이 한잔 하러 갈래?
>
> B: 그러지 뭐.
>
> A: 내가 일 끝나면 너희 사무실에 들를게.

03

A : That pizza was great.

B : Want some more?

A : I'd love another piece if there is any left.

> **우리말** A: 피자는 정말 맛있었어.
>
> B: 좀 더 먹을래?
>
> A: 남은 게 있으면 한 조각 더 먹었으면 좋겠는데.

04

A : Do you mind if I take a look around here?

B : Not at all, be my guest.

A : It's very beautiful.

> **우리말** A: 내가 여기 좀 둘러봐도 괜찮겠니?
>
> B: 그럼, 물론이지.
>
> A: 정말 멋지다.

05

A : How much do I owe you?

B : Give me twenty and we'll call it even.

A : Sounds good to me.

우리말 A: 내가 얼마나 주면 되니?

B: 20달러를 주면 우리 사이에 돈 문제는 깨끗하게 끝난 것으로 하지.

A: 알았어.

06

A : I think he's going to leave this company.

B : What makes you think so?

A : He can make much more money at another firm.

우리말 A: 그 사람이 이 회사를 그만둘 것 같애.

B: 왜 그렇게 생각해?

A: 다른 회사에 가면 돈을 훨씬 더 많이 벌 수 있잖아.

07

A : I'll have a club sandwich with fries.

B : Make it two.

A : I thought that you were on a diet.

우리말 A: 난 감자 튀김과 샌드위치 먹을 거야.

B: 같은 걸로 주세요.

A: 다이어트 하는 줄 알았는데.

08

A : Hello, are you still there?

B : Yes. There must be a bad connection.

A : I'll call you back from my home phone.

우리말 A: 여보세요, 듣고 있니?

B: 그럼. 연결 상태가 안 좋은가봐.

A: 집 전화로 걸게.

09

A : We got mail today and this is for you.
B : Please put it on my desk, I'm busy right now.
A : Alright, but don't forget to open it.

우리말 A: 오늘 우편물이 왔는데, 이건 당신 앞으로 온 거에요.

B: 제 책상에 두세요, 지금 바빠서요.

A: 그러죠, 잊지 말고 꼭 열어보세요.

10

A : Don't let me down.
B : Don't worry. I'll get it done for you.
A : I appreciate your help.

우리말 A: 실망시키지 마

B: 걱정마, 널 위해서 해낼테니까.

A: 도와줘서 고마워.

11

A : What brings you here today?
B : I have a pain in my neck.
A : Well, lie down and take off your shirt.

우리말 A: 오늘은 무슨 일로 오셨지요?

B: 목이 아파서요.

A: 자, 누워서 웃옷을 벗으세요.

12

A : La Scalla Restaurant... how can I help you?
B : I'd like to make a reservation for four at three
o'clock under the name "Davis."
A : Sure. Would you like smoking or non-smoking?

우리말 A: 라 스칼라 레스토랑입니다… 무엇을 도와드릴까요?

B: 데이비스라는 이름으로 3시에 4인석을 예약하고 싶습니다.

A: 좋습니다. 흡연석으로 하시겠습니까, 금연석으로 하시겠습니까?

13

A : I'm calling about the ad in last week's Job Search Magazine.

B : The position is still open, but we require a minimum of 3 years of experience.

A : No problem, I've got 10 years of experience in this field.

우리말 A: 지난 주 취업정보지에 난 광고를 보고 전화드리는건데요.

B: 자리가 아직 비어 있긴 합니다만, 최소한 3년의 경력이 있어야 합니다.

A: 문제없어요, 전 이 분야에서 10년 일했습니다.

14

A : I'm so upset that you forgot our anniversary.

B : I'm sorry. I won't let it happen again.

A : That's what you said last year, too.

우리말 A: 당신이 결혼 기념일을 잊어버려서 너무 속상해.

B: 미안해, 다신 그런 일 없을 거야.

A: 작년에도 바로 그렇게 말했잖아.

15

A : I'd like to propose a toast.

B : Oh, thanks. You don't have to do that.

A : Well, I want to. I'm so proud of your recent promotion. Here's to you!

우리말 A: 축배 들어요.

B: 아, 고마워요. 그럴 필요까지는 없는데.

A: 그래도 하고 싶어요. 얼마 전 승진한 거 정말 축하해요. 당신을 위하여!

16

A : How's it going with your new job?

B : I have to admit that it's pretty tough.

A : Don't worry. Things'll get easier.

우리말 A: 새로운 일은 어떠니?

B: 정말이지 상당히 힘들어.

A: 걱정마. 곧 익숙해질 거야.

17

A : Hello. What would you like?

B : Regular unleaded. Please fill it up.

A : No problem. Do you want the car wash with that?

> 우리말 A: 안녕하세요. 어떻게 드릴까요?
>
> B: 보통 무연휘발유로 가득 채워주세요.
>
> A: 알겠습니다. 세차도 해드릴까요?

18

A : I think my ex-boyfriend probably has a new girlfriend.

B : I don't think so. You just broke up last week!

A : Take my word for it. He's found another girl.

> 우리말 A: 내 옛날 남자친구가 새 여자친구를 만난 듯 해.
>
> B: 난 그렇게 생각 안 해. 니네들 헤어진 게 바로 지난 주잖아!
>
> A: 내 말 좀 믿어줘. 걔가 다른 여자를 찾았다니까.

19

A : Do you take checks?

B : Yes, as long as you have proof of identification.

A : Is a driver's license okay?

B : Yes, that will be fine.

> 우리말 A: 수표 받나요?
>
> B: 네, 신분증을 제시하시면요.
>
> A: 운전면허증으로 될까요?
>
> B: 네, 괜찮습니다.

20

A : Do you expect to hire any new employees in the near future?

B : Yes, as a matter of fact, we will be taking resumes for the busy summer season.

A : Then I'll send you a resume in July.

> 우리말 A: 귀사에서는 가까운 시일 내에 신입사원을 모집할 예정이신가요?
>
> B: 네, 사실 저희는 대목인 하계 시즌에 이력서를 받을 겁니다.
>
> A: 그럼, 7월에 이력서를 보내겠습니다.

21

A : Excuse me, can you tell me where the bathroom is?

B : Sure... it's just down the hall to your left.

A : Thanks, I'll be back soon.

B : We'll wait for you to get back before we start.

> 우리말 A: 죄송하지만 화장실이 어디 있나요?
>
> B: 네, 복도를 내려가다 보면 왼편에 있어요.
>
> A: 고마워요. 곧 돌아올게요.
>
> B: 당신이 돌아오는 거 기다렸다가 시작할게요.

22

A : Thanks for the lovely dinner party.

B : You're very welcome. How about some dessert?

A : Well, I think I'd better be going now.

B : Okay, then I'll see you tomorrow at the office.

> 우리말 A: 아주 멋진 저녁 파티였어요.
>
> B: 별 말씀을요. 디저트 좀 드실래요?
>
> A: 저, 그만 가봐야 될 것 같아요.
>
> B: 좋아요. 그럼 내일 사무실에서 봐요.

23

A : The number is 4-1-6-5-5-5-3-3-4-4.

B : Please, could you repeat that? I didn't hear it correctly.

A : Certainly... 4-1-6-5-5-5-3-3-4-4.

B : Thank you.

> 우리말 A: 4 1 6 5 5 5 3 3 4 4번입니다.
>
> B: 다시 한 번 말씀해 주시겠어요? 정확하게 듣지 못했거든요.
>
> A: 그러죠. 4 1 6 5 5 5 3 3 4 4번입니다.   B: 고마워요.

24

A : Look at all the stuff I bought!

B : Let me help you with your grocery bags.

A : Thank you, that's very kind of you.

B : My pleasure.

> 우리말 A: 내가 사온 물건들 좀 보세요!   B: 식료품 가방 들어줄게요.
>
> A: 고마워요. 정말 친절하시군요.   B: 뭘요.

25

A : Why are you so angry at me?

B : Because you said I was fat and ugly!

A : I didn't mean it. I was just kidding.

B : You were?

우리말 A: 왜 그렇게 나한테 화를 내는 거죠?

B: 나보고 뚱뚱하고 못생겼다면서요!

A: 진심이 아니었어요. 그냥 농담이었다구요.   B: 정말요?

26

A : Oh my God! How could I have done that?

B : Don't worry about it.

A : I feel like an idiot.

B : It could have happened to anyone.

우리말 A: 어머나, 세상에! 내가 왜 그랬을까?

B: 걱정하지 마세요.

A: 바보가 된 기분이에요.

B: 누구한테나 일어날 수 있는 일인 걸요.

27

A : May I speak to Bill, please?

B : He just stepped out for lunch.

A : How soon do you expect him back?

B : He should be back in about 15 minutes.

우리말 A: 빌 좀 바꿔 주시겠어요?

B: 점심식사하러 방금 나가셨는데요.

A: 언제쯤 돌아올까요?

B: 15분쯤 후엔 돌아오실거예요.

28

A : Good morning, I'd like to speak with Chris, please.

B : He's busy right now.

A : It's very important.

B : I'll get him for you.

우리말 A: 안녕하세요, 크리스와 통화하고 싶은데요.   B: 지금 바쁘신데요.

A: 굉장히 중요한 일이에요.   B: 바꿔드리죠.

29

A : May I help you?

B : Yes, I'm looking for running shoes.

A : You need to go up one more floor.

B : Thank you.

> **우리말** A: 도와드릴까요?　　　　B: 네, 운동화를 찾고 있는데요.
>
> A: 한 층 더 올라가셔야 해요.　B: 고맙습니다.

30

A : How much does it cost?

B : Which one, the black one or the white one?

A : The black one.

B : It costs $99.99.

> **우리말** A: 이건 얼마죠?　B: 어떤 거요? 검은 색이요, 아님 흰 색이요?
>
> A: 검은 색이요.　B: 99달러 99센트예요.

31

A : Can you give me any discount?

B : I can only give you a discount if you buy more than ten.

A : What kind of discount would I get?

B : I could give you a twenty-five percent discount.

> **우리말** A: 할인해 주실 수는 없나요?
>
> B: 10개 이상 사실 때만 할인해 드릴 수 있습니다.
>
> A: 어떻게 할인이 되는데요?
>
> B: 25% 할인해 드립니다.

32

A : Well, I've got to go now.

B : Okay, thanks for all your help.

A : Don't mention it. I'll see you later.

B : Okay, bye.

> **우리말** A: 저기, 지금 가봐야겠는데요.
>
> B: 그래요. 여러모로 도와주셔서 감사합니다.
>
> A: 별 말씀을요. 나중에 보죠.
>
> B: 그래요, 잘가요.

33

A : How would you like to pay for this?

B : With my credit card, if it's all right.

A : Yes, that'll be fine.

B : OK, I'll use my Visa card then.

우리말 A: 어떻게 계산하시겠습니까?

B: 괜찮다면 신용카드로 내겠어요.

A: 네, 괜찮습니다.

B: 좋아요, 그럼 비자카드로 내죠.

34

A : I'd like to buy this coat.

B : Will that be cash or charge?

A : I think I have enough to pay cash.

B : Great, that'll be $175.

우리말 A: 이 코트를 사고 싶은데요.

B: 현금으로 내시겠어요, 아님 신용카드로 하시겠어요?

A: 현금이 충분한 것 같군요.   B: 좋습니다. 175달러입니다.

35

A : May I make an appointment for tomorrow?

B : Yes, tomorrow is fine.

A : Are you free in the afternoon?

B : Yes. How about one-thirty?

우리말 A: 약속을 내일로 잡아도 될까요?   B: 예. 내일은 괜찮습니다.

A: 오후에 시간 있으세요?   B: 예. 1시 반이 어떨까요?

36

A : Are you ready to order your food?

B : No, I haven't decided yet.

A : That's all right, I'll just come back in a few minutes.

B : That would be perfect.

우리말 A: 주문하시겠어요?   B: 아뇨, 아직 못정했는데요.

A: 괜찮아요. 잠시 후에 다시 오겠습니다.

B: 그렇게 해 주시면 좋겠네요.

37

A : How do you like the steak?

B : It's the juiciest steak I have ever eaten!

A : I told you that this place was great.

B : I'm already planning to come back.

> 우리말 A: 스테이크 맛이 어때?
>
> B: 이렇게 맛있는 스테이크는 처음이야!
>
> A: 이 식당 좋다고 그랬잖아.
>
> B: 벌써부터 또 오고싶다는 생각이 들어.

38

A : What can I do for you?

B : Can I have a refund for this?

A : Certainly, if you have your receipt.

B : Yes, I do. Here you go.

> 우리말 A: 뭘 도와드릴까요?
>
> B: 이 물건을 환불받을 수 있을까요?
>
> A: 물론이죠, 영수증만 있으시다면요. B: 네, 있어요. 여기요.

39

A : Could I have the check please?

B : Do you want separate checks?

A : I would prefer that.

B : It will just take a few minutes.

> 우리말 A: 계산서 주시겠어요?   B: 따로 계산해 드릴까요?
>
> A: 그러는 편이 좋겠군요.   B: 잠시만 기다려 주십시오.

40

A : I would like to take tomorrow off.

B : Just leave your cell phone on in case we need to get in touch.

A : I'll charge it up and leave it on.

B : Enjoy your day off.

> 우리말 A: 전 내일 쉬고 싶은데요.
>
> B: 우리가 연락할 일이 있을지 모르니까 핸드폰은 켜놓고 있으세요.
>
> A: 충전해서 켜놓고 있을게요.   B: 그럼 잘 쉬어요.

41

A : My heart goes out to you.
B : I was really hoping that I'd get that promotion.
A : Another one will come along soon.
B : I hope so.

우리말 A: 진심으로 위로의 말을 전하겠습니다.

B: 저는 정말이지 승진하리라 기대했었거든요.

A: 곧 승진 기회가 다시 한번 올 거예요.

B: 저도 그랬으면 좋겠어요.

42

A : Come on, or we're going to be late.
B : I'm coming as quickly as I can.
A : I'll be out in the car.
B : I'll meet you out there.

우리말 A: 서둘러, 안그러면 우린 늦는다구.   B: 최대한 빨리 나갈게.

A: 밖에 나가 차안에 있을게.   B: 그럼 밖에서 보자.

43

A : I'm sorry I can't talk long.
B : I'll give you a call later when you have more time.
A : I'll be available after four o'clock.
B : Yes, I'll hear from you then.

우리말 A: 미안하지만 길게 얘긴 못해.

B: 그럼 나중에 시간될 때 다시 걸게.

A: 4시 이후엔 통화할 수 있을 거야.

B: 그럼 그때 다시 통화하자.

44

A : I think we're going to be late.
B : I'm sure we have a few minutes to spare.
A : What time do you have?
B : It is a quarter to nine.

우리말 A: 우리가 늦을 것 같은데.

B: 난 몇 분 여유가 있다고 보는데.

A: 몇 시니?   B: 9시 15분 전이야.

45

A : What do you think about the new office manager?

B : He's a nice guy, very friendly and easy-going.

A : Gee, that's great. It's difficult to work for uptight bosses.

B : Yeah, I feel that we are really lucky.

우리말 A: 새로 온 상사 어때요?　　　B: 좋은 분이죠. 정도 많고 털털해요.

A: 와, 잘 됐네요. 깐깐한 상사 모시기가 얼마나 힘든데요.

B: 맞아요, 우린 정말 운이 좋은 것 같아요.

46

A : So, what do you do for a living?

B : Right now I'm between jobs.

A : I see. What was your last job?

B : I was a personal assistant to an executive.

우리말 A: 그럼, 직업이 뭐야?　　　B: 지금은 백수야.

A: 아, 그래. 전엔 무슨 일 했었는데?

B: 어떤 기업체에서 중역의 비서로 일했어.

47

A : Where do you want to go?

B : I'm looking for the library. Is there one around here?

A : Yes, keep going straight and turn to the right when you come to the second traffic light.

우리말 A: 어딜 가시려구요?

B: 도서관을 찾고 있어요. 이 근처에 있나요?

A: 그럼요, 이대로 곧장 가셔서 두번째 신호등이 보이면 오른쪽으로 도세요.

48

A : I'm eager to start my vacation.

B : Where are you going?

A : I'm going to France for a few weeks.

B : Sounds like fun.

우리말 A: 어서 휴가를 갔으면 해.　　　B: 어디 갈 건데?

A: 몇 주 정도 프랑스에 가 있을려구.　　　B: 재미있을 것 같은데.

49

A : Is Jessy in the office today?

B : He is, but he is in a meeting right now.

A : May I leave a message?

B : Yes. Could I have your name and phone number first?

우리말 A: 제시 오늘 사무실에 있나요?

B: 네, 근데 지금은 회의중이신데요.

A: 메시지를 남겨도 될까요?

B: 그러세요. 성함과 전화번호부터 말씀해주시겠습니까?

50

A : Do you have any questions about the menu?

B : Yes. What's the special of the day?

A : Fried shrimp with a side of salad.

B : Okay, I'll have that.

우리말 A: 메뉴에 대해 뭐 궁금하신 거라도 있으세요?

B: 네. 오늘의 특별요리가 뭔가요?

A: 샐러드를 곁들인 새우튀김 요리예요.

B: 좋아요. 그걸로 하겠어요.

01

A : Hello Mr. Smith. I'm Ms. Kim.

B : Well, it's nice to finally meet you in person!

A : It is. It's nice to connect a name to a face.

B : Thanks for your expert advice on the phone.

A : Glad I could be of help. That's what our business is all about.

> 우리말 A: 안녕하십니까, 스미스씨. 저는 미즈 김이라고 합니다.
>
> B: 예, 드디어 당신을 직접 만나뵙게 되어 기쁩니다.
>
> A: 그래요. 이름만 듣다가 얼굴을 뵈니 반갑군요.
>
> B: 전화상으로 전문적인 자문을 해주신 데 대해 감사드립니다.
>
> A: 제가 도움이 되었다니 기쁘군요. 그게 저희가 하는 일이니까요.

02

A : I'm calling to talk to Mr. Shim in the marketing department.

B : I'm sorry, but he is out of the office right now. Would you like to hold or call back later?

A : I'll call back later.

B : All right. Would you like to leave a message?

A : No, thank you.

> 우리말 A: 마케팅 부서에 있는 미스터 심과 통화하려고 하는데요.
>
> B: 죄송합니다만 그분은 지금 잠깐 사무실에 안 계시는데요.
> 기다리시겠습니까, 아님 나중에 다시 전화하시겠습니까?
>
> A: 나중에 다시 전화하죠.
>
> B: 알겠습니다. 메시지를 남기시겠어요?
>
> A: 아뇨. 고맙습니다.

03

A : What's the purpose of your visit?

B : I'm visiting on business.

A : Can you tell me where you're going to be staying for the duration of your trip?

B : My company has booked me a room at the Park Plaza Hotel and I'll be staying there for the next week.

A : Enjoy your stay in Chicago.

우리말 A: 이곳엔 무슨 일로 오셨죠?

B: 사업차 왔어요.

A: 여행 기간 동안 어디에 계실 건가요?

B: 회사에서 파크 플라자 호텔에 방을
예약해둬서 다음 주에는 거기에 있을 거예요.

A: 시카고에 계시는 동안 즐거운 시간 되시길 바랍니다.

04

A : I'd like to check out now.

B : Could you tell me your room number please?

A : I was staying in room 703.

B : How would you like to pay for the room, Mr. Lee?

A : I'd like to pay by credit card.

우리말 A: 첵아웃을 하고 싶은데요.

B: 방 번호를 말씀해 주시겠습니까?

A: 703호에 묵었습니다.

B: 어떻게 지불하고 싶으십니까, 이 선생님?

A: 신용카드로 지불하겠어요.

05

A : Excuse me, do you know how many stops until the exhibition center?

B : I think it's about six stops from here.

A : Is this the correct bus to be on?

B : Yes, it is. When we get there, I will let you know.

A : Thank you very much.

> **우리말** A: 실례합니다만, 전시회장까지 몇 정거장인지 아세요?
>
> B: 여기서 여섯 정거장 정도 될 거예요.
>
> A: 이 버스가 거기로 가는 버스 맞나요?
>
> B: 네, 맞아요. 거기 도착하면 제가 알려드리죠.
>
> A: 정말 고맙습니다.

06

A : We're going to expand the business this year.

B : I thought you were going to go on leave.

A : I was thinking about that, but I changed my mind.

B : What are your expansion plans?

A : I thought we'd specialize in laptop computers.

B : Will you still carry regular computers?

> **우리말** A: 우린 올해 사업을 확장할 예정이야.
>
> B: 난 네가 쉴 거라고 생각했는데.
>
> A: 그렇게 생각했었는데 마음이 변했어.
>
> B: 네 사업확장계획을 좀 들어보자.
>
> A: 노트북 컴퓨터를 전문적으로 취급해볼 생각이야.
>
> B: 일반 컴퓨터도 계속 취급할 거니?

07

A : Hey Young-min, did you see that I sent you a text message?

B : No, I haven't had time to check my phone in the last hour.

A : You should look at it now.

B : Okay. I will check it and call you back, after I finish this work.

A : Great. It has to do with the insurance quote we talked about.

우리말 A: 영민, 제가 보낸 문자 메시지 보셨나요?

B: 아니요, 한 시간 전부터 전화 확인할 시간이 없었어요.

A: 지금 봐야 할 거예요.

B: 알았어요. 확인해보고 이 일이 끝나면 전화할게요.

A: 좋아요. 우리가 얘기했던 보험 견적과 관련이 있는 메시지예요.

08

A : Hello, Jason. Come on in. We've been waiting for you.

B : Thank you. Well, I know you're all anxious to hear our decision, so let's get started.

A : Great. What did you decide?

B : I have good news for you. We are ready to sign your contract.

A : Excellent. We couldn't be more pleased.

우리말 A: 안녕하세요, 제이슨. 들어오세요. 당신을 기다리고 있었어요.

B: 고맙습니다. 자, 여러분들이 모두 저희 회사의 결정을 몹시 듣고 싶어 한다는 걸 알아요. 자 시작하죠.

A: 좋습니다. 어떻게 결정이 났나요?

B: 좋은 소식이에요. 저흰 귀사의 계약서에 서명하기로 했어요.

A: 아주 잘 됐군요. 기분이 최고예요.

09

A : Hello, I am calling to talk to Mr. Kim.

B : I'm sorry, but he's not in at the moment.

A : May I leave a message for him?

B : Of course. What would you like me to relay to him?

A : Please tell him that I won't be able to make the golf game today.

우리말
A: 안녕하세요, 미스터 김과 통화하려고 하는데요.
B: 죄송합니다만 그분은 지금 자리에 안 계십니다.
A: 그분한테 메모를 좀 남겨주시겠습니까?
B: 물론이죠. 전하실 말씀이 뭔가요?
A: 오늘 골프를 치러 갈 수 없게 됐다고 전해주십시오.

10

A : I'd like a round-trip ticket to Chicago.

B : When would you like to depart and return?

A : I'd like to leave this Wednesday and return on Monday.

B : Do you want first class, business or coach class?

A : Business class, please.

우리말
A: 시카고행 왕복 항공권을 사고 싶은데요.
B: 언제 출발해서 언제 돌아오실 생각이십니까?
A: 이번 수요일에 출발해서 월요일에 돌아오려구요.
B: 일등석으로 해드릴까요, 아니면 비즈니스 클래스나 보통석으로 드릴까요?
A: 비즈니스 클래스로 주세요.

11

A : I have been trying to call you for over three hours! Why didn't you answer?

B : My cellphone was off.

A : You should leave it on so people can contact you.

B : I was in an important meeting. I couldn't.

A : I guess I have been a little impatient recently.

우리말 A: 당신과 통화하려고 세시간이 넘게 연락을 했었어요! 왜 전화를 안 받은 거죠?

B: 제가 휴대폰 전원을 꺼두었어요.

A: 사람들이 당신한테 연락할 수 있도록 휴대폰 좀 켜두세요.

B: 중요한 회의 중이었거든요. 켤 수가 없었어요.

A: 최근들어 제가 좀 참고 기다리지 못한다는 생각이 드네요.

12

A : We've been discussing this matter for about thirty minutes.

B : Yes, but we still haven't come to a decision.

A : Let's take a ten-minute break and continue the discussion later.

B : Good idea.

A : I think we could all use a stretch and some fresh air.

우리말 A: 이 문제를 가지고 벌써 30분 정도나 토론했군요.

B: 네, 하지만 아직도 결론에 이르지는 못했죠.

A: 10분 동안 쉰 다음에 토론을 계속합시다.

B: 좋은 생각이에요.

A: 모두들 스트레칭을 하고 신선한 공기를 좀 마시는 게 좋을 것 같아요.

13

A : How can I help you, sir?

B : I'm here for the International Media Conference.

A : Yes. Please take the elevator over there to the fifth floor.

B : Can I please have a copy of the schedule for today's meeting?

A : Certainly, sir.

우리말 A: 무엇을 도와드릴까요, 손님?

B: 국제 언론매체 회의때문에 왔는데요.

A: 네. 저쪽에 있는 엘리베이터를 타고 5층으로 가시면 됩니다.

B: 오늘 회의 일정표를 한 부 얻을 수 있을까요?

A: 물론이죠.

14

A : Mr. Kim, what's your feeling about the decision to cut down on spending?

B : I'm convinced that we made the right choice.

A : You seem sure about that. What makes you say that?

B : We'll save money for the company, and that's always a good idea.

A : That's true. You have a point there.

우리말 A: 김선생님, 지출을 줄이자는 결정에 대해 어떻

B: 옳은 선택을 했다고 확신합니다.

A: 그 결정에 확신이 있는 것 같은데요. 왜 그렇

B: 그렇게 하면 회사 차원에서 비용이 절감될텐

그런 게 안 좋을 리가 없죠.

A: 맞아요. 일리가 있는 말입니다.

15

A : I have a reservation. I'm Jin-su Lee.

B : OK. I have your reservation.
Are you still planning
to stay the third night?

A : I'm still not sure.

B : Just let us know before Wednesday
at 4:00 p.m. You can call down to the reception
at any time by dialing 0 on your phone.

A : Thanks. I'll let you know.

우리말 A: 예약을 했는데요. 저는 이진수라고 합니다.

B: 네. 예약되어 있네요. 3일간 묵기로 되어 있는데, 변함없으신가요?

A: 아직 잘 모르겠어요.

B: 수요일 오후 4시까지만 알려주시면 돼요. 방 전화기의 0번을 누르시면
언제든 접수창구와 통화하실 수 있습니다.

A: 감사합니다. 연락드릴게요.

16

A : How may I help you?

B : I'd like to change my flight to Paris.

A : Could I please have your name, flight number and
date of departure?

B : My name is Jane Marshall, the flight number is 097
and the date of departure is February 2nd.

A : I have your file in front of me. Let me know the
changes you want to make.

우리말 A: 어떻게 도와드릴까요?

B: 제 파리행 비행편 티켓을 바꾸려구요.

A: 성함과 비행편 번호를 말씀해 주시겠습니까?
그리고 출발일도요.

B: 제 이름은 제인 마셜이구요, 비행편 번호는
097, 2월 2일에 출발하는 비행기입니다.

A: 손님의 파일이 여기 있군요. 변경 사항을 말씀하세요.

17

A : What's the first item on the agenda?

B : Let's see. The first thing on the agenda is revising our hiring procedures.

A : Oh, yes. Does anyone have a proposal about this item?

C : I do. I've worked out a new system I'd like to run by the committee.

A : Great. Let's hear it.

우리말 A: 첫번째 안건이 뭐죠?

B: 어디보자. 첫번째 안건은 채용절차 개선 문제입니다.

A: 아, 그래요. 이 안건에 대해 제안하실 분 있나요?

C: 저요. 제가 새로운 제도를 마련해 봤는데, 위원회에서 검토해 주셨으면 좋겠습니다.

A: 좋아요. 어디 들어봅시다.

18

A : I want to reconfirm my reservation.

B : What is your flight number?

A : It is 492, to Washington.

B : Your reservation is confirmed, but the flight may be delayed because of bad weather.

A : I'll phone the airport ahead of time.

우리말 A: 예약을 확인하려구요.

B: 비행편 번호가 어떻게 되시죠?

A: 492번, 워싱턴행입니다.

B: 예약이 확인되었습니다. 그런데 날씨가 나빠서 늦게 출발할지도 모르겠어요.

A: 공항에 미리 전화를 해 보겠습니다.

19

A : Excuse me, sir. Is this the right road for Woodstock?

B : No, this road goes to Albany and then on to Canada.

A : Wow, I must be really lost.

B : Go back that way for ten minutes and take the road on your left.

A : Thanks for your time.

> **우리말** A: 실례합니다. 이 길이 우드스탁으로 가는 길 맞나요?
>
> B: 아니요. 이 길은 올버니로 가는 길이고 계속가면 캐나다로 통해요.
>
> A: 이런, 길을 완전히 잃어버렸네요.
>
> B: 왔던 길을 10분정도 되돌아간 다음 왼쪽 도로를 타세요.
>
> A: 시간내주셔서 감사합니다.

20

A : Do you have any prohibited items with you?

B : Not that I know of.

A : Did anyone ask you to bring anything into the country for them?

B : No, these are all my own personal belongings.

A : You may proceed.

> **우리말** A: 금지품목을 소지하고 계신 게 있습니까?
>
> B: 제가 알기로는 없습니다.
>
> A: 누군가가 손님에게 뭔가 가져다 달라고 부탁한 게 있습니까?
>
> B: 아뇨, 이것들은 전부 다 제 개인 물품들입니다.
>
> A: 지나가셔도 좋습니다.

21

A : Mr. Kim, do you have time to discuss the presentation tomorrow?

B : Sorry, but I have a hundred things to do.

A : Are you available on Thursday morning?

B : I think so. I'll call to confirm.

A : Alright, I'll talk to you later.

우리말 A: 김 선생님, 내일 그 프리젠테이션에 대해 의논할 시간이 있나요?

B: 죄송합니다만, 할 일이 너무 많아서요.

A: 그럼 목요일 오전에는 시간이 되세요?

B: 될 것 같은데요. 전화해서 확실히 알려드릴 게요.

A: 좋습니다. 나중에 이야기 하죠.

22

A : Could you tell me where the closest subway station is?

B : It depends. Where do you want to go?

A : I want to go to Millennium Plaza. I told Ms. Brown I would meet her there.

B : You don't need to take the subway. It's only about a ten-minute walk.

A : Great. Thanks a lot for your help.

우리말 A: 제일 가까운 지하철역이 어딘지 알려줄 수 있나요?

B: 경우에 따라 다르죠. 어디에 가실 건데요?

A: 밀레니엄 플라자에 가려고요. 브라운씨에게 거기서 만나자고 했거든요.

B: 그럼 지하철을 탈 필요가 없어요. 걸어서 10분밖에 안 걸리는 거리거든요.

A: 그렇군요. 도와줘서 정말 고마워요.

23

A : We need to get together to discuss the new contract.

B : You're right. How about tomorrow morning?

A : I'm in a meeting all morning, but I'm free after one o'clock.

B : That works for me.

A : I'll meet you in the boardroom at one o'clock tomorrow.

우리말   A: 새 계약건을 의논하기 위해 좀 만나야겠어요.

B: 그래요. 내일 오전 어떠세요?

A: 전 오전 내내 회의가 있지만, 1시 이후에는 한가해요.

B: 저도 그때가 괜찮아요.

A: 그럼 내일 1시에 중역회의실에서 뵙죠.

24

A : So, are we all in agreement on my proposal?

B : I support your idea completely.

C : Actually, I'm against the plan, Jim. It sounds too complicated.

A : What do you mean? I thought it sounded pretty straightforward.

C : Why don't I explain it again?

우리말   A: 그럼, 모두들 제 의견에 찬성합니까?

B: 당신 생각을 전적으로 지지합니다.

C: 사실, 전 그 계획에 반대합니다, 짐. 너무 복잡한 것 같아요.

A: 무슨 뜻이죠? 상당히 간단하다고 생각했는데요.

C: 제가 다시 한번 설명해드리죠.

A : Mr. Chairman, I'm afraid we can't seem to come together on this issue.

B : Do you think we should take a vote on it?

A : Yes, that might expedite this session.

B : We'll put it to a vote. The final decision on this matter will be made by majority rule.

A : Sounds fair.

우리말 A: 의장님, 이 문제에 대해선 합의를 보기 힘들 것 같습니다.

B: 표결을 해야 한다고 생각하십니까?

A: 네, 그러면 신속하게 처리될 것 같습니다.

B: 표결에 부쳐서 다수결 원칙에 따라 최종 결론을 내리겠습니다.

A: 그거 좋습니다.

Magic Talk

01

Seun-eh : Excuse me, but I seem to have lost my way.

John : Where is it that you are heading?

Seun-eh : I'm trying to find the National Art Gallery. Do you know where it is?

John : Sure, you have to take this road to the end and then turn right.

Seun-eh : Okay.

John : Then you have to continue for about five minutes until you reach an intersection. Are you with me?

Seun-eh : So far, so good.

John: Turn right at the intersection and it's on your right.

Seun-eh : Let me repeat the directions to you.

John : Shoot.

Seun-eh : I take this road to the end, make a right, go straight until the intersection, and then turn right.

John : You got it!!

우리말 순애: 실례합니다만, 제가 길을 잃은 것 같아서요.   존: 어디 가시는 길인데요?

순애: 국제 미술관에 가려구요. 어디 있는지 아세요?

존: 그럼요, 이 길 끝까지 가서 오른쪽으로 도세요.   순애: 알겠어요.

존: 그리고 교차로까지 한 5분 정도 계속 가야 해요. 아시겠어요?

순애: 지금까지는 알겠어요.

존: 그 교차로에서 오른쪽으로 돌면 오른편에 있어요.

순애: 제가 한번 말해 볼께요.   존: 그러세요.

순애: 이 길 끝에서 오른쪽으로 돌고 교차로까지 쭉 간 다음 오른쪽으로 도는 거죠.

존: 맞아요!!

02

Lydia : What do you usually like to do in your free time?

Danny : I enjoy just relaxing, but I love going for long bike rides.

Lydia : What kind of bike do you have?

Danny : I have two, a mountain bike and a racing bike.

Lydia : Which do you prefer?

Danny : I would have to say my mountain bike, because I can go many more places with it .

Lydia : Do you have any other hobbies?

Danny : Believe it or not, I really like fishing!

Lydia : What's the biggest fish you've ever caught?

Danny : I have caught a lot of big fish, but the biggest was a 10kg salmon.

 리디아: 여가 시간에는 대개 뭘 하십니까?

대니: 그냥 느긋하게 쉬는 것도 좋아하는 편이지만, 장거리 자전거 하이킹을 무척 즐깁니다.

리디아: 어떤 종류의 자전거를 갖고 계시는데요?

대니: 산악용 자전거랑 경주용 자전거, 이렇게 2대를 갖고 있습니다.

리디아: 어떤 게 더 마음에 드세요?

대니: 굳이 말씀드리자면 산악용 자전거인데, 그걸 타고 더 많은 곳을 다닐 수 있기 때문이죠.

리디아: 그밖에 다른 취미가 있습니까?

대니: 누가 뭐래도 낚시를 정말 좋아해요!

리디아: 지금껏 낚은 것 중에 가장 큰 고기는 어떤 거였죠?

대니: 전 대어를 많이 낚아봤는데 가장 큰 게 10kg짜리 연어였습니다.

03

Mike : What country are you from?

Ji-yeon : We are from South Korea.

Mike : How long do you plan to stay in Niagara Falls?

Ji-yeon : We were thinking of staying one or two nights, but we're not sure.

Mike : May I see your passports?

Ji-yeon : Here you go.

Mike : Are you planning on visiting any other Canadian cities while you're in Canada?

Ji-yeon : We might go to Toronto for a few days to do some sightseeing.

Mike : Here are your passports.

Ji-yeon : I'm looking forward to seeing what the Falls look like from the Canadian side.

Jin-woo : Maybe we can go on the Maid of the Mist boat while we're here. I've heard that the boat goes really close to the Falls and you get really wet.

Ji-yeon : As soon as I find parking, we can go on the boat tour.

우리말 마이크: 어느 나라에서 오셨습니까?

지연: 한국에서 왔습니다.

마이크: 나이아가라 폭포에서는 얼마나 계실 생각이죠?

지연: 하루나 이틀 정도 묵을 건데 확실히는 모르겠네요.

마이크: 여권 좀 보여주시겠어요?

지연: 여기 있습니다.

마이크: 캐나다에 계시는 동안 여기 말고 다른 도시에도 가실 건가요?

지연: 관광차 토론토에 며칠 갈 지도 몰라요.

마이크: 여권 여기 있습니다.

지연: 캐나다 쪽에서는 나이아가라 폭포가 어떤 모습일지 정말 보고 싶은 걸.

진우: 여기 있는 동안 안개 아가씨 호를 탈 수도 있겠네. 그 배는 폭포에 바짝 다가가기 때문에 사람들이 물에 흠뻑 젖는대.

지연: 주차할 곳을 찾으면 곧바로 그 유람선을 타자구.

04

Eun-hi : I can't believe how long it took me to get to work this morning. I was stuck in a traffic jam for almost an hour.

James : I understand what you mean. I was on the bus for an hour and a half this morning.

Eun-hi : Although the bus takes a little longer I think I might start taking it because I always arrive completely stressed.

James : At least I can do work on the bus and I don't have to concentrate on driving.

Eun-hi : I guess we just have to face it, the traffic situation in Seoul is terrible.

James : You've got that right. Something has to be done about it.

Eun-hi : I think I'm going to join you on the bus on Monday and start getting some work done.

James : At least we can make use of our time while we're stuck in traffic for an hour each way.

우리말 은희: 오늘 아침, 회사에 출근하는 데 얼마나 오래 걸렸는지 말도 못할 지경이야. 교통 체증 때문에 거의 한시간 동안이나 옴짝달싹도 못했어.

제임스: 무슨 말인지 이해해. 오늘 아침에 나는 한시간 반이나 버스에 있었다니까.

은희: 운전하는 것보다 버스를 타는게 시간이 좀더 걸리긴 하지만 출근할 때 차를 몰고 오면 완전히 스트레스를 받아서 난 앞으로 버스를 탈 생각이야.

제임스: 적어도 버스안에서 일할 수 있고 운전에 신경쓸 필요도 없으니까 말이야.

은희: 서울의 교통 사정이 끔찍하다는 사실을 감안해야 할 것 같아.

제임스: 네 말이 맞아. 무슨 대책을 세워야 해.

은희: 월요일엔 너랑 같이 버스안에서 일을 좀 해야겠는 걸.

제임스: 출퇴근길에 한시간씩 교통 체증에 묶여 있지만 시간은 이용할 수 있잖아.

05

Nam-su : I am calling to see if you are still accepting applications for the job?

Secretary : Yes we are. Have you had any specific training?

Nam-su : Well, I have taken several computer courses.

Secretary : That's good, but do you have any programming skills?

Nam-su : Yes, a few, and I have experience setting up web pages.

Secretary : We are also looking for somebody who can speak English.

Nam-su : What documents should I send to you?

Secretary : We need your resume and proof of training courses before the end of the week.

Nam-su : I'll send you it as soon as possible.

Secretary : Thank you. If we are interested in interviewing you, we will give you a phone call.

우리말 **남수:** 다름이 아니라 아직도 지원서를 접수받고 있습니까?

비서: 네, 그런데요. 뭐 특별한 기술이라도 있습니까?

남수: 음, 몇가지 컴퓨터 과정을 이수했는데요.

비서: 그거 괜찮군요. 그런데 프로그래밍은 할 수 있나요?

남수: 네, 조금요. 웹 페이지를 제작한 경험이 있습니다.

비서: 저희는 영어를 할 수 있는 분도 모집하고 있습니다.

남수: 어떤 서류들을 보내드리면 되죠?

비서: 이력서와 교육과정 이수증을 이번 주 안에 보내주시면 돼요.

남수: 가능한 한 빨리 보내겠습니다.

비서: 감사합니다. 면접이 결정되면 전화연락드리죠.

06

Kate : Hello, Mr. Drew's Dental Clinic. How may I help you?

David : I'm calling to reschedule my appointment. I have to go out of town on business.

Kate : Okay. What time are you scheduled for right now?

David : My current appointment is at 4 o'clock on Monday. I'd like to change it to Friday at the same time.

Kate : That would be fine. By the way, where are you going, sir?

David : I have to go to Hawaii to meet with some clients about a real estate deal.

Kate : Sounds like a lot more fun than sitting in this office and answering the phone.

David : It sounds fun, but it is actually very tiring. When you travel as much as I do, you relish being at home.

우리말　케이트: 여보세요, 드류 치과 병원입니다. 어떻게 도와드릴까요?

데이빗: 예약 날짜를 좀 바꾸고 싶은데요. 사업차 출장을 가야 하거든요.

케이트: 네, 그러세요. 지금 예약되어있는 시간이 어떻게 되죠?

데이빗: 현재 예약 시간은 월요일 4시인데요. 금요일 같은 시간으로 옮기고 싶습니다.

케이트: 그러세요. 그런데 어디에 가세요?

데이빗: 부동산 거래 일로 하와이에 갑니다. 고객들을 좀 만나봐야 하거든요.

케이트: 사무실에 앉아서 전화나 받는 일보다는 훨씬 재밌을 것 같은데요?

데이빗: 재미있을 것 같겠지만 실은 무척 피곤한 일이죠. 저처럼 많이 돌아다니다 보면 집에 있는 게 제일 좋아질 겁니다.

Bruce : Would you say you're more of an outgoing person or a more reserved kind of person?

Tina : I am most definitely an outgoing person.

Bruce : How would you make a more reserved person feel comfortable?

Tina : I guess I would try to find a common interest and find something that they like conversing about.

Bruce : Have you ever worked with people that are very quiet?

Tina : Yes, but I found that they eventually opened up and started talking to me.

Bruce : How would you communicate with someone who didn't speak your language?

Tina : I would probably use my hands and facial expressions until they understood what I said.

Bruce : Do you enjoy working with seniors?

Tina : I really enjoy working with them, they always have interesting stories to tell about the old days.

우리말 **브루스:** 당신은 외향적인 편인가요, 내성적인 편인가요?

티나: 저는 지극히 외향적입니다.

브루스: 내성적인 사람이 편안함을 느낄 수 있도록 어떻게 해 주시겠어요?

티나: 공통의 관심사를 찾으려 애써서, 그들이 얘기하고 싶어하는 대화거리를 찾을 겁니다.

브루스: 굉장히 말수가 적은 사람과 일해본 적이 있나요?

티나: 네, 하지만 결국엔 말문을 트고 저랑 얘기를 하게 되더군요.

브루스: 당신 나라 말을 할 줄 모르는 사람과는 어떻게 의사소통을 하실 건가요?

티나: 아마도 제 말을 이해할 때까지 손과 표정을 이용할 거예요.

브루스: 연장자와 일하는 건 즐거운가요?

티나: 정말 즐거워요, 그들은 항상 옛날에 있었던 재미있는 얘깃거리가 있거든요.

Dr. Lee : How are you today, Billy? I hear you've been having some stomach pain.

Billy : Yes, Dr. Lee. I've had a bad stomachache and diarrhea since last night.

Dr. Lee : Did you eat anything unusual yesterday that might have caused the problem?

Billy : Well, I had dinner at a buffet last night with my friends. I ate a lot at the buffet, but I can't remember all the different foods.

Dr. Lee : Did you have any meat that might have been bad?

Billy : No, I think it was fresh.

Dr. Lee : It's possible that you just ate too much. In the future, you might want to consider regulating the amount of food you eat for each meal. Overeating can lead to serious health problems.

Billy : I know. You're right, I should pay more attention to how much I'm eating.

우리말 **의사:** 안녕하세요, 빌리 씨? 배탈이 나셨다구요.

빌리: 예, 선생님. 어젯밤부터 배가 너무 아프고 설사도 심해요.

의사: 어제 문제가 될 만한 특별한 음식이라도 드셨나요?

빌리: 글쎄요, 어제 저녁에 친구들이랑 뷔페에 갔거든요. 거기서 엄청 먹었죠. 하지만 그 많은 음식들을 어떻게 다 기억하겠습니까.

의사: 상한 것 같은 고기라도 혹시 드셨나요?

빌리: 아니오, 고기는 신선했어요.

의사: 그렇다면 너무 많이 드셔서 그럴 수도 있습니다. 앞으로는 매 끼니마다 드시는 식사량을 조절하도록 신경을 좀 쓰셔야겠어요. 과식은 건강에 심각한 문제들을 초래할 수 있으니까요.

빌리: 저도 알고 있습니다. 선생님 말씀이 맞아요, 식사량에 좀더 주의를 해야 겠네요.

Server : Good afternoon, sir. Welcome to our restaurant. Would you like to see a menu?

Brian : No, that's all right. I think I know what I would like to order.

Server : Would you like to start off by ordering something to drink? Perhaps a glass of beer or some Coke?

Brian : Actually, I'd like a Shandy.

Server : That's fine. Would you like it mixed half with beer and half with ginger ale?

Brian : Yes, that's perfect and please put it in a tall glass.

Server : Okay, and what would you like for your main order? Are you interested in any of our house specials?

Brian : No, thanks, but I'd like a sirloin steak with mashed potatoes and onions.

Server : How would you like the steak done?

Brian : Medium-rare please.

Server : All right. I'll be back in a few moments with your drink, and the meal won't take long.

Brian : Thank you very much.

우리말 종업원: 안녕하십니까? 저희 식당을 찾아주셔서 감사합니다. 메뉴판 보시겠어요?

브라이언: 아니오, 됐어요. 주문할 걸 알고 있어요.

종업원: 음료수부터 주문하시겠어요? 맥주 한 잔이나 콜라로요?

브라이언: 어, 샌디로 할게요.

종업원: 좋아요. 맥주와 진저 에일을 반반씩 섞어 드릴까요?

브라이언: 네, 그럼 좋죠. 긴 잔에 담아주세요.

종업원: 네, 주 요리는 뭘로 하시겠어요? 저희 집 스페셜 요리는 어떠세요?

브라이언: 아니, 됐어요. 그냥 으깬 감자와 양파를 곁들인 등심 스테이크로 할래요.

종업원: 스테이크는 어떻게 해드릴까요?

브라이언: 약간 덜 익혀 주세요.

종업원: 좋아요. 음료수는 바로 갖다드리고 식사도 곧 준비하겠습니다.

브라이언: 고마워요.

10

Banker : Yes, how can I help you sir?

Robert : I'd like to open a new bank account.

Banker : You'll have to fill out some forms. Is it a personal account that you want?

Robert : Yes, one of the new accounts with the special interest rate.

Banker : Do you know that rate only applies if you maintain a balance over $1,000?

Robert : Yes, and that's all right with me.

Banker : Good, then you can fill in all the information on the form.

Robert : Do you need to see my identification?

Banker : You're one step ahead of me. Yes, I do.

Robert : Here is my driver's license and my passport.

Banker : I'll be back in one moment, I have to get my manager to sign the forms.

Robert : Does the account come with a cash card?

Banker : Only if you want one. Would you like me to provide you with an ATM card?

Robert : Yes, that would be great. Will the bank charge me a fee if I use the card to withdraw money?

Banker : Only if you use another bank's ATM machine.

우리말 은행원: 네, 무엇을 도와드릴까요, 손님?

로버트: 은행 계좌를 새로 만들고 싶은데요.

은행원: 용지를 좀 작성해 주십시오. 개인 계좌를 만드실 겁니까?

로버트: 네, 우대 이자를 주는 신상품 중에서요.

은행원: 1,000달러 이상 잔액을 유지해야만 그 만큼의 이자가 적용되는 거 아십니까?

로버트: 네, 그게 나한테는 좋을 거예요.

은행원: 좋습니다, 그럼 용지에 모든 사항을 기입하시면 됩니다.

로버트: 신분증 확인해야 되나요?

은행원: 저보다 한 발 빠르시네요. 네, 주십시오.

로버트: 운전면허증과 여권 여기 있어요.

은행원: 잠시만 기다리세요, 용지에 과장님 결재를 받게요.

로버트: 이 계좌에 현금카드도 나오나요?

은행원: 원하신다면요. 현금카드를 발급해 드릴까요?

로버트: 네, 그러면 좋죠. 카드를 이용해 현금을 찾으면 수수료가 붙나요?

은행원: 타은행의 현금인출기를 사용할 경우에만요.

11

Peter : I'd like to make a reservation.

Mona : Where are you departing from?

Peter : I am leaving from New York.

Mona : Where do you want to fly?

Peter : I need to fly to Miami.

Mona : What is the date of your departure?

Peter : I need to leave June 30th.

Mona : When do you want to return?

Peter : I need to be back in New York to catch an international flight on July 3rd at 4:00 p.m.

Mona : Do you have a preference for a particular airline?

Peter : No, but I would like my return to be in the late morning of July 3rd.

Mona : I have a business class seat available leaving June 30th at 8:10 a.m., and returning on July 3rd at 11:20 a.m.

Peter : I'll take it.

Mona : Thank you very much! How would you like to pay for this ticket?

Peter : Can I pay by credit card?

Mona : Yes. Do you want us to mail it to you or do you want to pick it up at the terminal?

Peter : I would rather pick it up.

Mona : If you have any questions or need more information, you can call our customer service.

Peter : Great!

피터: 예약을 했으면 하는데요.　　모나: 어디에서 출발하실 예정인가요?

피터: 뉴욕에서 출발할 예정입니다.　　모나: 어디로 여행하실 건데요?

피터: 마이애미로 갈 겁니다.　　모나: 출발 일자가 언제인가요?

피터: 6월 30일에 떠날 예정인데요.

모나: 언제 돌아오실 예정인가요?

피터: 7월 3일 오후 4시에 뉴욕으로 되돌아와서 국제선을 타야 합니다.

모나: 특별히 원하시는 항공사가 있나요?

피터: 아뇨, 하지만 7월 3일 오전쯤에는 돌아올 수 있었으면 좋겠어요.

모나: 6월 30일 오전 8시10분에 출발해서 7월 3일 오전 11시 20분에 돌아오는 비즈니스 클래스 좌석이 있어요.

피터: 그걸로 하죠.

모나: 고맙습니다. 티켓 요금은 어떻게 지불하실 건가요?

피터: 신용카드로 되나요?

모나: 네. 표를 우편으로 보내드릴까요, 아니면 공항에서 탑승하실 때 가져가시겠어요?

피터: 탑승하러 갈 때 가져가는 게 더 나을 것 같네요.

모나: 궁금한 점이 있으시거나 추가정보가 필요하시면 저희 고객상담실로 연락주세요.

피터: 그러죠!

12

Sera : So how was the birthday party?

Jun : Great! Since it was the baby's first birthday, everyone presented her with gold rings.

Sera : So the baby is already rich at the age of one?

Jun : No, the rings are just a traditional gift. But we did find out that she is going to become a millionaire.

Sera : How were you able to tell?

Jun : Traditionally, the baby has to make a choice between three objects.

Sera : What are the objects?

Jun : They are money, thread and a pencil.

Sera : I take it the kid grabbed the money! But what do the others mean?

Jun : The thread represents a long life and the pencil represents an educated person.

Sera : What did you grab when you were a child?

Jun : I grabbed the money.

Sera : So what happened?

Jun : I'm still waiting for the money to pour in.

우리말　세러: 그래, 생일파티 어땠어?

준: 굉장했어! 첫돌이라서 사람들이 모두 아기한테 금반지를 선물했지.

세러: 그럼 아기는 한살 밖에 안됐는데 벌써 부자가 되었네?

준: 아냐, 반지는 그저 전통적으로 주는 선물일 뿐인데 뭐. 하지만 그 공주님이 정말 백만장자가 될 거라는 건 알게 됐지.　세러: 어떻게 알았어?

준: 돌 잔치에는 전통적으로 아기가 세가지 물건 중에서 하나를 선택하는 순서가 있거든.

세러: 어떤 물건들인데?　준: 돈, 실 그리고 연필이야.

세러: 아이가 돈을 집었단 말이구나. 그런데 나머지 두개는 무슨 뜻이야?

준: 실은 오래 산다는 뜻이고 연필은 학식을 많이 쌓을 거라는 의미야.

세러: 너는 아기때 뭘 집었어?　준: 돈을 집었지.

세러: 근데 어떻게 된거야?

준: 아직도 돈이 쏟아져 들어오길 기다리고 있는 셈이지.

13

Gi-won : Where are you going to go today?

Bruno : I'm going back to Insa-dong.

Gi-won : That's the street of Korean culture and customs.

Bruno : Yeah, I was there yesterday, but I want to go back again today since there is so much to see there.

Gi-won : Did you go to any art galleries while you were there?

Bruno : Yes, but there are many more I want to go to, and also a lot of antique stores.

Gi-won : Do you like our antiques?

Bruno : I love them! I've already bought a reproduction of some antique ceramics.

Gi-won : You'd better be careful there today, you don't want to spend the rest of your travel money!

Bruno : At least it will be money well spent!

우리말 기원: 오늘은 어디에 갈 거야?

브루노: 인사동에 다시 가보려고 해.

기원: 한국의 문화와 전통의 거리지.

브루노: 그래, 어제 갔었는데, 볼거리가 굉장히 많아서 오늘 다시 가보고 싶어.

기원: 거기서 화랑(畵廊) 같은 데 갔어?

브루노: 응, 그런데도 가보고 싶은 데가 아주 많고 골동품상도 많더라.

기원: 우리나라 골동품 좋아하니?

브루노: 아주 좋아해! 이미 옛날 도자기 모조품도 하나 샀는걸.

기원: 오늘 거기 가면 조심해야겠다, 남은 여행비를 다써버리면 않되잖아!

브루노: 그래도 아깝진 않을 거야!

14

Michael : We strongly recommend that you take the offer.

Louise : I think we should think it over.

Michael : If I were you I wouldn't wait too long.

Louise : It might be a good idea to take this offer before they change their mind.

Michael : Is there an expiry date on the offer?

Louise : Yes. It can be rescinded at the end of the week.

Michael : That gives you a few days to think about it.

Louise : You're right.

Michael : Are we likely to get such an offer from another company?

Louise : You might, but it is really hard to say for sure.

우리말

마이클: 그 제의를 받아들여야 한다고 강력히 주장하는 바입니다.

루이스: 제 생각엔 꼼꼼하게 검토를 해봐야 할 것 같은데요.

마이클: 저라면 그리 오래 두고보지는 않겠습니다.

루이스: 그 사람들이 마음을 바꾸기 전에 제의를 받아들이는 것도 괜찮을 것 같군요.

마이클: 그 제의에 기한이 있습니까?

루이스: 네. 이번 주말이면 무효가 됩니다.

마이클: 그러면 생각할 시간이 며칠은 남아있는 거로군요.

루이스: 그런 셈이죠.

마이클: 다른 회사에서도 이런 제의가 들어올 가능성이 있을까요?

루이스: 그럴 수도 있겠지만, 자신은 못하겠습니다.

15

Paul : I am always surprised by the number of Koreans who are studying or want to study English.

Su-ji : Studying English is an obsession for many Koreans, but often the English that they study does not help them in real life situations with foreigners.

Paul : I don't understand what you mean.

Su-ji : Many Koreans only know text book English which is good for greetings, but it doesn't help them in real life business meetings.

Paul : Now I understand what you mean. They need some practical business English to help them interact with foreigners.

Su-ji : Exactly. They need to be able to use everyday expressions and greetings so that their foreign counterparts understand what they're talking about.

우리말 폴: 영어공부를 하고 있거나 하고 싶어하는 한국 사람들 수에 항상 놀란다니까.

수지: 많은 한국 사람들에겐 영어공부가 하나의 강박관념이 되고 있지만, 우리가 배우는 영어가 외국인들과의 실제 상황에선 도움이 안될 때도 있어.

폴: 무슨 말인지 모르겠어.

수지: 많은 한국인들은 인사할 때나 쓸 수 있는 교과서 영어만 아는데, 실제 비지니스 미팅에서는 도움이 안되거든.

폴: 이제야 네 말을 알겠어. 그들에겐 외국인들과 교류할 때 도움이 되는 실용 비지니스 영어가 필요하구나.

수지: 맞아. 일상표현이나 인사말을 배워서 우리가 하는 말을 외국인이 알아들을 수 있어야 돼.